Contents

2012 is a rather important year for London and the UK as we will be welcoming the world to our cities, so it is just as well that there has been something of a revolution in the UK – it is called the Café, Food and Restaurant Revolution. Even in these dire economic times they open every day of the week by keen, young people for whom food has become a religion – growing it and cooking it.

Of course opening and running a café and especially a restaurant can be hugely enjoyable when it goes well – you look around and the place is full of young people enjoying themselves and paying you for their enjoyment; you feel just like an actor with a full house.

But the great change has come about because serious entrepreneurial young people have seen that opening a café, food shop or small restaurant can get them on the bottom rung of the business ladder reasonably economically, and they hope they will have some fun setting it up too – and they will if they run their own place in a simple business way and find cheerful, experienced staff to build their team who don't mind working long hours.

The revolution began during that most depressing post-war period in 1953–4 when we were seriously rationed, spam sandwiches were the norm for most lunches occasionally highlighted with a spam fritter. Then along came Elizabeth David's marvellous cookbooks. As my generation read them and dribbled over them with pleasure, we made plans to go and visit France, Italy and Spain which was just possible in the early Fifties. So we came back from our travels and thought why can't we have food in the UK like they do in continental Europe? A few brave souls opened cafés and restaurants in the late 1950s with some success, and the success of the revolution is that now we do, and much more besides.

It seems to me and Peter that you can now eat food from every nation in the world, and that is why, as I hope this book will help to explain, London has at last become the restaurant 'capital' of the world. Part of the enormous diffusion is because the UK is home to a huge ethnic population from every corner of the world, and they want to eat their own national food.

When you think of the change in restaurants and cafés in London you can understand why the American magazine *Gourmet* nominated London as the Restaurant Capital of the World when, twenty years ago, the food in the UK was used as an excuse not to visit us.

So what Peter and I have tried to do is to select the cafés, restaurants and food stores in all London's villages that we hope you may enjoy as much as we do. We are both professional restaurateurs so have used our knowledge to select those places where we think food and service is good or even excellent.

As a designer I am also very interested in the environment and the graphics. I am particularly interested in café and restaurant chairs – their comfort and strength. Will there ever be a better chair than the bentwood Thonet? The archetypal café chair which can be thrown around and knocked off tables by the cleaners and it just bounces.

Foreword
Terence Conran

Above **Peter Prescott (left) and Terence Conran outside Lutyens, Fleet Street.**

The design of kitchens has also changed with new equipment such as fiercely-hot Japanese-style grills. The kitchen, I believe, should always be visible to the customer – this stops the ridiculous battles that used to take place between the chefs and the waiters and, even more importantly, it allows the kitchen staff to see the customers, the recipient of their hard work. It also encourages the kitchen to be kept clean and tidy unlike some basement kitchens I have worked in which are rather squalid to say the least. Not something you would like to see your food being prepared in.

Finally let me thank my co-author Peter who directs our restaurant, café and hotel – he is passionate about food, wine and service, and runs them brilliantly. If somebody tells him of a new food shop, restaurant or café, he is off like a shot. I always find when I go to a new place, he has been a couple of times already and he has a firm opinion about it – luckily we practically always agree. If not, we have a constructive discussion about it.

"

It seems to me and Peter that you can now eat food from every nation in the world, and that is why, as I hope this book will help to explain, London has at last become the restaurant 'capital' of the world. Part of the enormous diffusion is because the UK is home to a huge ethnic population from every corner of the world, and they want to eat their own national food and we do, too.

Introduction
Peter Prescott

I am not a writer or a journalist, but I do work in the restaurant and hotel business and have done so for over 20 years, more than half of this time spent working closely with my now business partner and co-author Terence Conran. Putting together my notes for this second edition of *Eat London* has been heavy weather at times, I confess. As a restaurateur, hotelier and keeper of a small food shop and bakery, I know I can always be doing more to improve things, and when I visit a new food store, farmers' market, café, bar or restaurant, it invariably makes me examine my own business. A dazzling experience might spark an idea, or a feeling of frustration that I haven't done it already, while a poor one will sometimes make me worry whether the same is also happening at our own properties. Of course a meal out or shopping for food is enjoyable, but for me it's also work. Being in the business makes it virtually impossible to stop thinking professionally about the daily process of eating and drinking. However, I do also love it: it's preoccupying in every sense, and I find it irresistible. Despite being around chefs, kitchens and dining rooms during my working life, if I hear about a new place, a great chef or a refurbished restaurant, I'll be rushing to visit. At the same time, I also try to stay loyal to my favourites and support past colleagues. The London restaurant scene is constantly evolving and improving. It's exciting and – I think – the best in the world.

This is not a totally comprehensive guidebook and isn't always objective. We've tried to offer a taste of the endless cuisines that are cooked in the capital, but cannot claim to include everything, especially when it comes to certain ethnic foods. To my knowledge, the excellent *Time Out London* magazine is the only publication that can claim to be really diligent in this regard. Instead, we offer an insider's opinionated view on the London restaurant scene. It's interesting to visit New York, Paris, Hong Kong, Moscow, Madrid or Rome, but in my view none of them come close to the excitement and variation that London has to offer on a plate. I am enormously proud of our great city and wouldn't want to live in any other place. I'm very interested too in the built environment, design, culture and the history of London, the finest metropolis on the planet. In almost every corner of the city there is decent food to be found now, and this book aims to tell you a little about the multitude of choices that are available. While east London, the City and the West End are the areas I know most intimately, I'll willingly travel across town to enjoy a great meal. Talking with colleagues and comparing notes and views with friends who are equally passionate about eating out is also part of the process. Rupert Taylor, our excellent head sommelier at Boundary restaurant, is particularly competitive in this regard: sometimes it seems like there's a race on between the two of us to see who can visit a new place first or most often.

We have a limited number of pages in this book, and sadly we have had to leave out some excellent restaurants and food stores for lack of space. We have focused on central London, which means that we haven't been able to include noteworthy food enclaves that lie further away from the heart of the city, such as the Korean food culture of New Malden, or the authentic Afro-Caribbean food in far-flung corners of north London. I would also like to stress that all of our comments are subjective and personal.

Right **Mise-en-place at Lutyens with the restaurant's cheese cabinet in the background.**

And unless we say otherwise, we pay for all of the meals in full and we do not give proprietors advance warning of our visits.

Perhaps more than any other trade or industry, the restaurant business is about personalities, unique experiences, and occasionally sheer good luck. What I love others might hate.

Certainly I harbour a bias towards humble, simple dishes, no-frills cooking, strong flavours and gutsy regional foods. I firmly believe in attractive presentation on the plate, but not to the point of contrivance or unnecessary manipulation of the ingredients. If a dish is over-dressed or fussily garnished, to me this signals that the chef is trying too hard, perhaps to compensate for a shortcoming elsewhere. I find myself looking for cooks who understand restraint, who know when to let the purity of good ingredients and a fantastic recipe speak for themselves. Equally, I try to seek out places that focus on seasonality, and that introduce the great highlights of the changing seasons with gusto. And I am always impressed by chefs who have garnered great knowledge, employ studious technique and respect their customers' desires.

Quirkiness, wonderful personalities, service, ambience, design, location and customer profile – all are factors that I have taken into account when selecting places to include. Consistency, history and a sense of tradition have also influenced my opinions. It is rare to find these characteristics in premises run by large companies, and you will find the majority of the entries are independently owned. Sometimes I have deliberately held back in my description, so that you can explore the restaurants and form your own judgement; sometimes it's better not to know too much before a visit, so that with luck you can discover assets and charms that I have missed. I'm sure there will also be occasions when you fervently disagree with me, or when things go wrong even though I have said a certain restaurant is renowned for its consistency. That's the food business for you.

The 2012 Olympics will see the eyes of the world on London, with a massive influx of visitors. It goes without saying that even the most exacting of food explorers will find something to surprise or delight in London. But not perhaps in or around the Olympic Park, sadly, where the centerpiece is to be the world's largest McDonald's, with ambitions to serve some 50,000 Big Macs over a 29-day period. Oh dear.

I hope that *Eat London* encourages you to travel to new areas of our great city, to experience different foods and to visit restaurants both new and long-established. While many new restaurants open each week, the failure and closure rates are also very high, so please do check before venturing across London.

Now that this edition of *Eat London* is complete, I'm looking forward to spending more time at Boundary, Albion and Lutyens – I can honestly say that these are my favourite places to eat in London, plus St. John, Moro, The River Café, Scott's, Terroirs, Brawn, Roka, Hereford Road and Hix Chop House. Cooking at home, when I get the chance, is my other great love. Please support your favourite restaurant; but please also – in measured fashion – explore the new.

Being in the business makes it virtually impossible to stop thinking professionally about the daily process of eating and drinking. However, I do also love it: it's preoccupying in every sense, and I find it irresistible. Despite being around chefs, kitchens and dining rooms during my working life, if I hear about a new place, a great chef or a refurbished restaurant, I'll be rushing to visit. The London restaurant scene is constantly evolving and improving. It's exciting and – I think – the best in the world.

Opposite **Grouse with liver toast, game chips and crumbs, bread sauce and a light gravy courtesy of Peter Weeden, head chef at Boundary Restaurant.**

Barnes
Chiswick
Hammersmith
Richmond
Teddington
Twickenham

Just eight miles from central London (a journey best made by train from Waterloo Station), Richmond is a beautifully green and leafy suburb. The Thames meanders through this part of London, where life is sedate and village-like, and most of the urbanization clusters around the bridges at Kew, Chiswick, Richmond and Barnes. Aeroplanes en route to Heathrow crisscross the air space and Twickenham rugby stadium may be glimpsed over the distant tree line, but otherwise the view from Richmond Hill is much the same today as it was hundreds of years ago. Beyond Richmond lie the picturesque and fabulously wealthy villages of Ham and Petersham.

In 1625, Charles I walled the open heathland to create the great hunting estate of Richmond Park, now Europe's largest urban enclosed park, roamed by wild red and fallow deer for all to see (but not to hunt). Cycling in Richmond Park is a popular pastime, with many cyclists adjourning afterwards to the numerous small restaurants and cafés to be found along this stretch of the river. Anyone interested in tracing the history of food back to Tudor times should visit Hampton Court Palace, with its vast kitchens which occasionally host cookery classes. The area's other great attraction is the Royal Botanical Gardens at Kew.

T. Adamou & Sons 124–6 Chiswick High Road, W4 1PU
020 8994 0752

You can be assured of friendly and knowledgeable service at this Cypriot family-run grocer's shop, where the emphasis is on Mediterranean foods, with a fine selection of feta cheese, vine leaves, tinned and dried foods and olive oils. The pavement display of fresh fruit and vegetables offers welcome relief from the more mundane offerings of neighbouring retailers. **O**

Angelsea Arms 35 Wingate Road, W6 0UR
020 8749 1291

Given the choice, we'd prefer a restaurant to a pub, but we also recognize that in the right hands a good public house can serve some very enjoyable food and drink – often better than the over-garnished and fussy food to be found in many restaurants. This excellent example of the type calls on proven classic dishes and earthy ingredients. Go for a pint of English ale and a slow, slow-cooked pork belly. **O**

Covent Garden Fishmongers 37 Turnham Green Terrace, W4 1RG
020 8995 9273 www.coventgardenfishmongers.co.uk

The leading independent fishmonger in the area can source any kind of fish or seafood and will prepare it and deliver locally. **O**

The Depot Tideway Yard, Mortlake High Street, Barnes, SW14 8SN
020 8878 9462 www.depotbrasserie.co.uk

The experience overall may not be worth writing home about, but when you live locally you don't always want something special, just honest food and sensibly priced wine. So if you find yourself in the area, I'd recommend a visit. The Depot has been around for over 25 years, and that counts for something: the locals vote with their feet and the bar remains buoyant. The food might not attain the high standards set at nearby Riva or Sonny's, but the view along the Thames far outstrips its competitors. And as you're behind glass, you can enjoy it all year round. **O**

Above **The relaxed and comfortable Angelsea Arms.**

The Gate 51 Queen Caroline Street, W6 9QL
020 8748 6932 www.thegaterestaurants.com

The Gate is considered by many to be the best vegetarian restaurant in London. We're probably not best qualified to judge, but the menu certainly includes some delicious ingredients, and the kitchen serves up a wide range of textures, colours and flavours that would satisfy any hungry visitor. ◐

High Road Brasserie 162–170 Chiswick High Road, W4 1PR
020 8742 7474 brasserie.highroadhouse.co.uk

Part of Nick Jones' über-cool Soho House Group and open to non-members, the Brasserie at High Road House is great for a long, lazy weekend breakfast or brunch, with newspapers, strong coffee, a croque monsieur, eggs Benedict or perhaps some waffles with blueberries and crème fraîche.

The design by Ilse Crawford is very agreeable, especially the zinc bar, the patchwork-style floor tiles and the light fittings. If you get a chance, try to visit other parts of this boutique hotel: given the space restrictions and the miniature bedrooms, the finished work is very comfortable in a summer-beach-house-meets-Shaker manner. ◐

Macken Bros 44 Turnham Green Terrace, W4 1QP
020 8994 2646 www.mackenbros.co.uk

If you buy your fish from Covent Garden Fishmongers, your meat course must come, after lengthy discussion, from butcher Rodney Macken. ◐

The Nutcase 352 Uxbridge Road, W12 7LL
020 8743 0336

This very unusual shop specializes in Arabic sweets, nuts and fruits that have been dry-roasted, some of them on the premises. Everything from mulberries to lupin or pumpkin seeds, plus baklava and Turkish jellies is to be found here, alongside a range of coffees from North Africa. ◐

Left **The Gate vegetarian restaurant.**

Petersham Nurseries Café and Teahouse Church Lane,
off Petersham Road, Richmond, TW10 7AG
020 8605 3627 www.petershamnurseries.com

Take the day off for this one. Jump on the train at Waterloo Station, and within 20 minutes you will be at Richmond Station. Then walk to the arcadia that is Richmond Hill, down the hill towards the meandering Thames and across Petersham Meadows in the full glare of the grazing cattle. For a townie, this is already bucolic bliss. And when you reach Petersham Nurseries it just gets better. Everything here – and we mean everything – has been done with an enormous helping of panache. Like no other garden centre (hardly the *mot juste* when it comes to Petersham), this is a botanical experience that far surpasses the paradigm.

Since Petersham Nurseries Café opened, chef Skye Gyngell has become a whirlwind success. The café has won numerous awards, including a Michelin star in 2011, and she has written three admirable cookbooks, writes on food for a national newspaper, and has generally been elevated to become one of the top food personalities in London. And it's all amply deserved.

The menu at the café is pitch perfect – just five first courses, five mains and five puddings. Everything is highly seasonal: go in the summer and you will find the menu strewn with ingredients grown in the gardens all round the kitchen.

In fine weather the café is without doubt the best al fresco dining experience outside central London, if not in the entire country. The setting is relatively informal, but it attracts serious and well-heeled local patronage, plus a few foodies on culinary pilgrimages. It's definitely worth the journey, no matter how arduous.

As at The River Café and Blueprint Café, no irony in the term 'café' is lost, and although each has its own style, they probably all share a similar food ethos. In the sea of restaurants that London offers this is a considerable accomplishment in itself, and the fact that the food on the plate is also so delicious merits added praise. ◦

17

This page
The meandering Thames and Petersham Nurseries.

Left **Alfresco dining at Petersham Nurseries Café.**

Strawberry Granita

Serves 4

For the sugar syrup

200 g (7 oz) caster sugar

475 ml (16 fl oz) water

3 punnets of English strawberries

juice of 1 lemon

Put the sugar and the water into a saucepan, and place it over a medium heat. Bring it to the boil, turn down the heat and then cook it for a couple of minutes to ensure that the sugar has dissolved. Remove the saucepan from the heat and allow it to cool completely.

Hull the strawberries, place them in a food processor and blend with the lemon juice until puréed and set aside.

When the syrup is completely cool, combine it with the strawberries. Pour the mixture into a freezerproof container, cover and leave it to chill. After 1 hour, remove it from the freezer and stir it up with a fork, dragging the mixture in from the sides. A granita's texture is not the same as a sorbet; it is meant to be icy and crunchy! Reseal the container, return it to the freezer and leave it to chill until it has set.

To serve, remove it from the freezer and scoop the granita into glasses.

Recipe featured in *A Year in My Kitchen* by Skye Gyngell, Quadrille

Right Tour the nurseries after a delicious lunch.

Princess Victoria 217 Uxbridge Road, W12 9DH
020 8749 5886 www.princessvictoria.co.uk

Overseas visitors to London (especially Americans) often ask their hotel concierge to recommend an archetypal British pub. Well, it's not so easy these days. There are now many different variants on the once omnipresent corner ale house; the classic example is closing at a rapid pace and new formats are emerging. As mentioned elsewhere, the era of the (ugly named) gastropub is well and truly with us; then you also find full-on restaurants in pubs, and even pubs with pizzerias and Thai food, to mention only a couple of the differing styles. Unless you are very informed and aware, it is all very perplexing. We have tried to make *Eat London* more than just a guidebook, and have given much thought to our criteria for inclusion, particularly when it comes to pubs. In general, a pub must demonstrate something that separates it from others or gives a reason for the tourist or hardened foodie to travel to an odd location to warrant inclusion. We were keen to include the Princess Victoria, a former gin palace dating back to 1829, on the strength of a number of interesting features, including its 350-bin wine list, its cigar and wine shop and its charming herb garden – not to mention its food. **○**

Riva 169 Church Road, Barnes, SW13 9HR
020 8748 0434

A small and basic dining room, probably with fewer than 40 seats, which also manages to be romantic, with purposeful Italian food that attracts celebrities and bigwigs who have all heard about this discreet restaurant's excellent reputation. Andrea Riva, the owner, hails from Lombardy, and the food follows a northern Italian style. While the room and table settings appear simple, the food is world-class. The qualities of this place are not always obvious, but on reflection you will realise that some of the best culinary treats in London are to be found here. **○**

19

Above **The pleasingly-understated Riva dining room.**

The River Café Thames Wharf, Rainville Road, W6 9HA
020 7386 4200 www.rivercafe.co.uk

Petersham Nurseries is one of the most original places to eat – in a greenhouse, full of flowers and quirky mismatched furniture – the best London restaurant for a romantic meal.

Chef patron, Tom Aikens

What started out mainly as a canteen for a neighbouring architectural practice is now one of most foodies' top five most admired restaurants. This was no ordinary architect's office, however: it was that of Lord Rogers, and the shell of the building was a nineteenth-century warehouse on the north bank of the Thames. Since those early days in 1987, the River Café has set the bar for modern Italian cooking in London. This is the kitchen where the television production company responsible for *The Naked Chef* first spotted Jamie Oliver, and where Hugh Fearnley-Whittingstall worked before his television career took off. Now it has a waiting list of chefs willing to work there for virtually no pay.

After 20 years of supreme consistency, the River Café has experienced some flux over recent years. A fire that started one Saturday night in early April 2008 closed the restaurant until the autumn of that year. During this time, it was reported that all the staff were retained and sent on training and research missions to enable them

to immerse themselves in Italian food culture, so that the reopened restaurant would further strengthen its commitment to quality at every level. When it did reopen, we were treated to several improvements on the already excellent design. The wood oven is now more prominent, a cheese room has been added, along with a private dining room, and the state-of-the-art kitchen is now fully open and visible. It's a triumph on every level, from the complementary colours – blue floor and flashes of yellow on the bar – to the industrial light fittings, the gently vaulted ceiling and the herbs and salad leaves in the garden outside, all make this a treat for both the fan of high design and the layperson alike.

The second major event in early 2010, came the very sad loss to cancer of co-founder Rose Gray. Ruth Rogers now continues the passionate search for the finest ingredients, especially from Italy – a continual and tireless effort that has helped earn the kitchen universal respect across the industry. The phenomenal success of the River Café cookbooks means their style of cooking has gained global renown. The River Café chocolate nemesis has entered chefs' vernacular and become a byword for flourless chocolate cake (even when the recipe in the book doesn't work). Another much-copied dish is their squid with chilli and rocket: somehow, others don't seem to deliver quite the same level of excellence. Menus always start with the aperitivo of the day, in the form of a variation on a Bellini made with Prosecco, with Charentais melon, pomegranate, strawberries, pear, blood orange or grapefruit sometimes substituted for the white peaches that usually form the core ingredient.

The all-Italian wine list follows the same earnest sourcing policies and is passionately promoted by the eloquent young staff. Service is impeccable, and all the staff seem merrily content to be part of a unique dining prodigy.

Fans and critics alike often comment on the high menu prices. But while the style might be *cucina povera*, the ingredients are far from 'poor kitchen'. Whatever the case, the diaries remain busy, and it's always difficult to get a table at short notice. Speaking for ourselves, we trust that the proprietors apply the same margins as other restaurants, and believe that the management would find cupidity vulgar. The high prices must surely be due to the quality of ingredients (and the generous portions) and the normal costs of running a high-quality restaurant. (PP) My only reservations about the costs are in relation to the cab fare to Hammersmith from the West End or east London, plus the fact they have to empty the restaurant by 11pm to satisfy local residents. Hence I don't visit as often as I would like, but maybe that's a blessing for the wallet. That apart, the River Café experience is without any faults or flaws. ●

Opposite and this page **The much-loved and admired River Café.**

Marinated Fresh Anchovies with Rosemary and Red Wine Vinegar

Serves 6

1 sprig of rosemary, finely chopped
1 tablespoon salt
1 teaspoon fennel seeds, ground
1 dried chilli, crumbled
juice of 2 lemons
extra virgin olive oil
500 g (1 lb) fresh anchovies
3 tablespoons red wine vinegar
freshly ground black pepper

Mix the chopped rosemary immediately with the salt. Scatter some of the rosemary, fennel seeds, chilli and black pepper over the surface of a serving dish. Drizzle with lemon juice and olive oil.

Place a layer of anchovies skin-side up in the dish, packing them closely together. Sprinkle them with a little more of the rosemary, fennel seeds, chilli, black pepper, lemon, red wine vinegar and olive oil. Make further layers, repeating the process. Make sure the final layer is submerged. Cover with clingfilm and leave to 'cook' in the marinade for at least an hour.

Serve on warm bruschetta.

Recipe featured in *The River Café Cook Book* by Rose Gray and Ruth Rogers, Ebury

Above **The outside terrace at The River Café is one of the best dining locations in London.** Left and right **Making fresh pasta.**

Zucchini Soup
Zuppa di Zucchine

Serves 6

1 kg (2 lb) medium courgettes, trimmed
25 ml (1 fl oz) olive oil
2 garlic cloves, peeled and chopped
500 ml (17 fl oz) chicken stock or water
140 ml (4½ fl oz) double cream
1 small bunch basil, chopped
1 small bunch flat leaf parsley, chopped
120 g (4½ oz) Parmesan, freshly grated
sea salt and freshly ground black pepper

For the crostini
6 slices ciabatta bread, cut at an angle
115 g (3¾ oz) black olives, pitted and chopped
1 large fresh red chilli, deseeded
extra virgin olive oil

Cut the courgette lengthwise into quarters, then into 2.5 cm (1 inch) pieces. Heat the oil in a heavy saucepan and cook the garlic and courgette slowly for approximately 25 minutes or until the zucchini are brown and very soft. Add salt, pepper and the stock and simmer for another few minutes. Remove from the stove.

Put three-quarters of the courgette in a food processor and purée. Return to the pan, add the cream, basil, parsley and Parmesan.

To make the crostini, toast the bread on both sides. Mix the olives and the chilli with some extra virgin olive oil and spread thickly on the crostini. Serve the soup with the crostini at the side of the plate.

Recipe featured in *The River Café Cook Book* by Rose Gray and Ruth Rogers, Ebury

Grilled Peaches with Amaretto
Pesche Gratinate con Amaretto

Serves 6

8 ripe peaches
1 vanilla pod
2 tablespoons caster sugar
120 ml (4 fl oz) Amaretto
crème fraîche, to serve

Preheat the oven to 190°C (375°F) Gas Mark 5. Preheat a char-grill or griddle pan. Slice the peaches in half and remove the stones, trying to keep the cut as clean as possible. Carefully place the peach halves cut side down on the griddle pan, and grill until each peach half has become slightly charred.

Thinly slice the vanilla pod lengthways and put into a mortar with the sugar. Pound with a pestle until broken up and combined.

Place the peach halves face up in a shallow ovenproof baking dish.

Scatter the vanilla sugar over the peaches and pour in some of the Amaretto. Place in the preheated oven and bake for 10 minutes or until the peaches are soft. Pour over the remaining Amaretto and serve hot or cold with crème fraîche.

Recipe featured in *The River Café Cook Book* by Rose Gray and Ruth Rogers, Ebury

Skye Gyngell

> The extraordinarily amazing River Café has got to be my favourite London restaurant. It's uniquely relaxed and convivial. The standards are maintained at all times, even after 20 years at the top of the business.

Chef and food writer, Petersham Nurseries Café and Teahouse

Above right **The dining room inside Sam's Brasserie.** Above **The communal table in the bar at Sam's.**

Sam's Brasserie Barley Mow Centre, 11 Barley Mow Passage, W4 4PH
020 8987 0555 www.samsbrasserie.co.uk

25

A true modern neighbourhood all-day brasserie, professionally run, comfortable and hard to fault: they seem to have thought of everything here, and to have addressed each and every point with sincerity and generosity. Whether you are seeking a simple late-morning croissant with a freshly squeezed juice or smoothie or a serious foodie experience, Sam's Brasserie provides the perfect setting. Located on a quaintly named narrow passage off the Chiswick High Road, the comfortable bar makes an ideal destination for lazy Sundays with a bloody Mary or a kedgeree and poached egg brunch. The central raised table is littered with newspapers, the music is suitably upbeat without being overpowering, and the young staff are trained to be both welcoming and technically proficient. On a sunny day they open the large doors and windows to allow a lovely breeze to waft through. After serving as Rick Stein's general manager, Sam Harrison has stepped out on his own with this relaxed and informal venture (although Rick is an investor). Sam patrols the tables with an omnipresent smile, confidence and pedigree that are rare in these parts. Prices are reasonable, the wine list touches all the key areas, children are welcomed with open arms, and they host an interesting programme of events, from jazz evenings to wine tastings. (PP) Oh, I do wish I lived next door. (TC) Oh, and so do I.

Sonny's 92–4 Church Road, Barnes, SW13 0DG
020 8748 0393 www.sonnys.co.uk

A Barnes staple for more than 20 years, Sonny's still feels fresh, modern and relevant. The menu consistently offers the good, solid and satisfying food that we all want to eat. The dining room is pleasant, and has interesting artworks on the walls. Local residents are lucky to have assets such as this restaurant and the adjoining food shop on their doorstep. If you're not a local, go for Sunday lunch before a saunter through Barnes village and along the river. ◐

La Trompette 5–7 Devonshire Road, W4 2EU
020 8747 1836 www.latrompette.co.uk

Owned by Nigel Platts-Martin, master of high-quality neighbourhood restaurants, and Bruce Poole, the Chez Bruce maestro, La Trompette was destined to become the leading high-quality restaurant in Chiswick. If Sam's Brasserie is our everyday all-purpose refectory then La Trompette is a once-a-month or celebration special treat. In reality, however, the prices are not too over the top. The menu is drawn from the cuisine of south and south-west France, although it does include a few diversions among the foie gras and confit de canard. The chateaubriand with chips and béarnaise must be eternally popular. As with all of Mr Platts-Martin's restaurants, the wine list is extensive: this one has over 600 bins. ◐

Le Vacherin 76–7 South Parade, W4 5LF
020 8742 2121 www.levacherin.co.uk

An impressive local restaurant brought to you by experienced chef patron Malcolm John, this French bistro offers an appetizing hint of Parisian under-designed style. The menu is a delight both to read and to eat. Put this delicious offering in central London and it would be one of the most popular eating places the capital could offer. We applaud Mr John for his commitment and confidence as a fine purveyor of chic France on a plate. ◐

Ray Neve

My favourite London restaurant has got to be Mosimann's. You can always be assured of a warm welcome from the manager. The place is timeless and holds so many happy memories.
Chef and proprietor, The Wharf

Left **Carefully selected art in the dining room at Sonny's.**

The Wharf 22 Manor Road, Teddington, TW11 8BG
020 8977 6333 www.thewharfteddington.com

After leading the kitchens at the Dorchester Hotel, Mosimann's, The Bankers Club in Kuala Lumpur and Conrad Hotels, Ray Neve, the proprietor and chef at this converted riverside boathouse, has started his independent career with a local favourite. The ground floor serves an eclectic European menu with several Asian specials, but – unlike other chefs who have tried to fuse these culinary styles – Ray doesn't confuse the two. You can expect cod brandade, moules marinière, duck confit or ham hock terrine with crusty bread on the one hand, or Thai-style beef, Chinese spiced pork belly and Morrocan lamb with couscous and charmoula on the other. The menu also includes a few brunch specials, such as a Caesar salad or a meaty hamburger. Upstairs, the bar and event space has fine views overlooking the River Thames and Teddington Lock, making it the perfect venue for a riverside wedding or celebration. ●

More places to visit in the area

● **Damas Gate**
81–5 Uxbridge Road, W12 8NR
020 8743 5116
A deli specializing in Middle Eastern foods.

● **Living Lab at Pizza Express**
Lion House, Red Lion Street,
Richmond-upon-Thames, TW9 1RE
020 8948 7460 www.futureexpress.co.uk
Long established and loved by the middle classes in the 1980s, Pizza Express is reinventing itself, bringing in a bevy of new talent, including Ab Rogers, to help restore their fortunes and experiment with the launch of a new concept. This left-field test site has probably gone too far, but it has provoked interest. The parabolic booths with their own lighting and music are just crazy.

● **Mortimer & Bennett**
33 Turnham Green Terrace, W4 1RG
020 8995 4145
www.mortimerandbennett.co.uk
A leading delicatessen and fine-food store with first-rate products from around the globe.

Above **The white-on-white approach at Sonny's is crisp and modern.**

Battersea
Brixton
Clapham
Putney
Wandsworth

The residents of Battersea, Clapham, Wandsworth and Putney are often characterized as people aspiring to live in Chelsea or Fulham. Young families whose finances do not stretch to property on the north side of the Thames (not really considered as north London) who settle for south of the river, rapidly fall for its charms – especially around Clapham Common – and gradually lose the desire to move. Although the residential population is massive, there doesn't seem to be much of a food and restaurant culture here. Yes, there are endless restaurants, but few of them offer any special quality or reason to travel to the area. A few star turns are worth it, notably Chez Bruce (see page 31) and Trinity (see page 36), but given the population, this is paltry.

Before the Industrial Revolution much of this area was farmland serving the City of London. A speciality at this time was lavender, hence Lavender Hill, one of the major roads just off Clapham Common. Towards the end of the 18th century, the area had over 300 acres of farmland and more than 20 market gardens. Today, New Covent Garden Market at Nine Elms serves a similar purpose, but now principally serving restaurants and hotels. The only reason for visiting is the adjoining flower market: go very early in the morning to see it at its best.

The defunct Battersea Power Station (the largest brick structure in Europe) continues to promise exciting change for the area. But – every south Londoner wants to know – will it ever happen? If we once thought the ivory chimneys of this great Sir Gilbert Scott building resembled the tusks of an elephant, sadly that elephant now seems to be a white one.

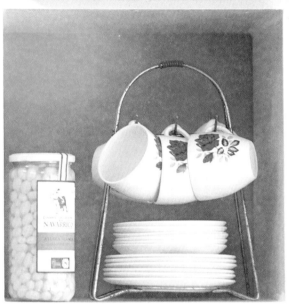

FRESHLY MADE
SANDWICHES
TO TAKE OUT

HOCOLAT

DELESPAUL-HAVEZ

Brady's 513 Old York Road, SW18 1TF
020 8877 9599 www.bradysfish.co.uk

This small café and takeaway fish-and-chip shop serves both grilled
(tuna, lemon sole, skate) and battered (cod, haddock, plaice) fish with
great chips and mushy peas. You can also get potted shrimps or half a pint
of prawns, plus treacle tart and apple crumble for pudding. The owners
buy fish direct from Cornwall and Grimsby and use mainly line-caught
fish. They are responsible in their buying and support the protection of
our seas and fish stocks – an approach we should all follow. ○

Brixton Market Electric Avenue, SW9
Daily 8am–6pm, Wednesday till 3pm; Sundays 10am–2pm

In April 2010, the Secretary of State of State for Culture overturned a
previous decision and confirmed the market's importance by giving it
a Grade II listing. Its covered arcades are interesting, but the listing was
granted not so much for its architecture as for its cultural importance. Over the years, this cluster of arcades and street markets has

provided a great deal for Brixton and become the epicentre of the symbolic
soul of black Britain. Best known as an African/Caribbean centre, it
actually offers much more. Electric Avenue, the street immortalized by
Eddy Grant's chart hit, is home to all manner of butchers, fishmongers
and greengrocers, plus an excellent supermarket selling Asian produce.
The huge displays of fish on ice, the vegetables and fruit from far-flung
places and the esoteric meats – think tripe, trotters, tails and tongues –
might not be the finest of produce, and there is certainly still a whiff of
illegal substances, but it is colourful and full of character.

To get the most from your trip, check the opening hours before
visiting. The farmers' market in Brixton Station Road on Sunday is one
of the best in town, and Saturday afternoon can get very lively. ○

Above right **The
menu at Brady's.**
Left **Brixton
Market.**

Chez Bruce 2 Bellevue Road, SW17 7EG

020 8672 0114 www.chezbruce.co.uk

This is by far the finest restaurant in the whole of south London, and has in the past been voted the best restaurant in London, eclipsing anything by Gordon Ramsay and the once unbeatable Ivy.

The restaurant's address has form: before becoming Chez Bruce it was the infamous and celebrated Harvey's, the restaurant that acted as a platform for the great Marco Pierre White and *White Heat* – the book that revealed a revolutionary kitchen and groundbreaking photography by Bob Carlos Clarke, who made chefs sexy for the first time. Bruce Poole (an alumnus of Bibendum in its heyday) and Nigel Platts-Martin have been the restaurant's owners since 1995, and you can therefore expect a copious wine list. Although this is principally a neighbourhood restaurant, it is virtually impossible to just call in; reservations need to be made some time in advance, and tables at sensible dinner times are usually unattainable.

The food is classic French, with a few Spanish and Italian excursions, and the cheese board is a delight. The ground-floor dining room has slender chairs and simple tableware, and the close proximity of the tables helps to relax the atmosphere. This is another restaurant with interesting and well-chosen art on its walls. ○

Above **All manner of ingredients, sometimes weird and often wonderful, at Brixton Market.**

32 **Franco Manca** Unit 4, Market Row, SW9 8LD
020 7738 3021 www.francomanca.co.uk

More than just a local favourite, this most modern of Neapolitan-style pizzerias is cooking up a reputation as the best of its type in the whole of London. Devised by the multi-talented Giuseppe Mascoli, the menu is straightforward, with pizzas numbered from one to six. All are made using a slow-rising sourdough base that is blast-cooked at 500°C, or nearly 1000°F. Wow, that's hot. This treatment locks in the flour's natural aroma and moisture, which gives both soft centres and crusty edges (cornicione). The toppings – from the tomato and mozzarella to the Gloucester Old Spot ham, wild mushrooms and organic chorizo – are sourced with assiduous care, and naturally the flour comes only from Naples. While the final product is fun and relaxed, Giuseppe and his team elevate the process of making an excellent pizza to something akin to a mystical art.

The dining experience isn't exactly the most comfortable, with tables flanking the Brixton Market arcade, but it doesn't matter. Equally, it shouldn't be a concern that you can expect to queue: don't despair, the service is quick, thanks to those tuff brick ovens that generate such a fierce heat. Once you've secured your perch, the staff will quickly bring your order, and you can enjoy organic lemonade or a decent organic Italian red with it.

Rumours are rife that we are soon to see Franco Manca outlets popping up all over London. Good news for us all. ○

Giuseppe Mascoli

The best restaurants in London I recommend are Galvin la Chapelle for French food, Bocca di Lupo for Italian, Moro for Spanish, and Dinings in Great Portland Street for great sushi.

Co-owner, Franco Manca

Above **Pure theatre, preparing the dough for the ovens at Franco Manca.** Right **Giuseppe Mascoli, owner of Franco Manca.**

Cherry Amaretti

by Bridget Hugo of Wild Caper and
joint founder of Franco Manca

Makes approximately 40 biscuits

720 g (1 lb 7 oz) ground almonds
400 g (13 oz) caster sugar
100 g (3 1/2 oz) glacé cherries, finely chopped
finely grated zest of 2 large lemons
2 heaped tablespoons honey
very small pinch of salt
300 g (10 oz) egg whites (about 8 large eggs)
plenty of icing sugar, for dusting

Combine the ground almonds and sugar in a large bowl. Add the chopped cherries and lemon zest and distribute within the dry ingredients using your fingertips (as for a crumble).

In a separate bowl, add the honey and salt to the egg whites and beat with an electric hand whisk until stiff. Fold this into the dry ingredients using a large metal spoon.

Cover 2 flat baking sheets with baking parchment. Put 2–3 cm (an inch or so) of icing sugar in a wide shallow bowl.

Spoon 25–30 g (1–1 1/2 oz) portions of the mixture into the bowl of icing sugar. Every few spoons, form these portions of mixture into balls. Toss the icing sugar over them, then pick them up with your fingertips and shake them very lightly around in the palm of your hand. (Be generous with the icing sugar so that the mixture does not stick to your hands.)

Gently drop the balls on to the baking tray from a low height (just enough to flatten the bottoms of the balls when they land). They should be evenly spaced.

After the breads have been baked and the temperature in my wood ovens has dropped significantly, the passive heat is enough to bake these biscuits. However, the baking trays are in direct contact with the oven's stone tiles, so there is a small risk that the residual heat may burn the bottoms of the biscuits. If using a convection oven you won't have to worry about this.

Bake in a preheated oven, 180°C (350°F), Gas Mark 4, for around 15–20 minutes, or until the amaretti start to turn golden. A slightly chewy centre is to be expected from this recipe, and it is a cross between a biscuit and a meringue that makes these amaretti so delicious.

However, there are occasions when I am after a crunchier version, so for this I twice bake the biscuits so they become very crunchy. Small chunks of these delicious amaretti are one of the ingredients in our Wild Granola.

Above **Delicious amaretti, ideal at anytime of the day.**

Gail's Bakery 64 Northcote Road, SW11 6QL
020 7924 6330 www.gailsbread.co.uk

Replacing the Lighthouse Bakery, Gail's continues the tradition of
excellent baking on this site, even superseding its predecessor in terms
of quality, which is a very high achievement. The area is known as
'Nappy Valley', thanks to the endless streams of buggies that traverse
Northcote Road, and Gail's is a firm favourite with both mothers and
children, who love the excellent biscuits and cakes. This is an artisan
bakery of some note, with an international range of breads all baked
without preservatives – just flour, yeast, water and salt.

    The adjoining cafe is a delight, with lots of young children
making for a lively clientele. Gail's has started to roll out across
London, and while this activity always makes us wary, there seems
to be no loss of quality. ◉

The Hive Honey Shop 93 Northcote Road, SW11 6PL
020 7924 6233 www.thehivehoneyshop.co.uk

This place is special, particularly at a time when the bee population is
declining and conservation groups are alerting the public to the perils of
collapsing bee numbers. The tiny store houses a glass-fronted hive with
20,000 bees, and James Hamill, the owner and head beekeeper, creates
his own honey from several apiaries around London. You can also find
beekeeping equipment, protective clothing, beeswax, honeycombs,
royal jelly and much more here. ◉

M. Moen & Sons 24 The Pavement, SW4 0JA
020 7622 1624 www.moen.co.uk

This excellent butcher's shop has a noteworthy history, but more
importantly has moved with the times: modern and forward-thinking,
it also offers cheeses, store cupboard essentials, marinades for barbecues,
potted things, oils, chutneys and much more. An essential resource for
local households. ◉

Above
**The charming
and homely
Rosie's deli cafe.**
Left **Outside
The Hive Honey
Shop in Clapham
Junction.**

Rosie's Deli Café 14e Market Row, SW9 8LD
020 7733 0054 www.rosielovell.co.uk

'Cute', 'adorable' and 'quirky' are some of the words that might come to mind when you step inside Rosie's. With Brixton Market on her doorstep, Rosie Lovell has created a lovely, understated café and deli with delicious and simple food. Baking is the highlight and the 'help yourself to a slice' service adds a homely spin. The background music and little trinkets and notices around this tiny single room add amusement and joy.

Rosie is a bit of phenomenon in achieving so much in such a short time. Her very personal book *Spooning With Rosie* tells the story, with charming anecdotes and illustrations. ●

Sophie Moody's Lemon Lime Drizzle Cake

Serves 8

125 g (4 oz) butter, plus extra for greasing
2 lemons
1 lime
225 g (7½ oz) golden caster sugar, plus 3 extra teaspoons
3 large free-range eggs
200 g (7 oz) self-raising flour
4 teaspoons natural yogurt
1 tablespoon poppy seeds, plus a pinch for the top
190 g (6½ oz) g icing sugar, sifted

Preheat the oven to 180°C (350°F), Gas Mark 4, and thoroughly grease a loaf tin 30 cm (12 inches) in length.

In a mixing bowl beat the butter with a electric hand whisk until soft. Finely grate in the zest of 1 of the lemons and the lime (keep the fruit for later). Beating continuously, gradually add the 225 g (7½ oz) caster sugar. Beat in the eggs one at a time. Discard your electric whisk in favour of a spatula and carefully fold in the flour, making sure you reach right to the bottom to combine it fully. Finally mix in the yogurt and poppy seeds.

Pour the batter into the tin and bake in the oven for 45 minutes. When it is cooked through, a toothpick will come out of the cake clean.

To make the drizzle topping, squeeze the juice of the zested lemon and lime into a small saucepan and add the remaining 3 teaspoons of caster sugar. Heat over a low heat until the sugar has dissolved, then pour over the warm cake immediately. Sophie suggests making a few holes with a toothpick to allow the syrup to sink into the cake. Set aside for 20 minutes to cool and absorb the syrup in the tin.

When the cake is cool, turn it out on to a wire rack to cool completely. To make the icing, finely grate the zest of the remaining lemon into a measuring jug, stir in the icing sugar and the juice of the lemon. Beat well to remove any lumps and then pour half the icing over the cake. Spread out to the edges with a palette knife before pouring over the remainder. Sprinkle with a few more poppy seeds and leave to set before serving.

Recipe featured in *Something Old and Something New* by Rosie Lovell, Kyle Books

Above **Rosie Lovell taking a deserved rest and enjoying a slice of cake and a cup of tea in her bijou café.**

Trinity 4 The Polygon, SW4 0JG
020 7622 1199 www.trinityrestaurant.co.uk

Adam Byatt has returned to the area where he first made his name with his much-admired Thyme restaurant. In the intervening years he moved up west to The Hospital, a flashy private members' club, but things didn't work out and he quickly became an outpatient. While the experience might have been painful for Adam, it has proved ultimately to the benefit of this part of south London, to which he has returned with a more confident and sophisticated offering.

The restaurant has already won two very significant awards, the AA's 'London Restaurant of the Year' *and* 'Best Local Restaurant in London' from *Time Out*. Some even claim that Trinity is rapidly coming to pose a threat to Chez Bruce's number one position in the area.

Looking at the menus, you might feel a little confused as to the direction of the food and find it hard to categorize the offering. Don't worry about it: just think of it all as an expression of Adam's personal culinary aspirations. That said, the best dish has got to be the slow-cooked bavette steak with béarnaise, roast bone marrow, land cress and triple-cooked chips.

The bright young staff are ultra-friendly, and a window seat on a warm summer's evening is a pleasure. For a neighbourhood restaurant the wine list is also admirable, if a little pricey. ◉

Above **The Trinity dining room.**
Right **Adam Byatt.**

Above and right **Iles Flottante service at the table at Trinity.**

Plaice, Mussels, Charred Leeks, Samphire and Monk's Beard

Serves 2

250 g (8 oz) mussels, cleaned
1 large plaice, filleted and skinned with bones reserved
100 g (3½ oz) samphire
5 g (½ oz) butter
1 bunch of monk's beard
salt and freshly ground black pepper

For the mayonnaise

1 cucumber
250 ml (8 fl oz) vegetable oil
2 egg yolks
1 teaspoon Dijon mustard
10 ml (scant ½ fl oz) Cabernet Sauvignon vinegar
juice of 1 lemon
salt and freshly ground black pepper

For the sauce

12½ young leeks
100 ml (3½ fl oz) olive oil
½ onion, roughly chopped
1 stick celery, roughly chopped
1 bay leaf
peppercorns
20 ml (1 fl oz) crème fraîche

First make the mayonnaise: place the cucumber under a grill to char the skin all over. Strip the charred skin from the cucumber and blend with the vegetable oil in a blender or food processor – discard the cucumber middle. Add the egg yolks, mustard, salt and vinegar and blend well (or whisk by hand in a bowl). Season with a little of the lemon juice to taste, and blend again. Reserve the rest of the lemon juice for the sauce. With the machine running or whisking vigorously by hand, very slowly pour in the rest of the vegetable oil until the mixture has emulsified, then adjust the consistency to your liking with a splash of cold water and season with salt and pepper. Store in an airtight container in the refrigerator (it will keep for up to 3 days).

To make the sauce, cut the dark green tops from the 2 whole leeks, slice the white parts finely and set aside. Put the green tops in a frying pan, add the olive oil and place over a high heat until charred. Season, cover with a lid and leave to cool.

Make a stock by roughly chopping the the remaining leek half, add to a large saucepan with the onion, celery, plaice bones, the bay leaf and peppercorns and sweat in a little butter over a gentle heat for 5 minutes. Add enough water to just cover

and place a piece of greaseproof paper cut to fit, on the surface then simmer for 30 minutes. Once cooked, strain the stock through muslin or a clean cloth into a small saucepan, then continue to cook over a high heat until it has reduced by a third.

Rinse the mussels and discard any that do not close when tapped. Take the plaice fillets and score the top-side lightly. Season and roll up each fillet, skin-side tucked inwards. Place the mussels, white leek rings, samphire, the stock, rolled plaice and a knob of butter in an ovenproof dish and cover with greaseproof paper.

Bring to the boil on the stove, then bake in a preheated oven at 190°C (375°F), Gas Mark 5, with a lid on for 4 minutes or until the fish is firm and the mussels have opened. Discard any mussels which do not open. Meanwhile, gently reheat the charred green leek tops and peel off the two outside layers to remove any grit.

Remove the fish, mussels and samphire from the dish and keep warm whilst you finish the sauce. Whisk the crème fraîche into the juices in the dish along with the remaining lemon juice to taste. Add the monk's beard and reduce the sauce over a high heat for 1 minute.

To serve, dress 2 plates with the cucumber skin mayonnaise. Arrange the samphire, leeks and mussels around the plates, then lay the plaice on top of the samphire. Place the charred leek on top and drizzle over the sauce.

Right **Large opening windows make Trinity a great location for lunch on a summer's day.**

More places to visit in the area

Above **Innovative presentation at Trinity for pigs' trotters on toasted sourdough with crackling and fried quail's eggs.**

Bennett's Oyster Bar and Brasserie
7–9 Battersea Square, SW11 3RA
020 7223 5545 www.bennettsbrasserie.com
A mini gastrodrome, with an all-day brasserie, bakery and shop selling wines, flowers and various groceries.

Bistro DéLICAT
124 Northcote Road, SW11 6QU
020 7924 3566 www.bistrodelicat.com
It's a pity there aren't more wines from the proprietor's homeland on the list at this small Austrian-focused bistro. Still, we can content ourselves with Viennese beef goulash, *wiener schnitzel*, sauerkraut and *apfelstrudel*.

Cantinetta
162–4 Lower Richmond Road, SW15 1LY
020 8780 3131 www.cantinetta.co.uk
A new modern Italian eatery with an ex-Locatelli chef that has risen from the ashes of the Phoenix. Go in the summer and sit in the garden.

Tom Ilic
123 Queenstown Road, SW8 3RH
020 7622 0555 www.tomilic.co.uk
Before establishing his own place, Tom worked his way around London gaining a reputation for his skill in breaking down a pig and charming diners with his gutsy offal dishes. A highlight on his current menu is braised pig's cheek with chorizo.

Upstairs Bar and Restaurant
89b Acre Lane, entrance on Branksome Road, SW2 5TN 020 7733 8855
www.upstairslondon.com
It might be small, with only 25 covers in the dining room, but its worth a visit. The menu is also confidently small, with just three first-course, three main-course and three dessert options to choose from, plus cheese and a few daily specials.

Wallace & Co
146 Upper Richmond Road, SW15 2SW
020 8780 0052 www.wallaceandco.com
Set up by Gregg Wallace, famed for his *MasterChef* television series, with John Torode, this is a simple café with many of the vegetables and salads sourced from chefs' favourite Secretts Farm in Surrey.

Wild Caper
11–13 Market Row, SW9 8LB
020 7737 4410 www.wildcaper.co.uk
Call in to this small café with great sandwiches as part of your trip to Brixton Market. They make their own bread using a Neapolitan mother sourdough starter that is allowed to ferment for a minimum of 24 hours, before being baked in the nearby Franco Manca pizza ovens using the residual heat. They also bake *panuozzi*, Italian flame bread.

Bayswater
Kensington
Notting Hill

Over the past 40 years or so, Notting Hill has risen from being an area of social deprivation to become one of the most affluent and desirable neighbourhoods in London. The annual Carnival started in 1965, initially in an attempt to help quell the race riots of the late 1950s. It is now one of the most colourful events in London: the Afro-Caribbean community embraced the Carnival, and Notting Hill hasn't looked back. During the last weekend in August, when the Carnival takes place, the streets are flooded with an influx of over a million people.

Outside Carnival, the area has gained global fame thanks to Richard Curtis's romantic comedy *Notting Hill*, which sent property values rocketing and put Portobello Market on every tourist's to-do list. Commercial property rents have undergone an equally stratospheric increase, and the number of independent traders is dwindling rapidly. We can only assume that the areas's restaurateurs and food retailers struggle to make any sort of profit. So please, support the independents and avoid the big groups.

Neighbouring Bayswater, a cosmopolitan zone with large Greek, Arab, Brazilian, Russian and American communities, has tried to share some of Notting Hill's success. One of the main efforts in this regard has been the re-launch of Whiteleys Shopping Centre. When it first opened in the late 19th century, Whiteley's was London's first department store, and even included a golf course on the roof. When the management swapped a huge McDonald's restaurant for the excellent Le Café Anglais, great hope and encouragement was abound, sadly, other transformative efforts have failed.

Kensington has never needed, nor wanted, to be regenerated.

Angelus 4 Bathurst Street, W2 2SD
020 7402 0083 www.angelusrestaurant.co.uk

A pleasant eccentricity runs through this small 'brasserie de luxe', from its Art Nouveau-styled interiors, spiked with modern and slightly outlandish flourishes and carefully retained elements of the listed building that was once a historic pub, to the patron himself, while incorporating the menu and a few other elements along the way. Thierry Thomasin, from Gascony, heartland of foie gras and Armagnac, was schooled at Le Gavroche and has achieved many accolades for his expertise in wine. An instantly recognizable figure, and he drives the service brigade towards excellence with passion and (some say) ferocity.

Even the position of this restaurant – next door to Hyde Park Stables and just a short trot from the park itself – is slightly odd. While the area boasts some very smart residential addresses and is also quite central, it also has some pretty dodgy hotels and unattractive elements. But despite all this, Angelus seems to work and has a distinct and enjoyable charm.

The signature dish is foie gras crème brûlée – sounds weird but again seems to work, like so many other aspects of Thierry's French refuge. ◉

Assaggi 39 Chepstow Place, W2 4TS 020 7792 5501

Although chef Nino Sassu is from Sardinia, the food at this discreet and special restaurant is more generally Italian. The portions are generous and the flavours full on. If you are not clear about any items on the menu, you can be assured that the delightful and knowledgeable staff can eloquently explain exactly how each dish is prepared, the component ingredients, and how wonderful it tastes. We particularly recommend the Pecorino con carpegna e rucola as a first course, followed by carre' d'agnello con fave. And the veal chop is pretty damn good. The taglionlini al granchio, made with nine different herbs and crushed walnuts, is a lovely pasta dish. They don't have a dessert menu: the staff simply visit your table and tell you what Nino has available that night. (PP) The bavarese with espresso coffee is a particular favourite of mine. Don't expect an over-designed dining room: part of the charm of this place is that it is simply a room above a half-decent pub. It's also reassuringly expensive. ◉

Above **Nino Sassu in the kitchen at Assaggi.**

Books for Cooks 4 Blenheim Crescent, W11 1NN
020 7221 1992 www.booksforcooks.com

If, as Janet Street-Porter claimed, cookery books are the new porn for the socially ambitious, then Books for Cooks is a hard-core sex shop. At the rear of the shop are a small test kitchen and a café, where you can enjoy a simple lunch or cake while you enjoy a cursory read through your new purchase. ◉

Wild Garlic Soup with Pan-Fried Frogs' Legs, Burgundy Snails and Roasted Garlic

Serves 4

1 garlic bulb, plus 1 clove
olive oil
1 shallot, finely diced
25 g (1 oz) unsalted butter, softened
15 g (1/2 oz) chopped parsley
6 pairs frogs' legs
300 g (10 oz) wild garlic leaves
1 onion, finely diced
1 litre (13/4 pints) chicken stock
1 baking potato, sliced
1 sprig of thyme
200 ml (7 fl oz) double cream
12 large cooked Burgundy snails
salt and freshly ground black pepper
crème fraîche, to serve

Preheat the oven to 180°C (350°F) Gas Mark 4. Season the bulb of garlic with salt, pepper and a little olive oil, then wrap in foil and bake in the oven for 45 minutes or until the garlic is very soft. Remove from the oven and allow to cool slightly. Once cooled, cut in half, squeeze out the roasted garlic and reserve.

Sweat the shallot in a little olive oil over a low heat until very soft but not coloured. Peel and crush the remaining garlic clove and add it to the shallot. Continue cooking for 1 minute then allow to cool. Once the shallot and garlic mixture is cool, mix with the softened butter and chopped parsley. Roll into cylinders in clingfilm and place in the refrigerator until needed.

For the frogs' legs, use a pair of scissors to remove the legs from the thigh joint. French trim the drumsticks to neaten, removing the flesh and skin from the bones.

To make the soup, wash and dry the wild garlic leaves and roughly chop them. Sweat the onion in a little olive oil until very soft but not coloured. In a separate pan, bring the chicken stock to the boil. Once the onion is soft, add the sliced potato, garlic leaves and thyme. Once the leaves have wilted, add the double cream and bring to the boil. Add the boiling chicken stock and simmer for 10 minutes. Taste and adjust the seasoning, then blend in a liquidizer until very smooth. Pass the soup through a sieve, adjust the seasoning again if necessary and keep warm.

Remove the shallot butter from the fridge, cut it into slices and melt in a frying pan over a medium heat. Add the frogs' legs and snails and pan-fry until golden brown and cooked through.

To serve, spoon 6 dots of the roasted garlic on to 4 large soup bowls or pasta plates. Top the garlic with 3 frogs' legs and 3 snails per plate. Warm the soup and pour it into the bowls.

Spoon a little crème fraîche into each bowl, drizzle over a little olive oil and serve.

Above **Wine expert and experienced restaurateur Thierry Tomasin at Angelus.**

Le Café Anglais 8 Porchester Gardens, W2 4DB
020 7221 1415 www.lecafeanglais.co.uk

The menu at Le Café Anglais is one of the most enchanting in London. It includes lots of lovely things that you want to eat, and is extensive without making it too difficult to choose. At the top of the carte is a selection of hors d'oeuvres including Parmesan custard with anchovy toast that the London food world now associates with this brasserie. Next comes a fine selection of oysters and a seasonal selection of first courses. The main course options include a range of ingredients cooked on the fiery rotisserie that can be seen from the dining room.

Rowley Leigh, the chef patron, is one of London's long-established restaurant personalities, highly regarded by his peers, by very hard-to-please critics, by past employees and by loyal customers alike. Every element of this place appears to have Rowley's stamp of approval, from the menu graphics and the wine list to the evocative name, which sends you on a journey of the imagination to 19th-century Paris.

The stylish Art Deco dining room boasts high ceilings, angular chandeliers that shed a soft light and huge windows that allow natural light to flood in. A recently added bar and oyster display now enables locals to visit more often without staying for lunch or dinner. (PP) I recently called in for a glass of wine and a few nibbles before heading off to dinner at the great Sally Clarke's restaurant just up the road.

Rowley is also one of the country's pre-eminent cookery writers. His weekly column in the *Financial Times* is unmissable. ◉

Above **The open kitchen and rôtisserie in the background at Le Café Anglais.** Below **Le Café Anglais' attractive Art Deco-inspired dining room.**

Parmesan Custard and Anchovy Toast

Serves 8

300 ml (1/2 pint) single cream
300 ml (1/2 pint) milk
100 g (3 1/2 oz) finely grated Parmesan
4 egg yolks
salt
white pepper
cayenne pepper
12 anchovy fillets
50 g (2 oz) unsalted butter
8 very thin slices of pain de campagne

Mix the cream, milk and all but 1 tablespoon of the cheese in a large bowl and warm gently over a pan of boiling water until the cheese has melted. Allow to cool completely before whisking in the egg yolks, salt, finely milled white pepper and a little cayenne pepper.

Lightly butter 8 china moulds or small ramekins 75 ml (3 fl oz) in capacity and divide the mixture between them.

Place the moulds in a deep roasting tray and pour in boiling water to come half-way up the side of the moulds. Cover the tray with buttered baking paper and bake in a preheated oven, 150°C (300°F), Gas Mark 2, for 15 minutes or until the mixture has just set.

Meanwhile, pound the anchovies and butter to a smooth paste and spread over 4 of the slices of bread. Cover with the remaining bread and toast in a sandwich maker or panini machine.

Sprinkle the remaining Parmesan over the cooked custards and brown the tops under a preheated hot grill.

Cut the toasted anchovy sandwiches into little fingers and serve alongside the custards.

46

Clarke's 122 and 124 Kensington Church Street, W8 4BH
020 7221 9225 www.sallyclarke.com

Following a four-year stint in California, where she became friends with
Alice Waters at the seminal Chez Panisse, Sally returned to London in
1984 and established Clarke's. Like Chez Panisse, the restaurant originally
offered a no-choice daily-changing menu based on what was good, fresh
and seasonal. Some years ago this policy was changed, presumably in
response to public tastes. In any case, after well over 20 years Sally had
proved her point.

(PP) Last year I enjoyed a very special evening at Clarke's with a menu
devoted to the great Elizabeth David. We were seated in the basement,
right next to the kitchen, which I thought was lovely and very homely,
especially when Sally herself shaved the white truffle on to my risotto.

In 1988 Sally opened the adjoining shop, which has flourished ever
since. The bakery is renowned across London, with many leading delis,
hotels and restaurants serving its breads and pastries. The shop stocks
an extensive range of excellent fruit, vegetables, larder essentials, sauces,
salads and much more. It also offers a seasonal menu (changing twice
weekly) of sweet and savoury cakes and tarts, from apricot clafoutis and
bitter chocolate cake to tarts of oven-dried vine tomato, goats' cheese
and basil, and asparagus, leek and Parmesan. ○

Left **The ground
floor restaurant
at Clarke's is
very popular
with London's
intelligencia.**

Right **Sally Clarke
continues to oversee
excellent standards
at her brilliant
restaurant.**

The Cow 89 Westbourne Park Road, W2 5QH
020 7221 0021 www.thecowlondon.co.uk

The Cow is a Notting Hill institution and helped fashion the original and best format of the gastropub movement, while the landlord, Tom Conran, is the evergreen local champion.

Downstairs is a great boozer, or saloon bar, with proper ales, bottled British and continental beers, and much more. The short-order kitchen on the ground floor is perfect for lunch. The menu includes fish stew, and sausages braised in beer and onions; or maybe a pint of prawns or a plate of oysters will hit the spot. It's all good grub at reasonable prices.

Upstairs, the small dining room serves some of the best food in Notting Hill. That doesn't mean that it is striving to chase stars, it simply has an attentively planned menu and first-rate cooks in the kitchen, while the ingredients are highly seasonal and come from the finest sources – Tom is passionate about provenance, good animal husbandry and artisan producers. The menu is proudly British, but with a few detours to the Continent. ◉

Tom Conran

" I would much rather shop in a specialist food store than a supermarket, although you may have a broader choice in the bigger shops the actual experience can leave you cold. There are a number of local shops that I love, the Athenian Grocer on Moscow Road for Greek provisions and fresh vegetables and salads imported direct from Cyprus. Tawana on Chepstow Road for eastern ingredients (it's a bit scruffy but always has what you need at the right price). I like the Lisboa Deli on Golbourne Road for Portugese cheeses, wine and charcuterie and their patisserie over the road for orgasmic custard tarts. But if I had to choose one shop as an all time favourite it would have to be Garcia's on Portobello Road.

Owner, The Cow, Crazy Homies

Have a
GUINNESS
when you're tired

Right **The upstairs dining room at The Cow.**

Crazy Homies 125 Westbourne Park Road, W2 5QL
020 7727 6771 www.crazyhomieslondon.co.uk

Inspired by the street vendors and taquerias of Mexico, Tom Conran
and his crew have created a neighbourhood hangout where you can
really let your hair down.

In a former life, this was the shebeen visited by Christine Keeler
(the infamous seductress of the Profumo affair) and Stephen Ward with
Lucky Gordon. Now the space has been sensitively reshaped to suit Tom's
idiosyncratic style, with plenty of help from Dutch artist Mr Wim. The
small tequila bar on the ground floor has cosy corners in which to enjoy
your totopos corn chips with salsa or a taquitos-rolled tortilla. The menu
in the subterranean dining space extends to burros, enchiladas, light
salads and shrimp cocktails. Every meal ends with churros (doughnuts)
with chocolate. The beer and tequila list is the best in town. ○

E&O 14 Blenheim Crescent, W11 1NN
020 7229 5454 www.eando.co.uk

This is another celebrity hotspot by Will Ricker, serving great Eastern
and Oriental (E&O) pan-Asian food and cocktails in glamorous and
sometimes noisy surroundings. ○

El Pirata Detapas 115 Westbourne Grove, W2 4UP
020 7727 5000 www.elpiratadetapas.co.uk

This impressive Spanish restaurant shot to the attention of Londoners
thanks to Gordon Ramsay's *Best Restaurants* television show, on which
El Pirata impressed the judges and beat off some very tough competition
to reach the final stages.

Though not the most inspiring of spaces, it's not drab, and some might
describe the dark colours and low lighting as sexy. In the front of the dining
room the tables are quite close together, which encourages conversation
with your neighbours and offers a sneak preview of the food before it
arrives at your table. The Spanish staff are of the young and funky variety,
informally dressed and liberally tattooed, which complements the setting.

The food is a combination of classic and contemporary Spanish fare,
including the now ubiquitous black risotto served with squid and prawns,
plus a choice of paellas and plenty of medium-sized dishes with gutsy
flavours. Pork cheeks with carrot purée and red wine shallots, wood pigeon
with fig, and rib eye skewers with romesco sauce are all deeply satisfying.

Great for a quick Cava with light tapas, El Pirata is equally suitable
for a leisurely supper with several healthy glugs of Rioja. ○

Tom Pemberton

The best restaurant in London for
great atmosphere and ambience –
St. John. They also have the best
cakes and pâtisserie.

Chef patron, Hereford Road

Top left **Relaxed
times at Tom
Conran's Crazy
Homies.**
Above and right
**Expertly carved
jamon at El Pirata
Detapas.**

Electric Brasserie 191 Portobello Road, W11 2ED
020 7908 9696 www.electricbrasserie.com

The Electric is an essential part of modern Notting Hill life. The landmark building includes an ornate cinema that is operated in a thoroughly up-to-date manner, with large and comfortable armchairs, footstools and side tables, where you can also get proper food and drinks before the movie. The ground-floor Anglo-French brasserie forms the epicentre of cool Notting Hill. Open for breakfast, lunch and dinner seven days a week, it has a menu that addresses every taste. The breakfast and brunch menus are particularly appropriate to the environment. Upstairs is a private members' club, as in other Soho House outposts. ●

Geales 2 Farmer Street, W8 7SN 020 7727 7528 www.geales.com

In the spring of 2011, the London launch of Champagne Salon 1999 was held at Geales – and that pretty much sets the scene for this posh chippy. Geales first opened in 1939, and in 2007 it was given a refit that confirmed its position as the original proudly swanky chip shop. Expect battered fish from the top drawer in the form of sea bass or Dover sole, or lobster and chips accompanied by a bottle of Krug or maybe Dom Perignon. Also on the wine list are fine white burgundies: Meursault, Montrachet and Corton Charlemagne. You can also enjoy decent potted shrimps, prawn cocktails, oysters and whitebait, followed by traditional old-school puddings. ●

Above **Battered fish, chips and mushy peas at Geales,** possibly the dish most synonymous with London, at least as far as the tourists are concerned.

Whole Grilled Plaice with Brown Shrimps, Nettles, Ramsons and Ramps

Serves 1

1 whole fresh plaice, trimmed
25 g (1 oz) butter
1 garlic clove, finely chopped
handful of cooked peeled brown shrimps
1 bunch of nettles, blanched by plunging into boiling water for 1 minute
small handful of ramps (wild leeks), finely chopped
small handful of ramsons (wild garlic), finely chopped
extra virgin olive oil
lemon juice, to dress
salt and freshly ground black pepper
a little grated nutmeg, to serve

Season the plaice with salt and pepper and place dark skin-side up in an ovenproof frying pan. Dot a little of the butter on top and place under a preheated hot grill. When the skin has browned nicely and crisped, turn over, dot with a little more butter and grill briefly until light golden in colour. Remove the fish from the pan on to a serving plate and set aside to keep warm.

Take the fish pan with its juices, add the remaining butter and the garlic, and sauté the brown shrimps over a meduim heat until hot. Add the blanched nettles, ramps and ramsons to the pan and wilt down, stirring lightly as needed for a couple of minutes.

Serve with the fish and dress with extra virgin olive oil and freshly squeezed lemon juice, and season with salt, freshly ground black pepper and grated nutmeg.

The Grocer on Elgin 6 Elgin Crescent, W11 2HX
020 7221 3844 www.thegroceron.com

While ready meals from supermarkets and corner shops are often full of preservatives and devoid of any discernible flavour, thankfully a more healthy and tasty alternative exists for the time-pressed workaholic in the form of the Grocer on Elgin. Here they prepare restaurant-standard meals and present them in sophisticated vacuum packs or sealed in parfait jars. Dishes such as Thai vegetable curry, duck leg confit or guinea fowl tagine can quickly be reheated to provide an ideal midweek sofa supper. ○

Hereford Road 3 Hereford Road, W2 4AB
020 7727 1144 www.herefordroad.org

If you order from the set lunch menu at this restaurant you will experience some of the best-value dining in London. At the time of writing, the price for three really excellent courses is just £15.50 – an exceptionally good price for cooking of this standard. The à la carte menu is also attractive and keenly priced. Everything about this restaurant shouts honesty and sincerity. Seasonal fare and a wide knowledge of delicious and often under-used ingredients are also conspicuous features. And the portions are generous without being daunting. There's a lot to like about this place. From the setting on a wide-ish and quiet street just off the main drag that is Westbourne Grove, to the mini-banquettes for two opposite the bar and the generous booth seating at the back of the room, the interior oozes a refreshing simplicity.

Tom Pemberton, an alumnus of St. John Bread and Wine, is the chef patron, and much of the menu at Hereford Road echoes the St. John idiom. On a recent visit, Tom was the only person in the entirely open kitchen. From his vantage point at the entrance to this former Victorian butchers' shop, Tom offers his guests an enthusiastic welcome and bids sincere thanks and farewells while at the same time preparing all the food. Very impressive!

A beautiful example both of a neighbourhood restaurant and of somewhere to journey to, especially if you want a great deal (in both senses). ○

Above
Tom Pemberton in his kitchen.
Right **The bar tables at Hereford Road.**

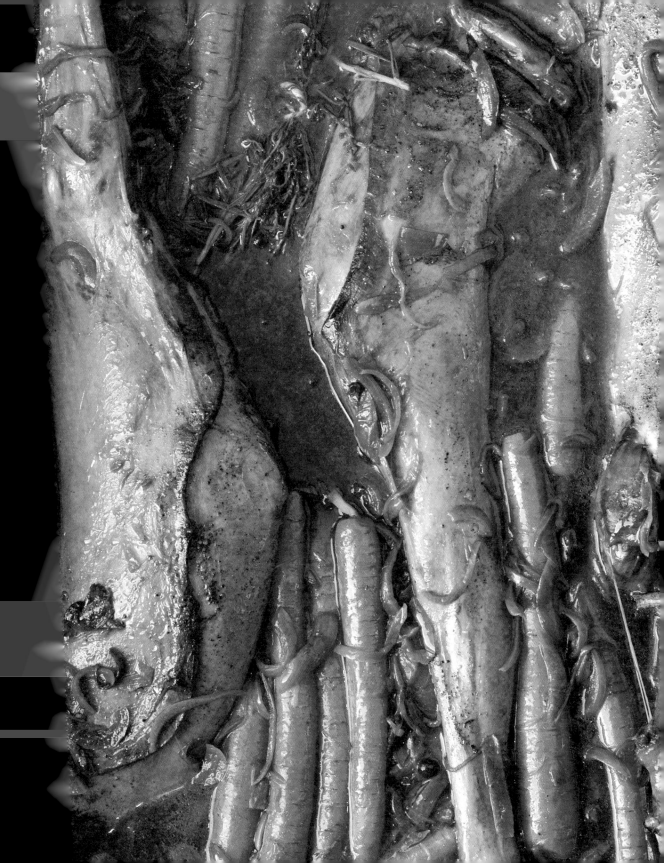

Lambs' Sweetbreads, Pearl Barley, Parsley and Mint

Serves 4

2 onions
2 leeks
6 celery stalks
1 bay leaf
juice of 1 lemon
12 large lambs' sweetbreads
200 g (7 oz) pearl barley, rinsed
1 bunch of thyme, tied with string
300 ml (1/2 pint) olive oil
1 bunch of flat-leaf parsley, leaves picked
1 bunch of mint, leaves picked
2 round shallots, peeled and sliced
1 teaspoon capers
approx 1/4 volume of olive oil to lemon juice used
1 garlic clove, finely chopped
oil and butter, for frying
splash of sherry vinegar
salt and freshly ground black pepper

Fill a large pan with cold, salted water. Slice 1 onion, 1 leek and 3 stalks of celery, and add to the pan with the bay leaf. Bring to the boil, squeeze in the juice of half the lemon, and blanch the sweetbreads for 4 or 5 minutes until firm. Remove the sweetbreads and peel off the fat and membrane while still warm, season with salt and pepper and set aside. Discard the stock.

Put the pearl barley in a pan with 750 ml (1 1/4 pints) water, the remaining onion, leek and celery, roughly chopped in large pieces so you can remove them easily at the end of the cooking time. Add the bunch of thyme and cook until the pearl barley is tender, following the packet instructions.

Drain, discard the vegetables and thyme, and dress the pearl barley in a little olive oil. Leave to cool, then toast briefly on a large flat baking tray in a preheated oven, 180°C (350°F), Gas Mark 4, for 20 minutes.

Roughly chop the parsley and mint leaves and place in a mixing bowl with the shallots, capers and pearl barley, and keep warm.

Make a dressing by mixing together the olive oil, remaining lemon juice and garlic.

Heat a large frying pan over a high heat, then reduce the heat to medium and quickly fry the seasoned sweetbreads in oil and butter until golden brown all over but still moist inside. Add a splash of sherry vinegar to the pan, briefly deglaze (by scraping and dissolving any deposits in the pan with a wooden spoon), stir, then take off the heat. Add the hot sweetbreads to the pearl barley mixture, dress with the olive oil and lemon dressing and taste for seasoning before serving.

Whole Braised Roe Shoulder and Carrots

Serves 2 hungry people

1 whole roe deer shoulder, approximately 1.25 kg (2 1/2 lb) in weight
vegetable oil
6 large onions. thinly sliced
1/2 bottle red wine
splash of port
1/2 star anise
1/2 stick of cinnamon
3 juniper berries, crushed
1 clove
1/2 garlic bulb, cloves left whole
bunch of organic baby carrots, trimmed
enough chicken stock to cover, approximately 2.5 litres (4 pints)
salt and freshly ground black pepper

Preheat the oven to 220°C (425°F), Gas Mark 7.

Take a large, deep roasting tray big enough to completely enclose the shoulder and add a little oil. Season the roe shoulder with salt and pepper, place in the tray and brown on the stove over a high heat. Put in the oven to brown further for 5 minutes. Remove from the oven and reduce the oven temperature to 180°C (350°F), Gas Mark 4.

Remove the shoulder from the tray and set aside while you prepare the braising liquid in the tray. Sweat the onions down in the tray on the stove over a medium heat. Add the red wine and a large splash of port, increase the heat and reduce the liquid by three-quarters. Season by adding the star anise, cinnamon, juniper berries, clove and garlic.

Turn off the heat, place the roe shoulder back in the tray with the baby carrots and add enough stock to cover two-thirds of the meat. Cover the roasting tray with foil and braise in the oven for 3 1/2 hours. Remove the foil and cook uncovered for a further 20 minutes or until browned.

Taste the sauce and season if necessary before serving.

Hummingbird Bakery 133 Portobello Road, W11 2DY
020 7851 1795 www.hummingbirdbakery.com

A high-quality American home-baking shop, the Hummingbird Bakery
specializes in cupcakes, brownies, New York-style cheesecake, apple pie,
pecan pie, key lime pie, Mississippi mud pie, banana bread, sweet and
savoury muffins and great cookies. Drop in and try the cupcake special
of the day on your way to Portobello Market. ●

Launceston Place 1a Launceston Place, W8 5RL
020 7937 6912 www.launcestonplace-restaurant.co.uk

Tristan Welch, the chef of this very chi-chi restaurant – in terms of
both its interior and its food – is definitely one to watch. His reputation
for creating seasonal menus based on traditional British dishes is
rapidly growing, and we're sure it won't be long before he finds a
larger berth. ●

The Ledbury 127 Ledbury Road, W11 2AQ
020 7792 9090 www.theledbury.com

Once relatively rundown, Notting Hill is now home to City bankers,
high-flying lawyers and successful entrepreneurs, all generously
represented among the habitués of the Ledbury.

Having trained under Philip Howard at The Square in Mayfair
(see page 280), chef Brett Graham opened The Ledbury kitchens in
2005 and has already scooped a string of awards, not least the Michelin
man's approval. The restaurant now has two stars.

The menu is very modern haute cuisine, perhaps a little too
architectural and precise for our liking, with all manner of endless
ingredients crowding on to every plate. This appears to be the style
favoured by young chefs and Michelin inspectors, as the Ledbury is
now one of the most admired restaurants in London.

The wine list is comprehensive, and the restaurant is known to
host more fine wine events than any other in London. ●

Brett Graham

" I love Ottolenghi on Ledbury Road.
They sell great pastries and their
croissants are some of the best you
can find in London.

Head chef, The Ledbury

Above left **Cupcakes
at the Hummingbird
Bakery.**
Above right **The
rather dark interior
at Launceston Place.**

Right **An elegant
drinks trolley in
the tiny bar at
Launceston Place.**

Saturday in Notting Hill

A great way to explore the best of Notting Hill in a day.

– Start with breakfast or early brunch at Tom's Deli.
– Do a little shopping on the strip either side of Tom's and up and down Ledbury Road – it's just like New Bond Street, so be prepared.
– Call in at Melt to see a chocolate demo and the finest truffles.
– Admire the stunning food displays at Ottolenghi.
– Buy an Italian gift for a loved one (or treat yourself) at Negozio Classica.
– Head to The Cow for oysters and a Guinness.
– Brave the crowds and head to Portobello Market (avoid buying overpriced junk).
– Read a few chapters at Books for Cooks with a strong espresso.
– Pick up some rare delights at The Spice Shop or Garcia & Sons.
– Take in a film: relax in the leather armchairs at the Electric Cinema.
– If you've had enough, head next door for great ice cream at Dri Dri.
– For those with more stamina, carry on to E&O for an Asian-inspired martini.
– Finish with a swanky dinner, fine wine and professional service at The Ledbury.

C. Lidgate 110 Holland Park Avenue, W11 4UA
020 7727 8243 www.lidgates.com

David Lidgate runs this fourth-generation family butcher's with his son, and together they understand customer service at its best, with nothing being too much trouble. The butchers, who sport straw boaters and bow ties, are unflappable as they courteously respond to every demand. They sell excellent quality meats, some from royal estates, poultry, game in season, sausages and much more. If you want heather-fed Shetland lamb, a haunch of wild boar, or teal and other wild duck, this is the place to come.

Shepherd's and cottage pies made on the premises are very tasty, while pre-marinated meats, meatballs, kofta kebabs and jerk chicken are all ideal for midweek meals when you don't have either the time or the inclination to roast a large piece of meat. ◯

Above **The window display at C. Lidgate's is reason alone to stop and call in.**

Anna Hansen

The best butcher in London has to be C. Lidgate in Holland Park.

Owner, The Modern Pantry

Above **The perfect hamburger, fries and shake at Lucky 7.**

Lucky 7 127 Westbourne Park Road, W2 5QL
020 7727 6771 www.lucky7london.co.uk

The classic hamburger is at the heart of Lucky 7, but it also delivers so much more. The patty is 100 per cent aged organic Aberdeen Angus, the bun is baked locally to a special recipe, the red onion, tomato and pickle are chosen for flavour and are sliced by hand. It seems simple, but so many 'hamburger joints' don't offer these essential basics.

Tom Conran has created this bijou, authentic but modern East Coast-style diner with sensitivity. Booth seating, an open kitchen, authentically eclectic 1950s-style fittings and diner tableware have all been fused with irreverent artwork to create a snugly informal environment. Lucky 7 bridges the gap between a café and a restaurant with fast service and cool music making the perfect all-day all-comers' destination.

Jumbo Wally (pickled dill cucumbers), 'homeslaw', spicy black beans, beer-battered onion rings and tasty French fries complement the extensive choice of burgers. The milk shakes are the best – try the five-dollar shake. ○

Malabar 27 Uxbridge Street, W8 7TQ
020 7727 8800 www.malabar-restaurant.co.uk

(PP) When visiting Malabar I was immediately taken by the array of metal tabletop equipment. The food is served in traditional Indian fashion on metal thalis, and beakers, platters, coffee pots and other items are all in stainless steel. Speaking from experience, the cost of buying and replacing operating equipment from plates to glassware is uncertain and expensive, but everything here is unbreakable and, I suppose, less desirable to the petty thief. I find this utilitarian approach certainly works in this setting, and everything seems to looks even better once it has acquired a dimpled surface and attractive patina. It appears that the restaurant owners are kindly passing on the cost savings, providing delicious Indian food at modest prices. On Sunday lunchtimes children eat for free, and there is a buffet with a variety of curries and tandoori dishes, with multicoloured aniseed sweets rounding off all meals. ○

Nicolas Garcia

My favourite butcher is in west London: H.G. Walter in Barons Court is a small butcher that provides for restaurants as well as having a street shop. The quality is fantastic.

Manager, Albion and Boundary Restaurant

Above **The Malabar dining room and booth seating.**

Lamb Curry

Malabar

Pilau Rice

Serves 2

Stage one

500 g (1 lb) diced leg of lamb, washed
1 onion, finely chopped
4 garlic cloves, finely chopped
5 mm (¼ inch) piece of fresh root ginger, finely chopped
3 tomatoes, roughly chopped
1 tablespoon vegetable oil
4 bay leaves
5 whole cloves
8 peppercorns
½ stick cinnamon

Stage two

4 fresh green chillies (optional)
1 green pepper, deseeded and roughly chopped
1 tomato, deseeded and roughly chopped
7 cardamom pods
1 teaspoon ground coriander
½ teaspoon ground cumin
1 teaspoon paprika
1 teaspoon turmeric
large handful fresh coriander, chopped

Add all the ingredients from stage one to a large, heavy-based pot set over a low heat, cover the pot and leave to cook for 35 minutes. Leaving the lid on during the cooking should cut out the need to add any extra liquid. However check every 10 minutes and add a drop of water if it looks dry.

Slice the green chillies lengthways (if using), removing the seeds if you don't want the curry too hot, and chop finely. After the 35 minutes cooking time add the ingredients from stage two, except the coriander, to the pot, stir and cook for a further 30 minutes over a low heat.

Scatter over the fresh coriander to finish.

Serves 4

450 g (1 lb) basmati rice
3 cardamom pods
2 tablespoons light oil
3 garlic cloves, finely chopped
2.5 cm (1 inch) piece of fresh root ginger, finely chopped
1 small onion, finely chopped
3 bay leaves
6 peppercorns
6 whole cloves
½ stick cinnamon
½ teaspoon cumin seeds
pinch of good saffron (soaked in a very little water)
salt, to taste

Wash the rice under cold running water and leave to drain in a colander for as long as possible while you prepare the rest of your ingredients.

Break open the cardamom pods to reveal the seeds and discard the shells.

Place a large saucepan over a medium heat, add a tablespoon of light oil and sweat the garlic, ginger and onion until translucent. Add all the spices, except the saffron, and cook for a further 2–3 minutes to help to release the spices' natural oils. Reduce the heat to low and add the drained rice, stirring to coat the grains as one would for a risotto. Finally stir in the saffron in its water, and top up the pan with water 2.5 cm (1 inch) above the rice level. Add salt, bring to the boil and simmer for 4 minutes with a lid on. Turn off the heat and tie a tea towel round the lid to retain the steam. The rice will continue gently cooking until you are ready to use it.

A final tip: if you cook your rice before preparing any accompanying dishes it will have the time to steam and absorb any excess liquid. Result: beautiful fluffy rice every time!

Above **Children are very welcome and eat for free on Sunday at Malabar.**

Louise Nason

"

I always make a delicious meal when I buy fish from this great fish shop attached to Kensington Place Restaurant. Park outside on the double yellows – but watch out for a ticket! They deliver, which is very useful when preparing for a party.

Founder, Melt

Opposite **The chocolatier's marble work surface is at the heart of the Melt shop where you can watch the chocolatiers at work (left).**

Melt 59 Ledbury Road, W11 2AA
020 7727 5030 www.meltchocolates.com
Chocolate contains phenylethylamine, a chemical related to amphetamines, which has been shown to make us feel more alert, and at the same time imparts feelings of contentment. Phenylethylamine is also known as the 'love drug', as it mimics the chemistry of our brains when we are in love. Which is why chocolate has a reputation as an aphrodisiac. So go to Melt to get your phenylethylamine high!

The all-white minimalist open-plan kitchen inside the shop allows the team to pour large quantities of chocolate on to the counter in front of shoppers who can watch them at work, filling the air with a strong chocolate hit.

The range and choice at this excellent chocolate boutique is exceptional. It should also be said that the creativity and integrity of the management is also highly praiseworthy. ○

Negozio Classica 283 Westbourne Grove, W11 2QA
020 7034 0005 www.negozioclassica.co.uk
This small store, bar and lounge is devoted to Italian high-end style, and sells a range of exclusive products including knives from Tuscany, balsamico from Modena, buffalo cheese, pesto and wildflower honey. Or you can just call in for a cappuccino, a glass of wine or a grappa. ○

Royal China 13 Queensway, W2 4QJ
020 7221 2535 www.royalchinagroup.co.uk
This is the original restaurant of probably the most highly rated and most reputable Chinese restaurant group in London, with five other branches around the capital. The two distinct black-and-gold dining rooms seat about 200 people, yet you can still expect queues for the strictly authentic dim sum at the weekend. The dim sum chef works from 8 am to 5 pm, so don't go after this time if you want the real thing – although the main menu is also very good. ○

The Spice Shop 1 Blenheim Crescent, W11 2EE
020 7221 4448 www.thespiceshop.co.uk

In 1990, while studying for an international business degree, Birgit Erath started a small weekend stall on the Portobello Road Market. The weekend project soon became a serious business, and in 1995 she opened a shop on Blenheim Crescent, a stone's throw from the original stall, which has now become one of the most inimitable spice stores in the UK. In many other parts of the world spice shops and market stalls are ubiquitous, but in London a store devoted exclusively to herbs, spices, salts, peppers, chillies, nuts and a few fresh herbs and beans is quite a novelty. Birgit now travels the world to find new spices, creating blends and mixes that are often based on ancient traditions. If you want to get serious about cooking dishes from the subcontinent or Asia, this is your starting point. Or you can simply call in for seasonings, as they stock a huge range of salts, from Maldon and fleur de sel to Diamant de Sel, a naturally formed and mined salt from Kashmir. ●

Tavola 155 Westbourne Grove, W11 2RS
020 7229 0571

Everything that makes it into this food store is of the highest quality, and the prepared foods made on site are simply superb. ●

Above left
The Spice Shop.
Left and right **Tavola offers some of the finest produce in London.**

Tom's Deli 226 Westbourne Grove, W11 2RH 020 7221 8818

Notting Hill is overloaded with delis, but Tom's was the first and still retains a prime position – not to mention the cool factor that most of those in the new crop don't even grasp. The adjoining café serves the best breakfasts and eggs Florentine in London, and the ready-to-eat meals and prepared foods are also first rate. A perfect place to begin the trudge through Portobello Market. **○**

More places to visit in the area

○ Athenian Grocery
16a Moscow Road, Bayswater, W2 4BT
020 7229 6280
A typical Greek Cypriot corner shop that's been established for more than 40 years, full of feta cheese, olives, pickled chillies, wines and spirits.

○ Dri Dri
189 Portobello Road, W11 2ED
020 3490 5027 www.dridrigelato.com
An authentic Italian gelateria located next door to the Electric Cinema.

○ The Fish Shop at Kensington Place
201–9 Kensington Church Street, W8 7LX 020 7243 6626
A still-impressive fish shop next door to a once-celebrated restaurant.

○ Four Seasons
84 Queensway, W2 3RL 020 7229 4320
Go for the Cantonese roast duck in this Chinese restaurant (but definitely not for the service or a friendly welcome).

○ R. Garcia & Sons
248 Portobello Road, W11 1LL
020 7221 6119
A slice of everyday Spain in the heart of Notting Hill, the deli and food store have been established since 1957, while the tapas bar and café next door opened in recent years. Pure pedigree España.

○ Kensington Wine Rooms
127–9 Kensington Church Street, W8 7LP 020 7727 8142
www.greatwinesbytheglass.com
A huge selection of wines by the glass is available here, thanks to the Enomatic machines that inject nitrogen into bottles to prevent oxidation of the wine after opening. The food is also pretty good.

○ Mandarin Kitchen
14–16 Queensway, W2 3RX
020 7727 9012
Specializes in lobster prepared in six different styles, as well as premium seafood such as sea bass, turbot and red snapper.

○ Maroush
21 Edgware Road, W2 2JE
020 7723 0773 www.maroush.com
The best place to soak up the Lebanese atmosphere has got to be Edgware Road. The Maroush group operates a few businesses: the original Maroush restaurant at no. 21, Ranoush Juice at no. 43 and the deli selling everything from fresh fish to sweets at no. 45–9.

○ Yashin Sushi
1a Argyle Road, W8 7DB
020 7938 1536 www.yashinsushi.com
A high-end modern Japanese restaurant located away from the hustle and bustle of Notting Hill.

Belgravia
Knightsbridge

With Her Majesty the Queen as its most famous resident, it comes as no great surprise that this area boasts hotels and restaurants that are uniformly of a five-star standard. Embassies, consulates and official residences of those connected with the Court of St. James abound; the Duke of Westminster owns much of the land; and His Grace's company, Grosvenor, protects the heritage of the area, from the paint colour on the building façades to who can (and who cannot) take a lease. With the arrival in London of billionaires and Russian oligarchs, the residential population has started to change. As the headquarters of charities and industrial institutions move out, so teams of builders move in, occupying the vacant premises on behalf of their super-rich clients, for whom they craft marble masterpieces and sumptuous interior designs. The largest of the area's gracious squares are Belgrave and Eaton, both the work of the revolutionary architect and builder Thomas Cubitt (1788–1855). Commissioned in 1824 to build most of the district's Regency and late Georgian buildings, Cubitt also reformed the building trade – a very good pub and dining room at 44 Elizabeth Street is named in his honour. The area is also known for its luxury shopping, with Sloane Street the home to many of the world's top fashion labels and jewellery shops.

Only five to ten years ago this corner of London was virtually devoid of any restaurants that we would feel comfortable in recommending. Things have changed for the better, but most places are expensive or located in five-star hotels, or both. You certainly won't find any foodie street markets or young entrepreneurs with start-up cafés and food shops here: this exclusive area is the preserve of well-funded and super-star chefs.

Pierre Koffmann

" My favourite place for breakfast is Raoul's on Clifton Road, but the best coffee in London is to be found at Sensory Lab on Wigmore Street.

Owner, Koffmann's

Amaya Halkin Arcade, Motcomb Street, SW1X 8JT
020 7823 1166 www.amaya.biz

The reputation of Indian food and restaurants has traced a near-vertical trajectory over recent years, and with the opening of Amaya in 2004 it scaled new heights. The focus at Amaya – unlike other modern high-profile Indian restaurants – is on grilled ingredients, rather than curries or spiced dishes with heavy sauces. The open kitchen focuses on three core methods of Indian cuisine: tandoor – cooking food in a really hot clay oven; sigiri – cooking over a coal flame; and tawa – cooking or griddling food on a hot, thick, iron plate. The food is designed to be eaten with your hands, if you feel comfortable doing so, and shared. The menu includes plenty of fish and shellfish, as well as game in season. ○

Above **The colourful interior at Amaya.**

Above **The open kitchen at Bar Boulud.** Left **Head chef Dean Yasharinn in the kitchens at Bar Boulud.**

Bar Boulud Mandarin Oriental Hyde Park, 66 Knightsbridge, SW1X 7LA 020 7201 3899 www.barboulud.com

While hailing from Lyon, it is in America, and particularly NYC, that Daniel Boulud has made his name as one of the planets super-chefs. Many say his flagship restaurant is the best in Manhattan. His first venture in the UK is a very welcome addition to the London dining-out scene. There are some great dishes on the menu, such as the coq au vin, but it is the charcuterie and de luxe burgers that have made headlines for this place. Parisian Gilles Verdot, one of France's top charcutiers, oversees all the terrines, pâtés, rillettes, saucissons and hams, and they can all be delicious. I'm no great burger expert, but AA Gill – acknowledged by many as an authority on the subject – described the three different burgers on the menu in the *Sunday Times* as 'supreme'.

Chabrot Bistro d'Amis 9 Knightsbridge Green, SW1X 7QL 020 7225 2238 www.chabrot.co.uk

The vermilion bands on the tablecloths and napkins set the tone perfectly for this bijou bistro. The combination of the scale of this place, its name and its signature roast chicken dish might put some in mind of the once great (now sadly less so) L'Amis Louis in Paris. Everything is here to remind us all of our favourite little piece of Parisian chic of yesteryear: crowded tables, bentwood chairs, the *prix fixe* menu written in a typically French hand on the wall mirrors, snails on the menu, and Serge Gainsbourg on the soundtrack – all present and correct in full, blatant pastiche mode.

With a very experienced chef in the kitchen and a team of owners with exceptional restaurant pedigree, the standards are very high. (PP) On a recent visit I enjoyed grilled langoustines, fantastic foie gras, and a full-on stuffed cabbage with veal, chestnuts and foie gras. The café gourmand idea at the end of the meal is a very good one, allowing diners who can't face a full dessert to enjoy a few decent petits fours with their coffee. I enjoyed an excellent canelé, along with a prune soaked in Armagnac.

Left and above **Bar Boulud is known in London and New York for its excellent burgers.**

Dinner by Heston Blumenthal

Mandarin Oriental Hyde Park, 66 Knightsbridge, SW1X 7LA
020 7201 3833 www.dinnerbyheston.com

Heston Blumenthal's London debut has proved to be the hottest and most eagerly awaited restaurant opening in recent years. As a result, unless you are fortunate enough to know an insider (and we do) it is extremely tricky to secure a booking. Since its opening the critics have swooned over it with praise, with one even claiming that it is the most important new restaurant to appear in over 20 years; national newspapers have devoted double-page spreads to it, and there is talk of its style of British food being elevated to such heights that it eclipses all else. Well, it's certainly a very good restaurant, but to redress the balance it could also be argued that it's just a must-try experience, like the Fat Duck, and not necessarily a place you would want to visit on a regular basis. But given the demand and the hype, the prices are quite reasonable and the food is extremely good. So maybe it *is* the best restaurant in London.

Prior to opening the big talking point was the name of the restaurant. Heston was quick to explain that dinner historically means the main meal of the day, whether it is at midday or in the evening. This is correct, but we're not sure this statement has silenced the doubters.

Don't expect Heston's trademark molecular gastronomy, famous from his Fat Duck restaurant in Bray; nor will you be able to try his egg-and-bacon ice or snail porridge. This is a new direction in food: new, but looking resolutely to the past. Heston and his head chef Ashley Palmer-Watts have extensively researched British gastronomy and looked to history books for inspiration. Each dish on the menu is given its approximate date of origin, and many are forgotten gems from the past that have been given a modern treatment.

There are some really creative dishes on the menu, yet at the same time most people agree that the kitchen manages to extract more flavour from the ingredients than you might think possible. This is truly the sign of a great chef. If the main function of the professional cook in today's world of globally available foodstuffs is to maximize the flavour of well-sourced ingredients, then full marks are due to this kitchen for achieving this feat with such aplomb.

It was a real treat on one of our visits to be given a tour of the kitchen and to meet the team. No expense has been spared when it comes to the kitchen equipment, especially the pulley system that operates the spit roast, a masterpiece that might well be envied by the finest Swiss watchmakers. Dining at the chef's table, next to the main service counter, has to be one of the most in-demand foodie experiences in London.

The main dining room is not too shabby either; in fact a window table can be one of the best in town. And naturally you can also be assured of excellent service. (PP) On the first of three visits, I was assured by the sommelier that the wine list would be respectful of Bar Boulud, located below Dinner, which specializes in Burgundy and Rhône wines. Instead Dinner focuses on the plethora of other great wines of the world, including several verticals of great Bordeaux and some exquisite Super-Tuscan wines. ●

Left and above
The interior at Dinner by Heston Blumenthal with ceramic jelly-mould shaped wall light fittings.

Bruno Loubet

London has the most exciting restaurant scene in the world. The variety of cuisine, the calibre of chefs, the quality of ingredients and the knowledge and enthusiasm of the diners make it the place to be.

Chef patron, Bistrot Bruno Loubet

Above **Spit-roast pineapple.**
Right **Heston's kitchen, probably the best in London, with a clockwork-operated spit roast.**

Above **Meat fruit (c.1500) – one of the signature dishes, is chicken liver parfait inside a mandarin jelly.**
Left **Ashley Palmer-Watts at work.**

The Goring Hotel and Dining Room

Beeston Place, Grosvenor Gardens, SW1 OJW

020 7396 9000 www.goringhotel.co.uk

Four generations of the Goring family have overseen the most British hotel in the capital. With the Queen as your next-door neighbour, indeed, it would be traitorous to be anything other than quintessentially British. The hotel is immaculately managed with every detail addressed with gentlemanly poise. The recently refurbished dining room (designed by David Linley, the Queen's nephew) is light, airy and pleasant, with heavy, comfortable armchairs and large tables with acres of space between them, while Swarovski crystal chandeliers add a more feminine note. This is a restaurant for grown-ups, celebrations and important luncheons.

Derek Quelch, who has previously worked at the Savoy and Claridge's, oversees the kitchens. His menus are sizeable but not overwhelming, with virtually all the ingredients procured from the most impeccable sources in the British Isles. Although the overall direction is British, there are also a few nods in recognition of the French culinary tradition. Between September and November a fine selection of the best game birds is available. ●

Harrods 87–135 Brompton Road, SW1X 7XL

020 7730 1234 www.harrods.com

(PP) In the 1980s, when I first arrived in London, I would visit Harrods as often as possible to learn more about food and marvel at the displays. Over recent years the Food Halls seem to have lost some of their grandeur, but you cannot deny the scale and range of produce available here. The endless counters offer every food possible, from meat, fish and Oriental foods to cheese, coffee and caviar. Harrods also has 32 restaurants, from the flagship Georgian Restaurant to American diners, sushi bars, a pizzeria, an oyster bar and tapas restaurants to mention just a few.

Across the road, Harrods have opened an upmarket convenience store called Harrods102. The opening hours are longer, with a range more focused on the time-pressed occupants of the nearby luxury apartments. ●

Derek Quelch

" I love Galvin on Baker Street because they consistently serve good food at sensible prices. It's always a pleasant atmosphere and an enjoyable evening out.

Head chef, The Goring Hotel

Above **Harrods food halls are legendary.**

Right
The Champagne trolley in the restaurant at Harvey Nichols 5th Floor.

Harvey Nichols Fifth Floor 109–125 Knightsbridge, SW1X 7RJ
020 7235 5250 www.harveynichols.com

Harvey Nicks, as it is affectionately known, is renowned for its street-level window displays and is considered as a more fashionable and younger version of Harrods, just a short walk along Brompton Road. When the Fifth Floor first opened, it transformed our conception not only of dining in a store but also of food retail areas within large department stores. Expectations were raised as new, modern interiors were merged with the deli, butcher's, fishmonger's, bakery and cheese counter, and all were wrapped up together in a busy café and excellent restaurant on an entire floor devoted to food and drink. The packaging, especially for own-label products, was also modern, and different from that in most other food halls and department stores. Before the Fifth Floor, restaurants in stores all too often involved appalling hot buffets, soggy foods and tray service.

Today, the format is still similar and a Yo! Sushi conveyor-belt sushi operation has been installed. The café, with its glass ceiling and rooftop terrace, is still an enviable place for a light lunch or afternoon break.

The adjoining restaurant interior was until recently a very civilized setting with comfortable armchairs and a semi-open kitchen. However, the design was given a radical overhaul and the new incarnation has got to be one of the most absurd restaurant interiors in London. The walls and ceiling are covered in light fittings that change colour according to the time of day, the weather and other factors. It is quite off-putting and must have cost an absolute fortune. (PP) I haven't met anybody who likes it. However, I don't know too many Ab Fab girls! ((TC) I do, and they don't like it either!) We recently heard rumours that they no longer use the light system. Although, not learning from prior experiences, the new look bar has been designed to look entirely outré.

Despite the bizarre interior, the food is still high in quality and the wine policy allows diners to take advantage of the adjoining wine shop. Ask for a window table so that you can focus on the great view towards the impressive architecture of the Mandarin Oriental hotel across the road. ○

Left **The extensive range of grocery items in Harvey Nichol's food halls all come in stylish packaging.**

74 **Koffmann's** The Berkeley, Wilton Place SW1X 7RL
020 7235 1010 www.the-berkeley.co.uk/koffmanns.aspx

'The Bear' is the soubriquet Pierre Koffmann has earned over 35 years toiling at the gastronomic peak in London. Back in 1972, Pierre was the head chef at the Roux brothers' Waterside Inn in Bray. In 1977 he opened his own place, La Tante Claire, which continued until the late 1990s on the site that is now home to Restaurant Gordon Ramsay. He then moved to the restaurant in The Berkeley Hotel that is now Marcus Wareing at The Berkeley. This first venture at the Berkely closed in 2003, but he is now back at the Berkeley in a different location, and whatever the hotel concierge might tell you this is now the pre-eminent restaurant in the hotel and (unlike the Marcus Wareing restaurant) an all-round pleasure.

The entire menu is a delight, but on a first visit we urge you to try the pieds de cochon aux morilles, the best pigs' trotter dish to grace a plate (see page 76). The boned-out trotter is stuffed with rich chicken mousseline, sweetbreads and morels and served with an unctuous sauce. Divine. Follow this with the pistachio soufflé, a signature Koffmann dessert (see page 77).

Marc Botes, the head sommelier, also deserves a very special mention for probably the finest all-French wine list in town.

Some restaurants offer a little more buzz and vibrancy, but if you are looking for a dignified and comfortable French supper you will struggle to find anything better than Koffmann's. ◗

Above **The stylish upper level of the dining room at Koffmann's.**

Coquilles St. Jacques à l'Encre

Scallops with Squid Ink Sauce and Cauliflower Purée

Serves 6

2 red peppers, deseeded and roughly chopped
300 ml (1/2 pint) double cream
1 whole cauliflower, chopped into florets
300 ml (1/2 pint) full cream milk
50 g (2 oz) butter
6 extra-large scallops with coral

For the squid ink sauce

6 shallots, peeled and finely chopped
knob of butter
300 ml (1/2 pint) Noilly Prat
200 ml (7 fl oz) double cream
6 tablespoons squid ink
salt flakes and freshly ground black pepper

First make a red pepper coulis: place the peppers in a saucepan with the cream and cook over a medium heat until the peppers are tender. Strain, reserving the cream, then whizz the peppers in a blender. Pour the blended peppers into a bowl and stir in the reserved cream gradually, until it reaches a purée consistency. Season with salt and pepper to taste, and set aside.

To make the cauliflower purée, place the cauliflower, milk and butter in a large saucepan and simmer over a medium heat until the cauliflower is tender. Strain, reserving the liquid, then whizz the cauliflower in a blender. Pour the blended cauliflower into a bowl and stir in the reserved milk gradually, until it reaches a purée consistency. Season with salt and pepper to taste, and set aside.

Clean the scallops, discarding the dark meat (sac). Separate the whites of the scallops reserving the outer membrane and coral. Wash each one gently in cold water.

Put a knob of butter in a saucepan over a medium heat, add the shallots and sweat down. Add the outer membrane and coral from the scallops, then the Noilly Prat. Cook gently for about 10 minutes, then strain over a bowl, discarding the coral and membrane. Return the liquid to the pan and boil over a high heat to reduce until it resembles the consistency of syrup. Add the double cream and cook again until it is reduced by half. Stir in the squid ink and season to taste.

Cut each scallop (the white meat) in half horizontally. Place a frying pan over a high heat and cook the scallops presentation-side down until golden brown. Turn over and cook the other sides for a further minute, keeping them tender. Add a sprinkle of salt flakes.

To serve, place some cauliflower purée on warmed serving plates and top with 2 scallop halves each. Garnish the plates with the squid ink sauce and red pepper coulis.

Pieds de Cochon aux Morilles

Pigs' Trotters Stuffed with Morels

Serves 4

4 pigs' hind trotters, boned
100 g (3½ oz) carrots, diced
100 g (3½) onions, diced
100 ml (3½ fl oz) Madeira
100 ml (3½ fl oz) port
30 ml (generous 1 fl oz) brandy
150 ml (¼ pint) veal stock
75 g (3 oz) butter
225 g (7½ oz) veal sweetbreads, blanched and chopped
20 dried morels, soaked until soft and drained
1 small onion, finely chopped
1 chicken breast, skinned and diced
1 egg white
200 ml (7 fl oz) double cream
salt and freshly ground black pepper

Place the trotters in a casserole with the diced carrots and onions, the Madeira, port, brandy and veal stock. Cover and braise in a preheated oven, 160°C (325°F), Gas Mark 3, for 3 hours.

Meanwhile place 50 g (2 oz) of the butter in a large frying pan and fry the sweetbreads for 5 minutes over a medium heat, then add the morels and chopped onion to the pan and cook for a further 5 minutes. Leave to cool.

Purée the chicken breast in a blender or food processor with the egg white and cream, and season with salt and pepper. Mix with the sweetbread mixture to make the stuffing.

When cooked, take the trotters out of the casserole and strain the cooking stock, keeping the stock but discarding the vegetables. Open the trotters out flat and lay each one on a piece of kitchen foil. Leave to cool.

Fill the cooled trotters with the chicken stuffing and roll them up tightly in the foil. Chill in the refrigerator for at least 2 hours.

Put the trotters in a casserole, add 100 ml (3½ fl oz) water and heat through in a preheated oven, 220°C (425°F), Gas Mark 7, for 15 minutes. Alternatively prepare a steamer, and when the water is simmering place the foil-wrapped trotters in the steamer until heated through.

Transfer the trotters to a serving dish and discard the foil.

Pour the reserved stock into the casserole and cook over a high heat until reduced by half. Stir in the remaining butter, pour the sauce over the trotters, and serve hot with mashed potato.

Soufflé aux Pistaches

Pistachio Soufflé

Serves 6

500 ml (17 fl oz) milk
125 g (4 oz) egg yolks
75 g (3 oz) caster sugar, plus 125 g (4 oz)
50 g (2 oz) flour, sifted
75 g (3 oz) pistachio paste
25 g (1 oz) softened butter
30 g (just over 1 oz) dark chocolate, grated
360 g (11½ oz) egg whites
icing sugar, to dust

Pour the milk into a large saucepan and bring to the boil. While it is heating, in a separate bowl whisk together the egg yolks, 75 g (3 oz) caster sugar, the flour and pistachio paste until smooth. Add half the hot milk and whisk to remove any lumps.

Return the mixture to the pan with the remaining milk. Bring slowly to the boil while stirring with a whisk. Continue stirring for at least 10 minutes or until the taste of the flour is cooked out. This should create about 600 g (1 lb 3 oz) of pistachio pastry cream.

Pour the pastry cream into a shallow tray, cover with clingfilm (making sure it touches the pastry cream) and chill.

Butter 6 ramekins. Sprinkle the grated chocolate inside each ramekin and rotate them so that the chocolate completely covers the insides.

Take a large clean bowl and using an electric hand whisk or freestanding mixer beat the egg whites until firm, then add the remaining 120 g (4 oz) caster sugar and whisk until stiff.

Spoon the pistachio pastry cream into another large bowl and warm slowly over a saucepan of barely simmering water, making sure the water does not touch the surface of the bowl.

Stir a small quantity of the whisked egg whites into the pistachio cream to soften, then gently fold in the rest of the egg whites until just combined. Pour the mixture into the ramekins and bake in a preheated oven, 180°C (350°F), Gas Mark 4, for 12–14 minutes or until well risen. Quickly dust the top of each soufflé with icing sugar and serve immediately.

Left **The shop interior at Ladurée.** Right **A beautiful box of Ladurée macarons makes the perfect gift.**

Ladurée at Harrods 87–135 Brompton Road, SW1X 7XL
020 3155 0111 www.laduree.fr

Much hype surrounded the arrival in London of this Parisian institution that serves an extensive range of French pastries, from éclairs to gateaux St. Honoré to millefeuilles. But it is the macarons, made from eggs, sugar and almonds plus a special Ladurée ingredient, then glued together with ganache-like fillings of various flavours, that attract most attention. Ideal in the afternoon with a cup of tea or after dinner as an alternative to a full dessert, they are indeed delicious, never failing to melt in the mouth. The very chic packaging also makes them a perfect gift. ○

Gary Rhodes

My favourite corner shop – that would have to be Harrods. This wonderful establishment holds the finest food halls in London, feeding you with great flavours which always result in a heavier carrier bag!
Chef and restaurateur

Above **The inspiring display counter at Ladurée.**

Right **Designer details inside Mr Chow.**

Mr Chow 151 Knightsbridge, SW1X 7PA
020 7589 7347 www.mrchow.com
When it opened in 1968, Mr Chow was possibly the first serious designer restaurant, renowned for its design details and art. The food is authentic Beijing, but some say it is now eclipsed by more modern Chinese restaurants. We still think Mr Chow is worth a visit. Its reputation may not be what it once was, but it is one of those places that you just must experience. It also has celebrity outposts in New York and Los Angeles. ⊙

Nahm The Halkin Hotel, Halkin Street, SW1X 7DJ
020 7333 1234 www.halkin.co.uk
Beyond the marble hall of this discreet and sophisticated Milanese-style hotel lies Nahm restaurant by David Thompson, the first Michelin-starred Thai restaurant in Europe. It's a relatively small and very cool space, but the cooking is fiery. David Thompson has modernized and mastered the flavours of royal Thai cooking, and done so with some note. Forget the phad Thai noodle dishes that have appeared elsewhere in London: Nahm operates on a level that is far superior. First courses might include hot and sour soup with wild sea bass or a salad of grilled squid and Middle White pork with chilli jam, followed by main courses such as chiang mai pork curry with shredded ginger, pickled garlic and shallots or stir-fried venison with chilli paste, onions and cumin. ⊙

Left **A David Hockney-designed matchbox at Mr Chow.**

Left **Yotam Ottolenghi.** Right **The imaginative and creative range of salads at Ottolenghi never fail to impress.**

Ottolenghi 13 Motcomb Street, SW1X 8LB

020 7823 2707 www.ottolenghi.co.uk

Islington and Notting Hill have had the benefit of branches of Ottolenghi for some time. Now the residents and office workers of Belgravia can enjoy some of the most attractively presented and best-tasting food of mostly Mediterranean inspiration in London. Yes it's not cheap, but in this location that is probably not a major consideration; in fact it's probably viewed as reassuring. ●

Left and right **the best food displays in London can be found at Ottolenghi.**

Poilâne 46 Elizabeth Street, SW1W 9PA
020 7808 4910 www.poilane.fr

Pierre Poilâne opened a small bakery in the St. Germain des Prés quarter of Paris in 1932. Today, Harvard graduate Apollonia Poilâne oversees an international multi-million-pound business. It was always Appollonia's intention to work in the family firm and she underwent a lengthy apprenticeship with her father Lionel at an early age. Following his untimely death, Apollonia was propelled into the role of CEO before her studies were even complete.

Some 3 per cent of all the bread consumed in Paris today is reputed to be by Poilâne, with daily exports to Milan, Brussels, Berlin, Tokyo and over 3,000 private clients in USA. The bakery in Elizabeth Street has attracted a loyal and distinguished client list for its now legendary sourdough. You can buy a small selection of other breads and punitions (literally 'punishments'), or butter shortbread sablés, but it is the large four-pound sourdough loaves with their trademark 'P' traced in the flour on top that are most certainly the real attraction for distinguished clientele.

Above left **Bread and pastries at Poilâne.**
Above right
The distinctive P for Poilâne can be seen on each of the sourdough loaves.

You can buy Poilâne bread at many fine delicatessens across London, and countless restaurants include the sourdough in their breadbaskets, but a visit to the shop is definitely a worthwhile experience. If you ask, they will also provide a quick tour of the bakery and office, where you can see a bread chandelier made by Salvador Dalí, a testimony to his great friendship with Lionel. ◉

Racine 239 Brompton Road, SW3 2EP
020 7584 4477 www.racine-restaurant.com

Racine has experienced some turmoil over recent years, with the two founders, Henry Harris (the chef) and Eric Garnier (front-of-house maestro), falling out and leaving to pursue other interests.

Henry is now back on the pans, and the cooking has returned to its original excellent bourgeois roots. The food is simple and tastes great, the presentation on the plate is attractive without unnecessary adornment, the familiar list of classic French dishes is perfect in size and balance, the prices are reasonable despite exceptional demand, and the service is friendly and efficient. The dining room seats about 75, with tables close together yet never too much so, the linen is pristinely white and pressed, the staff are sharply attired, and the ambience is always convivial. Meals start with French baguette and Echire butter, after which you can expect endive salad, Jésus de Lyon with cornichons, lapin à la moutarde, celeriac remoulade, pâté de foie de volaille and filet au poivre. All are dishes that we love when they are so well executed. This is what we call a *real* restaurant. ◉

Filet au Poivre

by Henry Harris © copyright 2005

Serves 2

2 fillet steaks weighing about 230–250 g (7¹/₂–8 oz) each
3 teaspoons cracked black pepper
salt
2 tablespoons clarified butter
50–75 g (2–3 oz) butter
50 ml (2 fl oz) Cognac
100 ml (3¹/₂ fl oz) veal stock

Preheat the oven to 100°C (210°F), Gas Mark ¹/₄. Take the 2 fillet steaks and place them on a dish. Place the pepper on to a cut side of each steak only and press it into the meat with the heel of your hand to ensure it is well attached. Then season the steaks with salt and set them aside.

Heat the clarified butter in a frying pan over a high heat and add the steaks pepper-side down. Cook them briskly for 3–5 minutes or until that first side is crusted and brown. Then turn over the meat and cook for 1 minute. Tip out the clarified butter from the pan and slip in half of the regular butter. Turn down the heat to a medium temperature and let the butter foam and cook to a gentle hazelnut colour. Baste the meat with the butter regularly. If the butter appears in danger of turning too dark then just lower the heat. Continue this process for 3–4 minutes. Add the Cognac and cook off the alcohol. Then add the stock, bring it to the boil and add the remaining butter. Reduce the liquid to a syrupy consistency.

Remove the steaks from the pan and transfer them on to a dish to rest in the oven for 8 minutes. Move the steaks to warm plates and add the juices that seeped out of the meat and into the dish. Adjust the seasoning, spoon the sauce over the steaks and serve immediately.

Left **Flambéing the Cognac and burning off the alcohol is all part of the fun in the filet au poivre recipe at Racine.**

Left and right
The interior at Zafferano has been spruced up and enlarged over recent years, but is still pleasingly modest.

Zafferano 15 Lowndes Street, SW1X 9EY
020 7235 5800 www.zafferanorestaurant.com

As we have mentioned elsewhere in this book, the River Café and Locanda Locatelli are our two top Italian restaurants in London. Michelin-starred Zafferano is definitely our number three, and for many it is number one.

Professional – but never overbearing – service from a mainly Italian team and the approach of a small and unassuming restaurant combine to produce an atmosphere of contentment. The room has been extended over the years and now incorporates a small bar and extra tables, yet it still retains elements that strike a modest note. This is especially evident in the private dining room, set in the brick-vaulted wine cellars.

Andy Needham, who has an enviable CV, cooks with fine ingredients such as burrata cheese (the more sophisticated version of mozzarella), truffles in season, cured pigs' cheeks, and excellent veal, lobster and fish.

In 2009, Zafferano won *Tatler's* highly prestigious 'Most Consistently Excellent Restaurant' award. ◉

Right **Zafferano's crab and asparagus salad.**

Yotam Ottolenghi

For my favourite specialist food shop experience in London, take me to La Fromagerie any day. Apart from the cheese, which is the best by far, there is a massive selection of quality European produce like nowhere else.

Owner, Ottolenghi and Nopi

Zuma 5 Raphael Street, SW7 1DL
020 7584 1010 www.zumarestaurant.com

(PP) Personally I find the atmosphere and clientele a bit loud (I prefer sister restaurant Roka, see pages 137 and 258), but the food is quite brilliant. Since Zuma, London opened in 2002 it has proved hugely popular, which has fuelled a global expansion. The chef and restaurateur Rainer Becker has created a contemporary version of a Japanese izakaya (an informal bar with simple food). Many of the dishes are designed to share among friends, and it's a great location for a small party. The sushi, sashimi and rolls are inventively prepared, and the fish and especially the pork and beef from the Robata grill are particularly good. The tasting menu is a full-on gustatory experience, but like most of the menu it carries a heavy price tag, especially if you go for the black cod or Wagyu beef.

The bar is wild and always busy as the cocktail staff create inspirational drinks, many including sake and Japanese spirits.

More places to visit in the area

Apsley's at the Lanesborough Hotel
Hyde Park Corner, SW1X 7TA
020 7259 5599 www.lanesborough.com
In Rome, Heinz Beck has been awarded three Michelin stars for his upmarket Italian food at La Pergola. His London restaurant, Apsley's, located inside the Lanesborough Hotel, is expensive and has a tendency to be pretentious, but the food can be very good. And those who enjoy a cigar can retire to the Garden Room, where they can smoke indoors thanks to some creative circumnavigation of the legislation.

Theo Randall at The Intercontinental Hotel
1 Hamilton Place, W1J7QY
020 7318 8747 www.theorandall.com
Another top-class chef in a five-star hotel setting. Theo is an ex-River Café chef, and his Italian food is thankfully more rustic than in some other restaurants in the area. As tends to be the case with hotel locations, the room and setting are a little off-putting, but the food is great.

Brick Lane
Hackney
Hoxton
Old Street
Shoreditch

From Dalston being voted the coolest place on the planet by *Vogue* to the arrival of the Olympic Village, east London is beyond all doubt the most exciting, diverse and creative district of London. The savvy have known this for some considerable time, of course, but things just keep getting better. The new East London train line has arrived, the area around Old Street roundabout is about to become Europe's equivalent of Silicon Valley, and the retail scene is booming, with the world's first pop-up mall – Boxpark.co.uk – opening just off Shoreditch High Street. Unlike other neighbourhoods that have experienced such injections of spirit, money and people, east London appears to be retaining much of its character. The edgy and slightly grubby corners remain and the massive graffiti scene is still vibrant. With their witty, creative and sometimes politically charged art, nocturnal street artists often bring wry smiles to the faces of those who live and work here. The area's bars, clubs and embryonic galleries are now being joined by smart hotels, posh restaurants and cool retail brands to generate an ensemble with a great buzz. East is most definitely the new west!

FENNEL &
WILD GARLIC

Albion 2–4 Boundary Street, E2 7DD
020 7729 1051 www.albioncaff.co.uk

We should start by declaring an interest. Albion is our version of a French all-day pavement café done in a British style, with an adjoining bakery and a small shop.

The menu is all about typical British caff foods, nothing challenging or complicated, just straightforward hearty ingredients and recipes. Breakfast is served throughout the day, alongside fish and chips, half pints of prawns, mussels cooked in cider, a minimum of three different pies (often more, including delights such as cottage pie, chicken and crayfish pie and game pie), plus Irish stew, kedgeree, devilled kidneys, doorstop sandwiches, fruit jellies, puddings and crumbles. There's nothing that you won't recognize and everything that you want to eat. The breakfast menu is eternally popular, whether with weekend shoppers or with the local creative community, who love to scoff everything from kippers to duck eggs on toast, or healthy organic yoghurt with poached fruits and muesli.

The bakery and pastry ovens are located in the café, so diners can watch the team at work and inhale the reassuring aromas. We now sell 16 different breads, an extensive array of viennoiserie and a full range of English cakes and bakery treats.

Our small shop stocks a range of British foods, from larder essentials and everyday basics, such as Maldon salt and Colman's mustard, to jams and Neal's Yard Dairy cheeses, regional specialities such as Kendal Mint cake and luxury chocolates, to mention just a fraction of what we cram into it. All of the fresh items, including a range of prepared meals, are made in our kitchen, and we stock a variety of meats and game in season. Gulls' eggs (despite their ridiculous price) and wild smoked salmon are popular. The kitchen garden at Barton Court, Terence's home in Berkshire, also provides vegetables and herbs.

Since it opened in January 2009, Albion has far eclipsed our wildest expectations, winning awards and local support. It just goes on growing. We hope you enjoy it. ○

Above **The Albion table setting complete with reclaimed bone-handle knives in reused syrup tins.** Right **The Albion shop is stocked with a range of British groceries and cook's essentials.**

Above **Inside Albion café.**

Kedgeree

Serves 4

thick slice of onion
1/2 carrot, roughly chopped
1 celery stick, roughly chopped
1 bay leaf
375 g (12 oz) undyed smoked haddock
25 g (1 oz) butter
5 shallots or 1 onion, finely chopped
1 garlic clove, finely chopped
1 teaspoon turmeric
1/2 teaspoon cumin
1/2 teaspoon curry powder
1/2 teaspoon fennel seeds
1 curry leaf
pinch of saffron
200 ml (7 fl oz) double cream
150 g (5 oz) basmati rice
small handful of parsley, finely chopped
3 eggs, hard-boiled and quartered
salt and freshly ground black pepper

Put 500 ml (17 fl oz) water into a wide, shallow saucepan, add the slice of onion, carrot, celery and bay leaf and bring to a simmer over a low heat to infuse the flavours. Place the haddock in the cooking liquor, then remove from the heat and leave the fish to cool in the liquid (it should just cook through).

To make the curry sauce, melt the butter in a medium saucepan, add the shallots and garlic, cook gently over a medium heat until soft. Add all the spices and cook for a further minute or two to release their flavours. Measure out 200 ml (7 fl oz) of the fish cooking liquor, add to the spices and bring to the boil over a high heat. Cook until reduced by half. Add the cream and reduce down until it is thick enough to coat the back of a spoon. Check and add seasoning if necessary, and set aside.

Rinse the rice in a sieve a couple of times in cold running water, then cook in plenty of boiling salted water for 12–15 minutes or according to the packet instructions. Drain, return to the pan, then put a lid on and leave off the heat to steam for a few minutes.

To serve, reheat the sauce, flake the cooked fish and stir into the sauce with the chopped parsley. Add the cooked rice, stir to combine and serve in shallow bowls (else it might be too hot to eat for a while). Scatter over the hard-boiled egg to finish, and serve with mango chutney.

Devilled Kidneys

Serves 1

100 g (3 1/2 oz) plain flour
10 g English mustard powder
5 g (1/4 oz) cayenne pepper
5 g (1/4 oz) paprika
3 lambs' kidneys, cut in half, with fat removed and cleaned
25 g (1 oz) butter
20 ml (3/4 fl oz) veal *jus*
1–2 thick slices of bread, toasted
small handful of parsley, finely chopped
salt and freshly ground black pepper

Mix the flour, mustard powder, cayenne pepper and paprika together and season with salt and pepper. Dust the kidneys with the flour mix.

Heat a frying pan over a medium heat and add the butter. When the butter has melted, add the kidneys and cook until golden brown on 1 side, then turn over to seal the other side. Add the veal *jus* and boil until it is reduced to a sauce consistency. Season with salt and pepper to taste.

To serve, place the kidneys on slices of toast, pour the sauce over and finish with a sprinkling of chopped parsley.

Bread and Butter Pudding

Serves 4

1 small loaf of crusty white bread,
sliced and buttered

125 g (4 oz) mixed currants, sultanas
and dates

50 g (2 oz) walnut pieces

50 g (2 oz) golden caster sugar,
plus extra for sprinkling

4 eggs

1.2 litres (2 pints) milk

Layer the bread and dried fruit and nuts in a
large ovenproof dish or 4 individual dishes.

In a large bowl, beat together the sugar,
eggs and milk, and pour all over the bread.

Allow the milk mixture to soak in for
half an hour or so before pressing down
gently to encourage absorption.

Sprinkle with more sugar and cook in a
preheated oven, 180°C (350°F) Gas Mark 4,
for 30–40 minutes (it will start to soufflé
once cooked).

Allow to cool a little before attempting
to eat. Best served with Ayrshire or Jersey
cream. Enjoy any leftovers straight from
the refrigerator.

Flâneur Sundays in east London

Charles Baudelaire defined a *flâneur* (a 'stroller', 'lounger', 'saunterer' or 'loafer', from the verb *flâner*, 'to stroll') as 'a person who walks the city in order to experience it'. Add a little shopping, sipping, snacking and dining, and you have the perfect Sunday in east London. A bicycle would add more pace, but might detract from the relaxed state of mind savoured by the true *flâneur*.

Ambala 55 Brick Lane, E1 6PU
020 7247 8569 www.ambalafoods.com

From swirls of jalebi to besan ladoo, made with gram flour, almonds, pistachios and brazil nuts, and luminous (thanks to food colourings) kaju fruits fashioned from cashew nut marzipan, Ambala stocks an impressive selection of traditional sweets from the Indian subcontinent, in addition to baklava in every possible shape and variety.

While the sweet counter is impressive, Ambala is even prouder of its rasmalai, ideal as an after-dinner dessert on a sweltering hot evening. ◐

Beigel Bake 159 Brick Lane, E1 6SB 020 7729 0616

Open 24/7, Beigel Bake serves everybody and has been doing so for decades. Go at four in the morning and watch the post-clubbing crowd, or on Saturday afternoons when London cabbies enjoy salt-beef sandwiches. The milky cholla still attracts the Jewish old-timers, and true East Enders come for the pastries. They bake over 7,000 bagels a day. ◐

Above left **A beigel after a night on the town, and doughnuts from Beigel Bake.**

A few suggested routes:
- Start with a stroll along the Regent's Canal, taking in Towpath Café.
- Buy some tulips or roses at Columbia Road flower market, and perhaps a few vintage plates or a teapot at the neighbouring bric-à-brac market.
- Call in at Albion for kippers or kidneys, or maybe the full Albion breakfast.
- Browse the shops on Redchurch Street – *Time Out* magazine voted it London's best shopping street.
- Head to Brick Lane for the vibe and for refreshing teas at the Hookah Lounge, then browse the design shops on Cheshire Street.
- Explore the labyrinthine markets, warehouse events, ethnic food stores and live music bars that line Brick Lane.
- Join the crowds at Spitalfields Market, with its great food and fashion stalls.
- Take a late lunch at St. John Bread and Wine – don't forget to buy a bottle of Pineau des Charentes before heading home.

Bistrotheque 23–7 Wadeson Street, E2 9DR
020 8983 7900 www.bistrotheque.com

Lying on a dark cobbled street, with no obvious sign to indicate its discreet entrance, this restaurant is not easy to find.

The downstairs bar is suave and usually full of Bethnal Green's coolest denizens. The owners have a previous life in the fashion world that has clearly influenced the whole operation. Alongside the restaurant, Bistrotheque is also known for its risqué and camp cabaret or drag-artist performances in the private area off the downstairs bar.

As you ascend the concrete staircase you may wonder if you have taken a wrong turn into a fire exit or staff area, but continue walking and you will arrive at the kitchen. We like the fact that you walk through the kitchen to get to your table! The dining room is set in the eaves of this old East End sweatshop, with polished white-tiled walls, nautical pendant lamps and steel-frame windows with mottled glass.

The menu has a mix of influences from brasserie staples, such as steak tartare, oysters, onglet and chips, plus crème brûlée and tarte Tatin to British ingredients such as potted shrimps or battered fish and chips. The weekend brunch menu includes porridge with honey, croque monsieur and madame, plus pancakes, eggs Florentine, Benedict and Royale, and, not forgetting an English breakfast. While the food and service is good, it is also fair to assume that most people go for the scene as much as the food.

This area is rapidly becoming the focus of the art scene that has migrated from parts of Shoreditch and is now centred on Vyner Street.

Above left
Bistrotheque's head chef Tom Collins.
Above and right
The industrial-style interior at Bistrotheque.

Caramelized Chicory with Roquefort Gratin

Serves 2

2 thick slices sourdough bread, crusts removed
2 garlic cloves
4 g (¼ oz) or a few stems of parsley
4 g (¼ oz) or a few stems of chives
10 g (½ oz) nibbed almonds
160 g (3 oz) chicory (2 small heads)
10 g (½ oz) butter
vegetable oil
pinch of demerara sugar
¼ head of celeriac, peeled
2 sprigs of thyme, leaves chopped
40 g (1½ oz) spinach leaves, roughly chopped
60 g (3 oz) Roquefort cheese
Maldon sea salt and cracked black pepper

Make a herb crust by blending the sourdough with garlic, parsley and chives in a food processor or blender. Turn out into a bowl, stir in the nibbed almonds and set aside.

Cut the chicory in half lengthwise. Heat a large ovenproof frying pan over a high heat. Add a quarter of the butter, a little oil and the chicory halves. Once the chicory begins to take on some colour, turn it over and add another quarter of the butter, the demerara sugar, and season with salt and pepper. Place in a preheated oven at 200°C (400°F), Gas Mark 6, for 10–15 minutes or until tender. Set aside.

Meanwhile slice the celeriac very finely into large roughly-shaped discs. Heat half the remaining butter in a saucepan over a medium heat and add the celeriac, thyme leaves, salt and pepper, and cook for about 4 minutes or until the celeriac is cooked.

To assemble the dish, warm the chicory and celeriac through in 1 saucepan with the remaining butter, add the chopped spinach and stir until the leaves wilt. Divide the chicory, celeriac and spinach neatly in the middle of 2 small heatproofserving plates and pour over any juices from the pan. Arrange slices of Roquefort on top of the vegetables, and sprinkle over the herb crust. Place under a preheated hot grill until golden brown. Serve immediately.

Boundary Restaurant & Rooftop 2–4 Boundary Street, E2 7DD
020 7729 1051 www.theboundary.co.uk

Boundary is our dream restaurant. It serves simple and delicious French recipes, both classic and traditional, alongside quintessential classics such as escargots à la bourguignonne and cuisses de grenouille, as well as more indulgent treats such as foie gras, Dover sole, côtes de veau and game in season.

Seasonal British-sourced ingredients, such as grouse, hare, asparagus, mushrooms, wild berries and gulls' eggs, together with truffles from France and Italy, are all served when available, and there is always a large selection of fruits de mer. Charcuterie, oysters, smoked wild salmon, daily-changing roast meats from the rôtisserie, and cheese are served from *chariots* in the dining room. The pudding menu always includes a glamorous soufflé and madeleines baked to order. You could say that we try to adhere to the ideals of Elizabeth David.

Wine is very important at Boundary Restaurant. The list includes more than 700 mostly French bins that range from aristocratic first growths and the finest grands crus from Burgundy to simple table wines from the Languedoc, with a good selection of large-format bottles. These magnums, jeroboams, methuselahs and rehoboams look very impressive and are ideal for large tables. The sommelier team also runs a very successful wine club, Château Boundary, which offers everything from regular tastings to wine holidays.

Alongside the restaurant is a small bar promoting purist versions of the great British and American cocktails. An exceptionally stiff Martini is the house speciality. A fine digestif selection, including a range of vintage Armagnacs, many different eaux de vie, and the very rare Louis XIII Cognac, is also available.

The charcuterie trolley is one of the restaurant's most popular features, with simple, rustic French flavours that deliver a perfect start to any meal. The trolley always offers jambon persillé, duck or rabbit rillettes, chicken liver parfait, terrine de campagne and three different saucissons, all accompanied by crusty baguette, cornichons and silver onions (see pages 98–9).

The rooftop cocktail bar and grill restaurant perched above the Boundary Hotel is open from April to October, and offers some of the most privileged panoramic views to be had of east London. The bar features rattan sofas and low-slung armchairs arranged around a huge open fireplace, and the space boasts a large sail-like canopy, heating, festoon lighting and Welsh blankets. ○

Peter Weeden

The best place in London for a late or post-theatre supper is Wong Kei, the 3-storey building at the end of Brewer Street. Paper table cloths, terrible – no – legendarily bad service, but green tea and Singapore fried noodles are always just the ticket later on in the evening.

Head chef, Boundary Restaurant

Top left **The fireplace on Boundary Rooftop.**

Above and left
Victorian brickwork alcoves now form cosy dining tables at Boundary Restaurant.
Right **A plateau de fruits de mer, and chefs shucking oysters at Boundary Restaurant.**

Left and right
Making passion fruit soufflé.

Terrine de Campagne

At Boundary, we line the terrine with sheets of lardo (thinly sliced salted back fat) or crepinette/caul (lacy fatty pig stomach lining) both of which you can get from a good butcher.

Makes 1 terrine mould about 23 x 7 x 7cm (9 x 3 x 3 inches)

20 ml (6 teaspoons) port
10 ml (3 teaspoons) brandy
800 g (1 lb 7 oz) pork shoulder
150 g (5 oz) smoked back bacon
250 g (8 oz) chicken livers
250 g (8 oz) pork back fat
1 tablespoon vegetable oil
400 g (13 oz) onions, chopped
1 garlic clove, crushed
sprig of thyme
pinch of ground cloves
pinch of mace
2 juniper berries, crushed
sprig rosemary
1/2 teaspoon black peppercorns, lightly crushed
4 bay leaves
2 teaspoons green peppercorns
handful of green pistachios
2 eggs, beaten
salt and freshly ground black pepper

Heat the port and brandy in a small saucepan over a high heat until reduced by a third, then set aside.

Mince the meat, fat and livers and season generously, then set aside.

Place a large saucepan over a medium heat, add the oil along with the onions, garlic, thyme, ground cloves, mace, juniper berries, rosemary, peppercorns and bay leaves. Cook until the flavours meld and mellow and the onion is almost cooked. Remove and reserve the bay leaves and allow the mixture to cool.

Add the port and brandy reduction to the cooled onion mixture along with the minced meats and remaining ingredients and combine well. In a small frying pan, fry a small sample of the mixture to check the seasoning.

Line the terrine mould with a double layer of clingfilm, fill with the mixture and arrange the bay leaves on top. Fold over the clingfilm and lightly cover with kitchen foil. Cook in a bain marie at 130°C (266°F), or in a preheated oven, 120°C (250°F), Gas Mark 1/2 for 1 1/2 hours or until the middle of the terrine reaches above 68°C (154°F).

Allow the cooked terrine to cool, and press the top down with a weight to compact it – just make sure the weight is well distributed to keep the terrine evenly pressed, and chill in the fridge. This terrine is best if allowed to rest for 48 hours before serving.

Rillettes

You need to take a cut of pork which has the required fat and flavour to make this dish work such as belly and neck cuts. The prep can be done the night before allowing the following morning for cooking, meaning it could be ready for supper that evening or lunch the following day (although it is also delicious for breakfast).

Serves 6-8 as a starter or for a picnic

1 kg (2 lb) pork without skin or bone, diced roughly (ask your butcher) – you can substitute up to 500 g (1 lb) with boneless rabbit or duck
500 g (1 lb) diced pork back fat
1 bouquet garni (1/3 celery stick, spring rosemary, 1 bay leaf and thyme sprigs, all tied together with string)
1 garlic bulb
150 ml (5 fl oz) water
100 ml (3 1/2 fl oz) white wine
sea salt and freshly ground black pepper

Rub the meat and fat cubes with sea salt, place in a dish, add the bouquet garni and garlic, cover and leave in the refrigerator overnight.

The following morning heat the oven to 140°C (275°F), Gas Mark 1, and transfer the salted meat and herbs to an earthenware (not metallic) dish. Stir in the water, wine and a couple of grinds of pepper, cover and cook in the oven for about 4 hours or until the meat is tender.

Allow to cool to room temperature, strain off the liquor into a bowl and go about shredding the meat and fat with 2 forks.

Pack the meat and fat back into a sterilized jar or serving dish and then pour over the strained cooking liquor and refrigerate until needed. It will keep for up to 10 days.

Chicken Liver Parfait

Makes 1 terrine mould about 23 x 7 x 7cm (9 x 3 x 3 inches)

500 g (1 lb) chicken livers
400 g (13 oz) butter, melted
(of which 200 g (7 oz) foie gras could be substituted for pure luxury)
4 eggs
4 shallots finely sliced
2 cloves of garlic finely sliced
sprig of thyme
50 ml (2 fl oz) Maderia
50 ml (2 fl oz) port
25 ml (1 fl oz) brandy
salt and freshly ground black pepper

Warm the chicken livers, melted butter and eggs to room temperature. Meanwhile boil and reduce the rest of the ingredients (shallots, herbs and booze) until the shallots are cooked and the liquid has reduced by half.

Trim the livers and discard any yellow/green tinges and blood vessels, then blend the livers with the eggs in a liquidizer, seasoning well with salt and pepper. Add the shallot reduction and pour in the melted butter a little at a time. Now, for the brave you can double check the seasoning by tasting a little of the raw mixture – alternatively place a drop on to a hot frying pan to cook before tasting, then add salt and pepper as necessary.

Pour the mixture into a terrine mould and set in a roasting tray filled two-thirds full with water (to come at least half-way up the side of the terrine). Cook in a preheated oven, 180°C (350°F), Gas Mark 4, for about 50 minutes or until middle of terrine reaches 68°C (154°F).

Brawn 49 Columbia Road, E2 7RG
020 7729 5692 www.brawn.co/

We should always be wary about describing any restaurant as the 'best'.
We all have different views on what makes the *best* gourmet experience
or all-round restaurant. But there can be little doubt that this small
neighbourhood wine bar and bistro is the apotheosis of its type.

All this talk of the 'best' is prompted by the controversy generated by
this charming offering when it received a (rare) maximum score from the
long-established restaurant critic of the London *Evening Standard*. Brawn
is a great place to visit, but the *ES* accolade was surprising for a number of
reasons, and ignited an interesting debate on Twitter. Notwithstanding,
almost all the national newspaper reviews have also been very positive.

Whatever the case, Brawn is certainly a very, very good example of a
friendly and welcoming local restaurant. There is much to admire, and it
manages to deliver its own inventiveness without being too gimmicky.
The owners (who also own Terroirs, see page 220) have an interest in a
successful wine company, Les Caves de Pyrène, specializing in 'real' wines
that are expressive of where they come from, made by hand with minimal
intervention, and with maximum respect for nature and the environment.
The wine list at Brawn therefore includes many natural, biodynamic
and organic wines, all at quite reasonable prices. Instead of being listed by
geographical location, they are grouped under headings such as 'Stones,
Shells and Sea', 'Clean Lines' and 'Aromatics From Eastern France'.
(PP) Some of my favourites come under the heading 'Vins de Soif'
('wines for thirsty drinkers' – a highly apt description for wines that
make the perfect accompaniment to much of the menu at Brawn).

Ed Wilson, formerly of some of London's top restaurants including
the Wolseley, is not only the head chef but also the patron, a shareholder in
the business, and even the DJ. The menu also has its own unique approach.
Forget first course, mains and puddings. Brawn is all about Taste Ticklers
(from oysters to brandade), Raw & Cured (Italian-style steak tartare, smoked
eel and salads), Pig (from excellent saucisson to pork rillettes), Plancha
(from foie gras and clams to artichokes and quail, all cooked directly on
a very hot metal surface) and Slow Cook (think choucroute, baked
Vacherin Mont d'or and gratins). As these ingredients indicate, there is
a strong French influence to the menu, which also includes treats from
Italy and Spain, as well as from British fields, farms and waters.

All in all, Brawn is a fine example of simple and delicious food paired
with excellent wines in a relaxed setting – probably London's best wine bar,
best neighbourhood restaurant, and quite simply one of London's best. ⊙

Cervelle de Canut

Makes 500 g (1 lb)

500 g (1 lb) fromage blanc or quark
1 shallot, very finely diced
1 tablespoon chopped chives
1 tablespoon chopped tarragon
1 tabelspoon chopped chervil
3 tablespoons cider vinegar
2 tablespoons walnut oil
(plus extra to serve)
salt (optional)

Put the fromage blanc in a bowl and add the
diced shallot, chopped herbs and vinegar.
Mix together thoroughly, then add the
walnut oil. Taste. The vinegar should bring
enough acidity to enliven the fromage blanc
but should not mask the flavours of the herbs
and shallot. The walnut oil should bring a
little depth of flavour. You may also want to
add a little salt. An artisan fromage blanc will
also add flavour.

To finish, drizzle a little extra walnut oil
over the top and serve with bread with
aperitifs or as a starter.

Right **The Lyon
speciality: cervelle
de canut.**

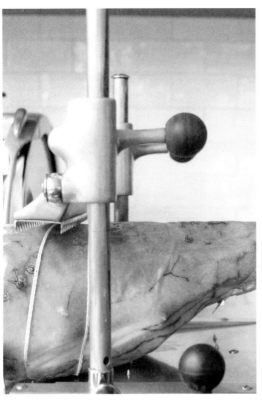

'TIS TRUE MY FORM IS SOMETHING ODD,
BUT BLAMING ME IS BLAMING GOD,
COULD I CREATE MYSELF ANEW
I would NOT fail in pleasing YOU.

IF I COULD REACH FROM POLE to POLE
OR GRASP the Ocean WITH A SPAN
I WOULD BE MEASURED BY THE SOUL.
The MIND's the Standard
the man.

JOSEPH MERRICK

Above **A beautiful old mechanical slicer and charcuterie at Brawn.**

NUL
n'est
cense
ignorer
la loire

Left and right **The back bar shelves at Brawn are full of interesting things.**

Broadway Market Broadway Market, E8
www.broadwaymarket.co.uk Saturdays 9 am–5 pm

There have been barrow boys at Broadway Market since 1890, but it was in 2004 that the market was re-established in its present form. Every Saturday, a narrow road between the oft-forgotten greenery of London Fields and Goldsmiths Row comes to life. Broadway is not a farmers' market, but rather welcomes all styles of food. Ghanaian fast food or fried wild mushrooms on toasted sourdough with a hefty slug of garlic are both great, and there is even the odd fashion, music or small objets stall. Nestling among a few small galleries, a florist's and a couple of bookshops, artisanal food retailers offer an ideal excuse to avoid ghastly supermarket fare and a great opportunity to shop locally in the community.

The crowd is quite modish, but you will also see many cheerful young families in this evolving corner of Hackney. Its location and the lack of major transport links nearby mean that this food market is thankfully mainly for locals. The Cat and Mutton makes a convenient spot for refuelling or a hang-out when the market is over. Although the market is only open on Saturday, there is also a happy buzz here on Sunday over the summer months.

(PP) This is my favourite London food market, for many reasons. Hackney is also developing other smaller satellite markets: a recent visit to the still quite small Chatsworth Road Market nearby was an uplifting experience. ○

Peter Weeden

The best fishmonger in London is The Fin & Flounder on Broadway Market, as they buy fish direct from the Helford day-boat fleet.

Head chef, Boundary Restaurant

Above **The bustling and lively Saturday Broadway Market.** Right **Many different types of street food are available Broadway Market.**

Left **F. Cooke** is one of the last few remaining pie and eel shops in London at Broadway Market.

Left **Mrs King's** Melton Mowbray pies – the best pork pie in the world.

Right and left **Lunch** at Broadway Market is always delicious.

E Pellicci Bethnal Green Road, E2 0AG
020 7739 4873

We love Pellicci's because it's a family business and an East London institution, housed in premises partly listed by English Heritage. The English breakfast will satisfy all comers, from locals on a budget to tourists and those in search of a hint of Italian Formica café nostalgia. ◉

Jones Dairy 23 Ezra Street, E2 7RH
020 7739 5372 www.jonesdairy.co.uk
Fridays and Saturdays 8 am–1 pm (shop), 9 am–3 pm (café)
Sundays 9 am–2 pm (shop), 8 am–2 pm (café)

The best day to visit Jones Dairy – open only for three half-days a week from Friday to Sunday – is definitely Sunday, when you can also enjoy the thronging cobbled streets of the East End and Columbia Road flower market in full bloom. Look out for the small antique market, a few independent furniture retailers, a handful of quirky clothing shops and a smattering of nearby art galleries that also add to the pleasure.

Jones Dairy consists of three small elements: the front shop, a small caff at the rear and an occasional oyster shucker down the adjacent alley; just what you need on a Sunday morning. A glass of stout at the Royal Oak pub next door could follow.

The shop window showcases the extensive range of handmade breads, including cholla, rustic rye, walnut cob, organic spelt, black rye, pain au levain and much, much more. Inside, you'll find the best unpasteurized British cheeses, cakes, artisanal preserves, honey, chutneys and condiments. The attention to detail in this tiny room is impressive, and the old-fashioned scales are redolent of an age when food retailing of this ilk could be found on every street corner.

The caff serves hot, strong tea and coffee served in heavy white mugs, with breakfast buns, toast, freshly-squeezed English apple juice and a few choice sarnies. If you go on a winter's morning you can huddle against the coal-fired heater and its impressive steel chimney. ◉

Left **A local enjoying a hearty lunch at E Pellicci.**

Right **The bar and mini deli at Pizza East.** Far right **Reclaimed furniture is part of the industrial interior at Pizza East.**

Leila's Shop 15–17 Calvert Avenue, E2 7JP
020 7729 9789

The quality of produce at this bijou café and neighbouring food store is second to none. The range is sometimes a little sporadic, probably because only the best is permitted, and is therefore ideal for impulse purchases with a particular culinary creation in mind. Whether it is artichokes, blood oranges, chocolate, cheese, pulses, rice or Ortiz products, they are all – always – exemplary. The café is a favourite weekend breakfast spot, serving an interesting range of egg dishes, all brought to the table in the pan. ◉

Pizza East 56 Shoreditch High Street, E1 6JJ
020 7729 1888 www.pizzaeast.com

Located on the ground floor of the Tea Building, Pizza East is a design triumph and makes a very enjoyable night out for the young, cool crowd in and around Shoreditch. Great credit is due to Nick Jones, founder of the Soho House Group, and the designers involved. The exposed concrete, reclaimed floors and furniture, leather banquettes and sharing tables combine with polished tiles, attractive bars and an open kitchen with inferno-like wood ovens to create the perfect fit for Shoreditch. For a pizzeria, this place has made a huge splash on the scene. It's no ordinary pizzeria, of course – you need to add the 'gourmet' tag – it offers much more than just pizza. The kitchen also gives serious attention to antipasti, salads, baked items and desserts. There is also a small deli, a late-night gig venue and club. (PP) The veal meatballs, prosciutto, cream and sage pizza is my favourite. ◉

Left and right **The ground floor of the Tea Building has been expertly transformed into a cool stripped-back dining area.**

Right
Gourmet pizzas.

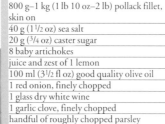

Salt Pollack with Artichokes

Serves 4-6

800 g–1 kg (1 lb 10 oz–2 lb) pollack fillet, skin on
40 g (1 1/2 oz) sea salt
20 g (3/4 oz) caster sugar
8 baby artichokes
juice and zest of 1 lemon
100 ml (3 1/2 fl oz) good quality olive oil
1 red onion, finely chopped
1 glass dry white wine
1 garlic clove, finely chopped
handful of roughly chopped parsley
freshly ground black pepper

Two days before, take the pollack fillet and check for bones, removing these with tweezers if necessary. Mix 20 g (3/4 oz) of the sea salt with 10 g (1/4 – 1/2 oz) of the caster sugar and rub this mixture into the flesh of the pollack. Let it rest for 2 hours, then repeat. Leave in the refrigerator for 12 hours.

Soak the pollack in cold water for 24 hours, changing the water after 12 hours. Remove it from the water and leave it to rest.

To prepare the artichokes, cut the stems 5 cm (2 inches) from the base. Using a vegetable peeler, remove the outer layer of skin from the stem and trim the harder outer petals. Cut the artichokes in half down the middle and remove the choke. Once cut, drop the artichokes into water with some of the lemon juice to prevent oxidization.

Pour a little of the olive oil into a heavy-based saucepan, add the artichokes, and cook gently over a medium heat for a few minutes until they take on a golden colour. Turn them with a spoon, add the chopped onion and cook for a further 3 minutes. Stir in half the white wine to deglaze the pan, cover with a cartouche (greaseproof paper cut to size to sit on the surface) and cook for a further 10 minutes until the artichokes have softened.

Put a splash of olive oil in a separate pan with the garlic. Cook until the garlic infuses the oil, then add the pollack (skin down), the remaining white wine and 2 tablespoons water. Cover and cook for 5–6 minutes, until the fish starts to flake.

Stir the pollack into the artichokes with the roughly chopped parsley, lemon juice and 1 teaspoon of zest, season with salt and pepper and serve.

Lamb Cutlets with Goats' Cheese, Chicory and Watercress Salad

Serves 4

4 racks of lamb, French trimmed (ask your butcher)
25 g (1 oz) shelled walnuts
1 teaspoon olive oil
2 heads of red chicory, leaves torn
1 bunch of watercress, leaves torn
150 g (5 oz) goats' cheese or a creamy Italian variety such as a carina fresco.
juice of 1 lemon
salt and freshly ground black pepper

Cut the lamb racks into individual cutlets, season with salt and pepper, and cook in a frying pan over a high heat or on a barbecue to your liking.

In a separate large pan, toss the walnuts in olive oil over a medium heat to toast them lightly, remove from the heat, then add the chicory and watercress and toss together.

Divide the chicory, watercress and walnuts between serving plates and arrange the cutlets on the side. Scatter over big creamy chunks of goats' cheese, season with lemon juice and serve.

Alyn Williams

"

Beigel Bake in Brick Lane sell the world's best salt beef bagels, 24 hours a day.

Head chef, The Westbury Hotel

Poppies of Spitalfields 6–8 Hanbury Street, E1 6QR
020 7247 0892 www.poppiesfishandchips.co.uk

Poppies is a wonderful new addition to the dining scene in this corner of east London, on the edge of Spitalfields Market: a retro-looking 'chippy' (complete with jukebox), with proper service values, all underpinned by experience and tradition. Pop has been serving the East End with fish and chips since 1945. You can eat in or take away, the latter being wrapped in newspaper. There is a full range of fried or grilled fish, from cod to Dover sole, with homemade mushy peas and pickled onions, plus saveloys, whitebait and jellied eels. You can wash it all down with a glass of Sauvignon Blanc or a ginger beer. ●

Ridley Road Market Dalston, E8 www.ridleyroad.co.uk
Monday to Wednesday 9 am–3 pm, Thursday 9 am–12 pm,
Friday and Saturday 9 am–5 pm

Hackney is a melting pot of different ethnicities, and one of the best examples must be this market. Jewish immigrants, followed by Asian, Greek, Turkish and West Indian communities (hence the reggae music), have dominated the stalls over the years. All can rub shoulders here in this loud and raw vibe. If you are preparing an exotic feast or a Turkish delight, this is the only place to buy the comestibles. ●

Left and above
Battered fish and chips served in paper, no longer old newspaper, but still evocative.

Above **Melanie Arnold and Margot Henderson in the Shaker-esque former bicycle shed that is Rochelle Canteen.** Left **Melanie and her dog.**

Rochelle Canteen Arnold Circus, E2 7ES
020 7729 5677 www.arnoldandhenderson.com

This used to be a little-known canteen principally for occupants of the adjoining former Victorian school, now studio space for various designers including Giles Deacon. Established in the late 1990s by James Moores, the project also includes an interesting gallery and event space.

The canteen is now one of the coolest must-go locations for the fashionistas of east London. Entering via the solid metal gate and secret club-like entry buzzer, you cross the grassed-over former school playground and head towards the converted bike shed, where you will find a very simple Shaker-style interior with seating for about 20, alongside a fully open kitchen. When weather permits, dining extends to the outside area, which is also within a watering can's distance of the herb garden and plant pots.

Fans of the St. John 'nose to tail' argot will love this simple menu. The business is run by Margot Henderson (wife of Fergus) and Melanie Arnold, who also operate a very successful outside catering business that specializes in feeding London's burgeoning art crowd.

(PP) I remember visiting this place when it first opened. The menu was much shorter then, and the bills were presented on scraps of paper. While setting up Boundary nearby (see page 96), I visited the canteen about once a week and enjoyed every mouthful. The choice and range of drinks has moved on since those early days, but thankfully it has retained all its beguiling mannerisms. The only negatives are no wines and limited opening hours (just breakfast and lunch, Monday to Friday). ●

Saf 152–4 Curtain Road, EC2A 3AT
020 7613 0007 www.safrestaurant.co.uk

Saf is an acronym for simply authentic food; it also means 'pure' in Turkish – the parent company is based in Istanbul. This is a very special and rare type of restaurant, specializing in plant-based ingredients and raw foods. 'Raw' is often used to denote food cooked under 48°C (118.4°F), so that the flavours are preserved and the nutritional value is maximized. Preparing food in this way also means that the enzymes on which the body relies for healthy digestion are largely unharmed. With this background you might think that you lose an essential part of visiting a restaurant. But you would be very wrong. The food here is special; the cocktails, natural wines and organic teas are all excellent.

(PP) I have a confession and interest to declare with regard to Saf, as I was a general consultant on the project when it first opened. The whole experience was eye opening. The technique, knowledge and passion displayed by the whole team were amazing. This is an entirely different way of viewing food, respecting the fundamental link between what you put into your body and your personal wellbeing. Even if I don't practise it, I believe in it. ◗

St. John Bread and Wine 94–6 Commercial Street, E1 6LZ
020 3301 8069 www.stjohnbreadandwine.com

A sibling of the seminal St. John (see page 190), Bread and Wine opened in 2003 in a former bank building. The St. John aesthetic prevails, with white walls, a reclaimed parquet floor, a few pendant lights, Shaker-style coat hooks, counters clad in stainless steel and an open kitchen with a huge baker's oven.

Fergus Henderson continues the 'nose to tail' cooking, though over the years Bread and Wine appears to have developed its own identity. The menu is set out according to the time of the day. From 9 am, you can indulge in porridge and prunes or an Old Spot bacon sandwich; from 11 am, seed cake and a glass of Madeira provide a fillip; and the always intensely seasonal best of St. John is rolled out after midday.

(PP) I recently called in for a late Monday afternoon lunch and had the most delicious blood cake with a duck egg followed by a blancmange. Although the menu is slightly shorter and simpler than at the main St. John restaurant, you can still expect the highest-quality seasonal British cooking, plus a fine selection of feasting options for groups of eight or more. Whole suckling pig has always been a favourite and recently they have added whole sea bass with kohlrabi and sorrel for four; chicken and leek pie; braised lamb; and Black Angus flank for eight. Perfectly ripe Lancashire cheese and Eccles cakes, and madeleines baked to order end most meals.

Some people prefer Bread and Wine over its older sibling for its more edgy and arty crowd. Expect queues for lunch at the weekend, when it can get very busy, but it's certainly worth any wait. The staff, in their signature uniform of chef-style white jackets, also deserve an appreciative mention. ◗

Above **A proud baker at St. John.**

Right **St. John B&W is housed in a former bank.**

Taj Stores 112 Brick Lane, E1 6RL 020 7377 0061 www.tajstores.co.uk

If you thought your knowledge of rare and unusual fruit and vegetables could match that of most chefs, try naming the ingredients as you enter this cornucopia of foods from India, Bangladesh, Malaysia and Thailand, Greece, Jamaica, Lebanon and Japan to mention just a few of the sources. Chow chow, turia, ravaja, gourds, muki, and eddoe are just a few of the unusual products displayed in large crates alongside a profusion of peppers and chillies.

At the rear of the store you will find large chest freezers filled with up to 12 different types of prawns set in blocks of ice. There are also 3 cm-long, deliciously oily, translucent keshi fish and metre-long and very ugly rita fish.

The halal meat counter includes pheasant, duck, pigeon and goat, alongside lambs' brains and chicken hearts. This is a specialist food supplier at its best. If you're thinking about cooking an Indian supper for friends, your starting point has to be a visit to Taj Stores. Even if you only buy a tarva pan for your chapati, it will certainly impress your guests. **○**

Up Market Ely's Yard, Old Truman Brewery, E1 6QL
www.sundayupmarket.co.uk Sundays 10 am–5 pm

The local carrom league (carrom is an easy-to-understand board game believed to have originated in India hundreds of years ago, often compared to billiards, marbles or air hockey) meets here every Sunday, so pick up a herbal lassi and wait your turn. Everybody is welcome.

Street food rules at the Up Market, from sushi, paella and empanadas to falafel and Sri Lankan curry. You can even buy a healthy jungle juice from Caribbean Momma's. The Ethiopian stalls are a personal favourite: soya shuroh and gomen (Ethiopian greens) are wrapped in soft injera bread, made with four different flours while Ethiopian coffee is roasted in small pans over charcoal, crushed, and then placed in a jebena pot with hot water.

A trailer kitchen outside the market sells cheap Lao and Thai staples such as tom yum, phad thai and red curries. **○**

Above **Exotic food displays at Taj Stores.**

Left and right **Sunday afternoon at Up Market.**

Viajante Patriot Square, Bethnal Green, E2 9NF
020 7871 0461 www.viajante.co.uk

Viajante, meaning 'traveller' in Portuguese, is not the type of restaurant we would usually recommend. But there are more than a few things to admire here. Equally, for people who enjoy 'real' food, there is much to dislike. It's one of those restaurants that is worth trying just for the experience and to open your mind, but few people would choose to come here on a regular basis. It's a one-off, not least because there is no menu: everybody is expected to have the chef's tasting menu, the only option being between three, six or nine courses.

(PP) I had the six-course option, but when you add the appetizer, the bread course – yes, there's a bread course – the pre-dessert and other extras, you find yourself at the receiving end of apparently endless volleys of bizarre food combinations, served by efficient and well-informed acolytes of the Nuno Mendes cult. Some of the chef's creations work and are utterly delicious, some are absolutely horrible. I enquired about the nine-course option: apparently it takes at least three hours to complete the exercise – not my idea of a convivial meal. But the sexy bar and Danish modernist furniture are very pleasant. ○

Viet Grill 58 Kingsland Road, E2 8DP
020 7739 6686 www.vietnamesekitchen.co.uk

On a stretch of Kingsland Road known for its Vietnamese restaurants, Viet Grill is renowned as a favourite among those who appreciate great food. The prices are very reasonable, the food authentic and the service sweet – unlike some of the other restaurants on the 'strip' – and they are also serious about matching wine with food to ensure you have a truly enjoyable experience.

(PP) I'm no expert on Vietnamese food, traditional or modern, but I can't think that there is a better Vietnamese restaurant to be found in London. Their sister restaurant, Cay Tre on nearby Old Street, is also excellent. ○

Above, top
Nuno Mendes, chef at Viajante.
Above **The sexy bar at Viajante.**
Left **Beautiful Scandinavian-style furniture in the Viajante dining room.**

Pear Crumble Muffins

More than anything else, these muffins are a vehicle for perfectly ripe pears. At Violet we change the fruit as new and wonderful types come into season. In the summer, strawberries, raspberries, cherries and then plums feature in the moist crumb of the muffin, topped with buttery crumble. Muffins are best when made by hand, as over-mixing ruins the texture. At Violet, we make all our muffins in small batches without the aid of electric mixers.

Makes 12 muffins

275 g (9 oz) plain flour
2¹/2 teaspoons baking powder
¹/2 teaspoon bicarbonate of soda
¹/4 teaspoon salt
2 eggs
175 g (6 oz) caster sugar
75 g (3 oz) unsalted butter, melted
140 ml (4³/4 fl oz) buttermilk or natural yogurt
¹/2 lemon
3 ripe pears such as Comice (or about 200 g/7 oz other fruits in season)

For the crumble topping

100 g (3¹/2 oz) cold unsalted butter
150 g (5 oz) plain flour
4 tablespoons light brown sugar

Preheat the oven to 170°C (340°F), Gas Mark 3¹/2, and line a 12-cup muffin tin with paper cases.

In a large bowl combine the flour, baking powder, bicarbonate of soda and salt and use a balloon whisk to mix it all together. We find this much easier than sifting, and it works in the same way to distribute the baking powder and bicarbonate of soda evenly through the flour. Set aside.

In another bowl, whisk together the eggs and caster sugar. Gradually drizzle in the melted butter, and finally whisk in the buttermilk or plain yogurt. Zest the lemon straight into the bowl to that you catch the aromatic oils that are released. Pour the liquid into the dry ingredients and stir together until the dry ingredients are only just incorporated into the liquid so as not to overmix – the batter will be quite thick.

Spoon the batter into the paper cases. Quarter and core the pears and cut each quarter into bite-sized pieces. Push about a quarter of a pear into each pape case.

Quickly mash all the crumble ingredients together and sprinkle generously over the muffins. The topping can be made in advance and kept in the refrigerator for up to a week or in the freezer for up to a month.

Bake the muffins for 25–30 minutes or until a skewer inserted in the middle comes out clean. Serve warm with a pot of fresh coffee.

Violet 47 Wilton Way, E8 3ED
020 7275 8360 www.violetcakes.com

Claire Ptak is one of the most talented pastry chefs, bakers and food stylists working in London today. Having arrived in London after serving as pastry chef at Alice Waters' legendary Chez Panisse in California, in 2005 Claire started baking from her flat in Hackney to supply her weekly stall at Broadway Market.

(PP) I used to live in the same building, and the pervading smells were glorious. Things have moved on since those early days. Claire is now a full-on London food personality. A visit to her stall at Broadway Market is a weekly ritual for many, and she is also involved with the new Maltby Street Market project. The tiny shop and production kitchen are a precious blessing for local residents.

The house speciality is seasonal American-style cupcakes with butter cream icing, including rhubarb in the spring, berries and cherries in the summer, figs and quince in the winter and lots of lovely things like the very best vanilla and chocolate. You can also enjoy sticky hot cross buns at Easter, cookies, Christmas cake and many other delights. Claire's books, particularly *The Whoopie Pie Book*, are also admirable. ◐

Above **Outside Claire Ptak's modest premises in Hackney.**

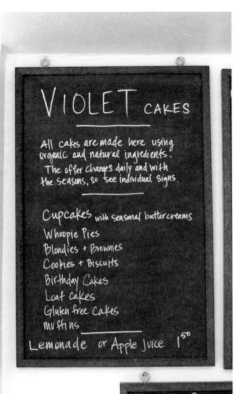

More places to visit in the area

Above **Violet's cakes and baked goods are some of the best in London.**

Androuet
Old Spitalfields Market,
107b Commercial Street, E1 6 BG
020 7375 3168
A name with resonance for Parisian cheese-lovers is now to be found on the edge of Spitalfields Market. The adjoining restaurant isn't for us, but the range of French cheese in perfect condition is definitely worth it. Not as atmospheric as La Fromagerie or Neal's Yard Dairy, but the cheese is carefully matured.

Fifteen
15 Westland Place, N1 7LP
020 3375 1515 www.fifteen.net
(St) Jamie Oliver's first restaurant in London is still very popular. (PP) I prefer the ground-floor Trattoria, where they make fresh pasta in the bar and there is always a pronounced aroma of garlic.

Ginger Pig
99 Lauriston Road, Hackney, E9 7HJ
020 8986 6911 www.thegingerpig.co.uk
If you find yourself near the splendid Victoria Park, don't leave before exploring the nearby Lauriston Road 'village', where you'll find the Ginger Pig butchers. (PP) You can usually find me here on a Saturday morning, before heading next door for my wine at Bottle Apostle and on to Jonathan Norris for some fresh fish. Broadway Market is just up the road.

The Grocery
54–6 Kingsland Road, E2 8DP
020 7729 6855 www.thegroceryshop.co.uk
Very popular with the local Shoreditch residents, thanks to its extensive range of health foods and daily staples.

Sedap
102 Old Street, EC1V 9AY
020 7490 0200 www.sedap.co.uk
(PP) I was introduced to this unassuming Malaysian eatery by a fellow restaurateur. I now find myself recommending it more often than other Asian restaurants. Food is fantastic; the service is pure family charm.

Towpath Café
42 De Beauvoir Crescent, Dalston, N1 5SB
An ideal stop-off and coffee injection with dainty carbs for anyone exploring east London. The patron has a smile and positive outlook that are so rare (especially when the service is so chaotic). Watch out for joggers and cyclists – somebody's bound to fall in the canal one day.

Whitechapel Gallery
77–82 Whitechapel High Street, E1 7QX
020 7522 7896 www.whitechapelgallery.org
Angela Hartnett (see Murano page 274) has recently been appointed as restaurant consultant. A good opportunity to enjoy art and a good plate of food on a more modest scale than the Tate experiences.

Camden
Hampstead
Highgate
Primrose Hill
St. John's Wood
Stoke Newington

Home to numerous thespians and awash with actors from the big screen, it is rather surprising that the restaurant scene in this area of London is not more exciting than it is. Maybe over-discerning residents are deterring entrepreneurial restaurateurs from trying their luck in this high-minded corner of London. Hampstead is by reputation the intellectual, literary and liberal heart of London, with a large proportion of its residents professing to be dedicated foodies. This doesn't seem to show on the High Street, however, which offers very little choice other than the ubiquitous café and coffee shop chains.

With their history, large residential properties and proximity to Hampstead Heath and Parliament Hill (and its amazing view over the London skyline), Hampstead and Highgate are lovely places to live, but the restaurant and food options here are underwhelming. Although quality restaurants might be in short supply, there are some decent traditional pubs conveniently close to the Heath. Great for bracing winter walks, the Heath is even better for a summer stroll and a restorative lunch in a cosy pub.

There can be no better place to picnic in London than historic Hampstead Heath. It is more enjoyable if you prepare the foods yourself and pack a rug, proper plates, cutlery and glassware, a bottle of Champagne and a few English strawberries. Failing this, The Bull and Last pub can cater to your every whim with an excellent range of takeaway foods and hampers (see opposite). The open-air concerts at Kenwood House organized by English Heritage are another classic highlight of summer in the city.

Left and below
Brew House.
Right **Kenwood
House on the edge
of Hampstead
Heath.**

Brew House Kenwood, Hampstead Lane, NW3 7JR
020 8341 5384 www.companyofcooks.com

Set in landscaped grounds on the edge of Hampstead Heath, Kenwood
was remodelled by Robert Adam in the 18th century, and remains one of
the most elegant and palatial of all grand English houses. It is also home to
masterpieces by Turner, Vermeer, Rembrandt and Gainsborough. After a
tour of the house, the Brew House terraces and café make an ideal place to
linger over tea and cake. ◐

Joël
Antunes

The current food scene in London
is amazing and I do think it's one
of the best places in the world for
eating out. British chefs have found
their own way in the last 10 years.

Chef patron, Brasserie Joël

Left **Hampstead
Heath on a rare
fine day.**

Above **Oxtail and bone marrow, and the fish board (above right) from the menu at The Bull and Last.** Left **The Bull and Last is one of the most hospitable places in London, for man and his dog.**

Brian Lay-Jones 36 Heath Street, NW3 6TE

020 7435 5084

This traditional local greengrocer's offers a wide array of fresh and exotic produce at very reasonable prices.

The Bull and Last 168 Highgate Road, NW5 1QS

020 7267 3641 www.thebullandlast.co.uk

(PP) I walked into this excellent example of a British pub on a hot summer's day, and sitting on the bar were two faultless Scotch eggs with molten yolks alongside two cold beers. You couldn't ask for more, but The Bull and Last will certainly supply it all the same. Ollie and Joe, who run the pub, are highly affable, something both Lisa, our brilliant photographer, and I discovered and that their regular customers report. It's a slightly quirky place, which is exactly what you want, and the food is tasty, seasonal and wholesome. Ollie and Joe have also cleverly developed a range of picnic hampers that are ideal for the Heath.

This page **Ice cream made in seconds at Chin Chin thanks to the chilling effect of nitrogen.**

The Chin Chin Laboratorists 49–50 Camden Lock Place, NW1 8AF
www.chinchinlabs.com Tues-Sun 12–7 pm

Europe's first nitro ice cream parlour is great fun for the kids, and interesting and indulgent for adults. Essentially, it offers fast-track and ultra-fresh ice cream made to order in front of you. In fact, it is all rather simple: they pour the custard mix into a table-top blender, add liquid nitrogen, and hey presto, there's your creamy ice cream. The flavours are seriously tempting and use highly prized ingredients. (PP) The flavour of the week when I visited was 'Cajeta – Mexican caramel', a rich caramel flavoured with cinnamon, vanilla and goats' milk. Yum, and much better than the ubiquitous salted caramel.

Beware: Chin Chin Lab is on the edge of the Camden Market, so on Saturdays you can expect to queue – all the more fun and anticipation for little ones. ◖

Right **Expectant queues at Chin Chin.**

REVER...

...EAT FOR FUN

...putumayo
world music
cds on sale here

guaranteed to ...

Ahrash & Nyisha

"

For us, the single best thing about the London food scene is the variety of cuisines on offer. London has everything, and even the haute restaurants are affordable.

The Chin Chin Laboratorists

Gaucho Grill 64 Heath Street, NW3 1DN
020 7431 8222 www.gaucho-grill.co.uk

We have consciously avoided 'multi-site' branded restaurants (those with the same menu and similar interior designs) in this book, not because we disagree with the approach, but quite simply because the food and service in such restaurants – in London and throughout the UK generally – are habitually dreadful. Nevertheless, there are a few groups of cafés and restaurants – Leon, Carluccio's (now losing it a bit), Giraffe and Gaucho Grills – that have done much better than others. While some concepts are simply not suited to being rolled out on every high street in the country, others are eminently so. The critical factors are the motivation and experience of the management, as what starts in London as a new and exciting concept invariably ends up being over-managed by financiers.

Gaucho Grills are serious restaurants, slightly more expensive than most other branded operations and not always found on the high street. They have integrity, as well as an interesting concept. The first site opened well over a decade ago, and they do not seem to be mandated by investors. Instead, they have expanded gradually and in a controlled manner. While the design at each restaurant shares a common thread, including high-quality furnishings, there are also significant differences.

The main reason for their success is the excellent quality of the Argentinian beef they use. The moist and mild climate, rich soil and vast terrain on which the cattle graze, combined with the process by which the meat is aged, ensure that Argentinian beef develops its own distinctive flavour. The Argentine Aberdeen Angus that graze freely over grassland contains less cholesterol and has less intra-muscular fat. At Gaucho Grill steaks are cooked in the traditional Argentine manner, turned just once for greater caramelization: this forms a delicious crust and enhances the flavour. The menu also has many other facets, not least an all-Argentinian wine list. ○

Giraffe 46 Rosslyn Hill, NW3 1NH
020 7435 0343 www.giraffe.net

This was the first site of the Giraffe chain that serves a globally popular menu and is now a highly successful group and brand. The owners clearly have a soft spot for this property, and have recently tweaked the concept to give it a little more café style. It is very much a family restaurant and brilliant for kids – ideal for the area. Go for brunch and enjoy stacked pancakes with strawberries and bananas with maple syrup or a brekkie burrito. ○

Above **Giraffe has a deserved reputation as a family-friendly café.**

Harry Morgan 29–31 St. Johns Wood High Street, NW8 7NH
020 7722 1869 www.harryms.co.uk

You need to know about Harry M's, but you don't necessarily need to eat on the premises. The room is hardly the greatest attraction and the service is pretty poor, especially from the young kids (the slightly more mature staff aren't bad). But this long-established diner, deli and takeaway service is a perennial attraction for the great and the good of the north-west London Jewish community, as well as many other religious faiths and communities. Their chicken soup and salt beef are said to be the best in London. Other heimishe foods include pickled tongue, chopped liver, gefilte fish, pickled cucumbers, potato latke, lokshen pudding and apple strudel. The hot salt-beef sandwich and the smoked salmon bagels are also good to go. ◉

Louis Patisserie 32 Heath Street, NW3 6TE
020 7435 9908

A Hungarian café with old-fashioned pastries and endearingly grumpy old ladies. The interior hasn't changed over the years, and makes a welcome change from the bland coffee shops now found on every high street. ◉

Market 43 Parkway, NW1 7PN
020 7267 9700 www.marketrestaurant.co.uk

Sandwiched between dodgy kebab shops and the tanning salons of Camden (a notable exception being the very good Whole Foods store a few doors down) is the tiny Market restaurant. Market is not a restaurant to travel to, but it's one of the best in the area. Simple and quite small, it has zinc-topped tables, oak floors and exposed brick walls, with pleasant staff and a menu offering six or seven options at each course.

(PP) I thoroughly enjoyed my visit to Market, although one dish – the delicious and extraordinarily generous chicken and ham pie – needed to be countered by three glasses of wine. I found myself comparing it to the version we always include on the menu at Albion (see page 88), but the Market version had a more creamy gravy that is a little floury for my liking. Some people may prefer the Market pie filling, but the pastry topping doesn't compare with the Albion pie. As I debated the virtues of each, people at the tables all around me were oohing and aahing about their food, and it all looked fantastic. ◉

Bryn Williams

London is great because it's so diverse. For example it offers anything from an £8 curry on Brick Lane to an £80 curry at Benares, and everything in between.

Chef patron, Odette's

Melrose and Morgan 42 Gloucester Avenue, NW1 8JD
020 7722 0011 www.melroseandmorgan.co.uk

This embryonic chain is distinguished by its modern design and slightly clinical styling. The range of store cupboard stocks is more toffee-nosed than essential, but they offer excellent fresh *traiteur* dishes. ◉

Above **A salt beef sandwich with mustard at Harry Morgan's.**

Above left and right
The classy interior at Odette's.
Left **Bryn Williams at his fabulous restaurant, Odette's.**

Odette's 130 Regent's Park Road, NW1 8XL
020 7586 8569 www.odettesprimrosehill.com

With its colourful interior, chi-chi menu, extensive wine list, chef who is an emerging star (with a famous rock-star girlfriend, it is rumoured), and cosy corners for lovers' trysts, this restaurant is perfect for Primrose Hill, and attracts many young flirting couples.

Odette's has been around since 1978, and in 2006 was acquired by the concert promoter and legendary Irishman Vince Power, who installed Bryn Williams as the chef. Bryn now owns the joint, and has introduced a sprinkling of ingredients from his native Wales to the menu.

(PP) I was a little sceptical about one of Bryn's signature dishes, the pig's head and black pudding terrine with crispy ears, apple jelly and pickled mushrooms (see page 125); then I tried it, and happily revised my views. ○

Odette's

Braised Oxtail, Turbot and Cockles

This is based on the dish that won me the BBC's *Great British Menu* competition in 2006, and which was served at Her Majesty the Queen's 80th birthday banquet. It's never off the menu at Odette's. There are quite a few components to this recipe, so read it through carefully before you begin. You'll need to start at least a day ahead because the oxtail has to marinate for a full 24 hours.

Serves 4

1 kg (2 lbs) oxtail, chopped
1 large onion, peeled and chopped
1 large carrot, peeled and chopped
2 bay leaves
750 ml (1 1/4 pints) red wine
3 tablespoons vegetable oil
50 g (2 oz) plain flour
2 litres (3 1/2 pints) chicken stock
400 g (13 oz) cockles, cleaned (discard any that remain open)
125 ml (4 fl oz) white wine
1 tablespoon olive oil
20 g (3/4 oz) samphire
pinch of nutmeg
juice of 1 lemon
4 pieces of turbot, about 125 g (4 oz) each, skinned
50 g (2 oz) butter
2 tablespoons crème fraîche
salt and freshly ground pepper

Put the oxtail into a large, heavy-based saucepan with the onion, carrot, bay leaves and red wine, and set aside to marinate for 24 hours.

Next day remove the oxtail and the vegetables and set aside on separate plates. Preheat the oven to 140°C (275°F), Gas Mark 1. Place the red wine marinade, in its saucepan, on to the heat and bring it to the boil. Reduce it hard by three-quarters of its volume – you only want about 200ml (7 fl oz) left in the pan. Skim off any scum or foam that rises to the surface. Set aside.

Heat a heavy-based flameproof casserole on a medium flame and add 1 tablespoon vegetable oil. Season the flour with some salt and pepper and use it to dust the oxtail. When the oil's hot, add the oxtail pieces allowing each one to colour until golden brown all over. You may have to do this in batches to avoid the meat steaming instead of browning. Remove and set aside.

Add the marinated vegetables to the pot and fry until golden brown. Add the red wine marinade and deglaze the casserole, bubbling to reduce the liquid by half.

Return the oxtail to the pot. Cover with chicken stock and bring to the boil.

Skim again, removing any excess fat or scum. Place it in the oven for 2 1/2 hours. You want the meat to be coming off the bone. Set aside to cool in the liquid. When completely cool, remove the oxtail from the liquid and pick the meat from the bones, trying to keep the meat in large pieces. Strain the liquid through a fine sieve into a clean saucepan and bring to the boil. Simmer and reduce by half. Then set aside to keep warm.

Put the cockles into a large, warmed saucepan with the white wine. Immediately cover with a lid and cook on a high heat for 1–2 minutes, or until the shells have opened. Discard any that remain closed.

Strain the cockles through a colander, reserving the liquid. Pick most of the cockles from their shells, saving a few of them in their shells for garnish. Set them aside to keep warm.

In a another saucepan, gently warm the olive oil. Add the samphire. Season with salt, pepper, the nutmeg and lemon juice. Cook for 30 seconds, then remove from the heat. Set aside.

Heat a non-stick pan over a medium heat. When hot add the remaining vegetable oil. Place the turbot into the pan and cook until the underside has browned (2–3 minutes). Turn the turbot pieces over and cook for a further 2–3 minutes over a lower heat. Add the butter to finish the cooking.

To serve, place the wilted samphire onto each plate, and arrange the cockles and picked oxtail around it. Drizzle with the oxtail jus, then position the turbot on top of the samphire. Bring the cockles' cooking liquid to the boil and whisk in the crème fraîche. Pour this on to each plate and serve immediately.

Bryn's tip:
Here's a trick for cleaning cockles: place them in a large bowl of cold water. Add a handful of wholemeal flour, and leave them for an hour. They'll then clean themselves in the clean water. When the time's up, rinse the cockles, and they're ready to use.

Recipe featured in *Bryn's Kitchen* by Bryn Williams, Kyle Books

Odette's

Pig's Head Terrine with Pig's Ear Cubes and Pickled Mushrooms

You'll need to start this recipe a day ahead to soak the meat. At Odette's we cook this using a sous vide machine (a machine that cooks food in a water bath at controlled temperatures).

Makes 1 large terrine

1 pig's head cut in half
2 ham hocks
10 g (pinch) 5-spice powder
10 g (pinch) cumin
10 g (pinch) chilli flakes
10 g (pinch) ground ginger
5 star anise
5 cloves
3 cinnamon sticks
sprig of thyme
1 bay leaf
500 ml (17 fl oz) cold chicken stock
3 sticks black pudding, 100 g (3½ oz) each
500 ml (17 fl oz) apple juice
salt and freshly ground black pepper

For the pickled mushrooms

1 kg (2 lb) button mushrooms
600 ml (1 pint) white wine vinegar
300 g (10 oz) sugar
2 tablespoons sea salt
1 red chilli (split)
1 garlic clove (crushed)
1 sprig thyme
1 bay leaf

The day before, singe the pig's head to remove all the fine hair, and cut off the ears. Soak the pig's head and ears in cold water for 6–8 hours.

Soak the ham hocks in a separate bowl of cold water for 8 hours.

The next day, drain the pig's head and set the ears aside. Place the head in a large saucepan, cover with cold water and bring to the boil. Pour away the water, cover with clean cold water and bring back to the boil. Repeat this process once more, then bring to the boil again and skim off any scum that forms on the surface.

Add all the spices, thyme and bay leaf, lower the heat and cook gently for 8 hours or until cooked and the meat shreds easily.

Drain the ham hocks, then place in a sous vide bag. Pour in the cold chicken stock, vacuum seal and place in a water bath or sous vide machine to cook at 80°C (176°F) for 6 hours.

Pick the meat from the pig's head, place in a bowl and season with salt and pepper.

Pour the chicken stock from the cooked ham hocks into a small saucepan and place over a high heat to reduce until the mixture is just sticky enough to bind the ham.

Pick the meat from the ham hocks and place into a large saucepan. Stir in the reduced chicken stock and season with salt and pepper.

Peel the skin from the black pudding, and place the black pudding in a saucepan to warm up until you are ready to assemble the terrine.

Line a terrine mould, 20 x 10 cm (8 x 4 inches), with clingfilm and fill it with alternate layers of ham hock, pig's head meat and a spreading of black pudding, finishing with a layer of ham hock. Wrap over the clingfilm and press it down with a weight (a good option is a can of baked beans), then leave to set until cool.

For the pig's ears

Place the apple juice in a saucepan over a high heat until it reduces down to 100 ml (3½ fl oz), then leave to cool.

Place the pig's ears into a sous vide bag and pour in the apple juice. Vacuum seal the bag and place in a water bath or sous vide machine to cook at 80°C (176°F) for 6–8 hours.

When cooked, chop the meat into small cubes, fry in a hot pan in a little oil until golden, then serve with the terrine.

For the pickled mushrooms

Wash and dry the mushrooms, then place on a tray or in a wide shallow container that you can cover with a lid.

In a saucepan, boil the vinegar with the sugar, salt, chilli and garlic for 2 minutes, then add the thyme and bay leaf. Pour the mixture over the mushrooms, cover, and leave to cool.

When cold, strain off the liquid and pour the mushrooms into sterilized preserving jars and seal.

To serve

Serve slices of the terrine with a few pickled mushrooms and pig's ear cubes on the side.

The Old White Bear Well Road, NW3 1LJ
020 7794 7719 www.theoldwhitebear.co.uk

This pub is a little distance from the Heath, but certainly worth the extra weary walk after a morning constitutional. While the concept of a pub is resolutely British, this one has more than a hint of Europe about it. The colourful patterned tiles on the floor and tabletops, the Jieldé light fittings and various menu options all point to our cousins across the Channel. But the pleasures of Albion are restored by a crackling fire. ●

Raoul's Deli 8–10 Clifton Road, W9 1SS
020 7289 6649 www.raoulsgourmet.com

This great local deli opposite Raoul's Café offers *traiteur*-style prepared foods, different breads including Poilâne loaves, charcuterie, organic fruit and vegetables and innumerable cheeses and continental specialities. A selection of goodies from the Raoul's menu is on sale to take away, or you can sit at the pavement tables and enjoy a coffee and a piece of cheesecake. ●

Sushi-Say 33b Walm Lane, NW2 5SH
020 8459 2971

Although Sushi-Say is a bit off the beaten track, and not exactly in one of the finest areas of the capital, the ambrosial food is certainly worth the effort so forget the car or a cab and take the tube.

This small, traditional and authentic Japanese restaurant is run by a husband-and-wife team: Yuko is the manageress, while Katsuhara presides over the sushi bar. The menu offers beautifully executed age-old classics from the Japanese repertoire. After one really excellent lunch I enjoyed there, Yuko began to reflect on the new wave of Japanese restaurants and the modern dishes that, thanks to Nobu (see page 270), have entered the vernacular of Japanese menus. She was adamant that the furthest Katsu would go in this direction is California rolls and soft shell crab tempura – so not very far, thankfully.

Katsu's recent recommendations have included razor clam, whelk and freshwater eel nigiri sushi, plus a really excellent *o-toro* – fatty tuna belly. The lustre on all of the fish is testimony to its extreme freshness, and – unlike in many other Japanese restaurants – the proportion of rice to fish is just right. The fish is far more dominant than the rice, which is also excellent and not overpowered by the wasabi, but instead reveals a subtle sweetness. If you don't like sushi, there is also a fine choice of tempura, yakitori, pickled vegetables, bean curd and grilled fish, along with rice and noodle dishes. The gyoza and shumai are excellent appetizers. In short, Sushi-Say has some of the very best sushi in London. ●

Left **Some of the best traditional-style sushi in London is served at Sushi-Say.**

XO 29 Belsize Lane, NW3 5AS
020 7433 0888 www.rickerrestaurants.com/xo

The Orient is brought to the doorstep of north London in this branch of Will Ricker's collection of cool and trendy restaurants and bars offering the full gamut of foods from the region. Miso, dim sum, Vietnamese salads, tempura, maki rolls, sashimi and Asian curries: all are to be found here, complemented by sexy cocktails. A successful and winning formula. ●

More places to visit in the area

Above and above right A little out of the way, but worth the trip for the intimate dining rooms at The Old White Bear.

Carluccio's
St. John's Wood High Street, NW8 7SH
020 7449 0404
32 Rosslyn Hill, NW3 1NH
020 7794 2184 www.carluccios.com
These two branches of the now-national chain of Italian caffès and delis are extremely popular.

The Hampstead Butcher and Providore
56 Rosslyn Hill, NW3 1ND
020 7794 9210
www.hampsteadbutcher.com
Alongside the butcher's display you can also buy a range of deli and store cupboard essentials, while the back of the shop holds a cheese and wine room.

The Horseshoe
28 Heath Street, NW3 6TE
020 7431 7206
This is a stripped-back modern gastropub with equally stripped-back food and an on-site micro-brewery. Fish and chips are generally the order of the day.

Jin Kichi
73 Heath Street, NW3 6UG
020 7794 6158 www.jinkichi.com
A long-established Japanese restaurant in the heart of Hampstead.

Trojka
101 Regent's Park Road, NW1 8UR
020 7483 3765 www.trojka.co.uk
Simple Eastern European food, with a buzzy evening scene and live musicians on Friday and Saturday. The extensive menu includes Russian, Ukrainian, Polish and Jewish dishes.

The Wells
30 Well Walk, NW3 1BX
020 7794 3785
www.thewellshampstead.co.uk
A good pub with food. The classic Georgian building perched about halfway between the sedate, semi-rural charms of the Heath and the village high street makes a good place to stop for a light lunch and a beer (cold or warm, according to taste).

Canary Wharf
Dulwich
Greenwich

In 1984, the late Michael von Clemm, then chairman of Roux Restaurants, and Reg Ward, chief executive of the London Docklands Development Corporation, met for lunch on board the boat *Res Nova*, close to the then defunct West India Docks. Comparing the derelict warehouses with those of Boston Harbor, which had been developed for office use, von Clemm dreamed up a transformative scheme for this part of London. Luck, good fortune and enthusiastic support from the government all played their part, and construction work started in 1988. Today it is doing rather well, thanks not least to the Docklands Light Railway. The trees are nearing maturity, and there is a multitude of restaurants and a series of lively retail arcades.

Between 1802 and 1980, West India Docks was one of the world's busiest docks, employing up to 50,000 people. Today, the working and residential population has eclipsed this figure – a perfect example of redevelopment. In recent years, however, the global collapse of Lehman Brothers and the waning spirits (and spending at local restaurants and bars) of the many banks located in the wharf have had a significant impact.

Since quality food options in this corner of London are in short supply, this chapter covers a large geographical area, including – in addition to Canary Wharf and the Docklands area – Dulwich and Greenwich, across the Thames (not that it's easy to cross the river at this point). We have included these areas in order to highlight some hardworking local heroes who deserve recognition, so you know exactly where to head should you find yourself in their neighbourhood.

Billingsgate Market Trafalgar Way, E14 5ST
020 7987 1118 www.billingsgate-market.org.uk
Tuesday–Saturday 5–8.30 am

The largest inland fish market in the country covers a 13-acre (173-sq km) site that is open to the public from Tuesday to Saturday (though you have to get up early, as trading is from 5.00 to 8.30 am). This pungent, fascinating place is an essential experience for any aspiring young chef, and given the fact that fish stocks in our oceans and seas are declining at a rapid rate is something that should interest us all. The market is open to the public, and educational private tours are also available, but no kippers for breakfast. Children under 12 are not permitted. ○

East Dulwich Deli 15–17 Lordship Lane, SE22 8EW
020 8693 2525 www.eastdulwichdeli.com

A firm favourite among locals, with friendly staff, excellent displays and first-class fresh produce including fine cheeses, salami and prosciutto to great pastas, oils and vinegars. ○

Frank's Café and Campari Bar 10th floor, Peckham multi-storey car park, 95a Rye Lane, SE15 4ST 0758 288 4574 www.frankscafe.org.uk
Thursday–Sunday, 11am–10 pm

Peckham (a short drive from Dulwich) is probably one of London's edgiest neighbourhoods, and this project follows suit. It is located on top of an ugly and unwelcoming concrete car park, without any refinements or enhancements (but plenty of parking spaces); when you reach the wide-open top level, however, you are greeted by an amazing view of the capital, from Westminster to Canary Wharf. Neither the food nor the drink is anything to write home about, and it's all rather scruffy (less noticeably so when the sun goes down), but despite all this it's a red-hot venue on a high summer's day. The bar is part of the Bold Tendencies sculpture project, though it has to be said that most people bypass the installation and head for the bar. ○

Green and Blue 38 Lordship Lane, SE22 8HJ
020 8693 9250 www.greenandbluewines.com

The small deli section and bar food are well sourced, but the true focus here is on wine. This is a wine retailer at the leading edge, and a haven for wine lovers. (PP) They also stock my favourite brand of Breton cider. ○

Adam Byatt

My favourite butcher is M. Moens and Sons in Clapham. For fish I go to Moxons in Clapham South or Dulwich. And the best cakes and pâtisserie are to be found at St. John.
Owner and head chef, Trinity

This page **Fresh catch of the day at Billingsgate Market.**

The Gun 27 Coldharbour, E14 9NS
020 7515 5222 www.thegundocklands.com

Located on the east side of Canary Wharf as you travel from the City, amid ever-expanding new residential developments, The Gun dates back over 250 years. It takes its current name from the cannon that was fired to celebrate the opening of the West India Import Docks in 1802; before that even, in the late 18th century, Lord Horatio Nelson enjoyed assignations with Lady Emma Hamilton in an upper room there.

Following a fire in 2001, the new owners have painstakingly restored and refurbished the listed building, and have installed a serious head chef and high-calibre general manager. The menu of the small dining room reflects the experience of its management, and includes an eclectic array of high-quality ingredients. The pub menu features a pint o' prawns, oysters, fishcakes, bookmakers' steak sandwiches, devilled whitebait, Scotch egg made with black pudding, burgers and sausage rolls, and Scotch egg bangers and mash with onion gravy. ○

Hope and Greenwood 20 North Cross Road, SE22 9EU
020 8613 1777 www.hopeandgreenwood.co.uk

They call themselves 'Purveyors of Splendid Confectionery', and they're not wrong. Established as a sweet shop since 1955, Hope and Greenwood is nostalgically British, with shelves displaying 175 glass jars filled with sugar sweets, sherbet lemons, cola cubes, chocolate mice, liquorice and the like. It makes the ideal special treat for any five-year-old on a Saturday morning (perhaps followed by a trip to the dentist), and there is also a small selection of handmade chocolates in elegant gift boxes for adults. ○

Jamie's Italian Unit 17, 2 Churchill Place, E14 5RB
020 3002 5252 www.jamieoliver.com/italian

Canary Wharf has too many branded restaurants, and Jamie's Italian is destined to become the country's most popular restaurant in this category. (PP) I found the service over the top and too American and the menu descriptions cringe-worthy, amid a number of other toe-curling features – but if you ignore all this, the food is OK and reasonable value for money. ○

Leon Promenade Level, Cabot Place West, E14 4QS
020 7719 6200 www.leonrestaurants.co.uk

Dairy-free, good carbs/good sugar only, no or low animal fat, vegetarian, wheat-free, lactose-free, Fair Trade, organic, locally sourced, fresh and just made, antioxidant-high, naturally low GI, superfoods: just some of the many politically correct labels that appear on the menu at this really excellent fast-food takeaway/quick-service restaurant. And it is all done with an enormous helping of style and relevance. The quality doesn't end with the written menu. The Mediterranean food with a splash of British is fresh, seasonal and reasonably priced.

Move over McDonald's, the new phenomenon to hit the high street is Leon. This is one branded chain restaurant that we would like to see expanded. ○

Above **Leon is a chain of restaurants that continue to enjoy a decent reputation for its styling and its food.**

Smoked Eel with Beetroots, Pea Shoots and Horseradish Cream

by Jamie Younger

Serves 2

For the horseradish cream

50 g (2 oz) freshly grated horseradish
1 tablespoon lemon juice
3 drops Tabasco sauce
1 tablespoon white wine vinegar
1 tablespoon caster sugar
150 ml (¼ pint) whipping cream
salt and freshly ground black pepper

For the smoked eel

4 tablespoons olive oil
1 bunch (about 8) baby beetroots, cooked in salted water with a splash of red wine vinegar
150 g (5 oz) smoked eel
2 spring onions
1 punnet of pea shoots
½ lemon
freshly ground black pepper

First make the horseradish cream by blitzing the horseradish in a food blender with all the ingredients except the cream and salt and pepper. When smooth, lightly whip the cream and gently fold it through the horseradish. Season the sauce and set aside.

Heat a heavy-bottomed frying pan with the olive oil. Sauté the beetroots until they are lightly coloured. Add the smoked eel and when warm take the pan off the heat and add the spring onions, pea shoots, a squeeze of lemon juice and a twist of pepper.

Divide the eel into 2 shallow bowls. Add a spoonful of horseradish cream and enjoy.

Priscilla Carluccio

New Tayyabs 83–9 Fieldgate Street, E1 1JU
020 7247 6400 www.tayyabs.co.uk

Although this isn't exactly in the Docklands area, it lies en route from the City to Canary Wharf and is definitely worth including here. So roll up your sleeves and enjoy Tayyabs for what it is – a very busy, 100 per cent halal, old style Pakistani Punjabi restaurant. The restaurants on Brick Lane nearby have long offered similar experiences, but recently seem to have lost some of their allure. New Tayyabs, meanwhile, has remained truly authentic.

Unless you are going as a group, don't bother making a reservation, as you'll still have to join the queue. The menu is not an arduous read, being just a laminated card with rather unflattering photographs. Most of the first courses are tikka-marinated chicken, mutton or lamb chops – chew them to the bone – or paneer, all presented on sizzling-hot skillets, plus the ubiquitous samosa, pakora and shami kebab. The main courses are mostly stir-fried in a karahi (a bit like a wok) and brought to the table in steel balti-style dishes. The karahi dhal gosht (lamb) is probably the best meat main course, and the menu includes a good selection of vegetarian main courses.

Don't forget to bring your own Tiger beer or wine, otherwise you'll be drinking London water or a daily-changing lassi. They don't charge corkage, but you need to take your own corkscrew or bottle opener.

When the staff start to re-lay your table before you've paid your bill or left your seat, you become only too aware of the high turnover, such is the popularity of this place. Given this caveat, it might seem surprising that New Tayyabs is considered one of the best restaurants in its category – but it's the food and the value for money that matter. ○

The Old Brewery The Pepys Building, The Old Royal Naval College, SE10 9LW 0203 327 1280 www.oldbrewerygreenwich.com

Greenwich has lots to offer tourists and history-lovers, but little for the hungry traveller and voyager. The Old Brewery, located within the grounds of the Old Royal Naval College, is half-decent and – as the name suggests – has an excellent range of beers and brews. ○

The Palmerston 91 Lordship Lane, SE22 8EP
020 8693 1629 www.thepalmerston.net

Outside the West End, gastropubs are very often the best places to eat decent food at reasonable prices. Sometimes they can be a bit hit and miss, but that is certainly not the case at The Palmerston, where local residents can benefit from chef Jamie Younger's experience at Bibendum. The dining area is very small, with extra seats in the pub section, but the food delivers huge flavours, good provenance, seasonality and excellent combinations of ingredients. The breadth of the menu also reflects Jamie's experience and knowledge, including foie gras, aged beef, the finest cured meats, whole baked sea bass, and wild salmon served *en papillote*. (PP) I had a delicious rabbit leg oozing with garlic and served with pancetta and an excellent mustard sauce. For a pub, this place is welcoming to families and kids, while also retaining its stout-loving old regulars. ○

Above **Ex-Bibendum chef Jamie Younger at his pub and dining room in East Dulwich.**

Far left
Tulip chairs designed by Eero Saarinen, and table bases with marble tops together with an Arco light and a Terence Conran-designed conical ice bucket form stylish details in the restaurant at Plateau.

Left **The bar and grill at Plateau, designed by Terence Conran.**

Plateau 4th floor, Canada Place, Canary Wharf, E14 5ER
020 7715 7100 www.plateau-restaurant.co.uk

From the outset, Plateau has been the destination of choice for the senior bankers, lawyers and newspaper people of Canary Wharf. It's certainly the top ticket in Canary Wharf during the working week, and it also has a thriving weekend business. Located on the top floor of an incongruously low building, the restaurant benefits from a half-glass ceiling and an entire glass wall overlooking the lawns and sculpture of Canada Square Park. At night, when you look up towards the surrounding 40- and 50-storey buildings, you can't help being reminded of New York or even Gotham City (in fact part of *Batman Begins* was filmed at the restaurant).

There are two dining options: a grill and bar area, plus the smarter restaurant. The interior design is iconic 1950s, with Arco lamps, Eero Saarinen tulip swivel chairs, and tables with beautiful marble tops and wavy eau-de-nil upholstered banquettes. The silver cutlery is designed by David Mellor and the other table accoutrements are also very stylish. ●

Rivington Grill 178 Greenwich High Road, SE10 8NN
020 8293 9270 www.rivingtongreenwich.co.uk
Part of the burgeoning Richard Caring restaurant empire, this is all about solid no-fuss British food in a simple whitewashed space. ○

Roka 1st floor, 4 Park Pavillion, 40 Canada Square, E14 5FW
020 7636 5228 www.rokarestaurant.com
(PP) If I worked in Canary Wharf, this is where I would have lunch every day. It is sister to the excellent original Roka in Charlotte Street (see page 258). (TC) Roka also has an outside terrace with very comfortable armchairs and sofas where I can sit and smoke a cigar. ○

Sea Cow 37 Lordship Lane, East Dulwich, SE22 8EW
020 8693 3111
Battered fish and chips have long been popular in the UK. The simple format was apparently inspired by a trip to Sydney, Australia: as you enter the premises, the fish and a small range of crustaceans are displayed on crushed ice, awaiting your selection. Everything comes from Billingsgate Market (see page 130) and is cooked to order, from cod and chips to red snapper, bluefin tuna or gilthead bream. You can also order a tiger prawn salad, crab cakes or calamari with tartare sauce.

The spacious room, with its chunky bench seats and interesting modern art, makes a civilized setting. Sea Cow also has a small wine list. ○

Wapping Food The Wapping Project, Wapping Wall, E1W 3ST
020 7680 2080 www.thewappingproject.com
London has seen restaurants spring up in old smokehouses, banks, car garages, boating sheds and warehouses. The Wapping Project was formerly a hydraulic power station. The space is huge and retains many of its industrial features, with Ron Arad and Eames furniture creating the restaurant area. The adjoining art gallery adds further interest before or after a meal.

An historic area that was once one of the most industrialized shipping-warehouse districts in London, and probably the world, Wapping Wall has now been transformed to provide high-quality residential accommodation. The cooking here is as contemporary as the warehouse apartments around it, and the exclusively New World wine list is inspired. ○

William Rose Butchers 126 Lordship Lane, East Dulwich, SE22 8HD
020 8693 9191 www.williamrosebutchers.com
This traditional butcher offers an extensive selection of free-range and organic meats, including rare breeds and poultry such as Sutton Hoo chickens from Suffolk and a selection of French birds, all at reasonable prices. The pork pies are an excellent fillip on the journey home. ○

Left **The former hydraulic power station is now the Wapping Project dining room.**

Chelsea
Fulham
South
Kensington

Several centuries ago, about the time when Charles II would travel from Whitehall to Hampton Court along a specially constructed private road – known as the 'King's Road', and later to become the retail mecca that we know today – this area was known as a village of palaces. In recent years, with the arrival of Roman Abramovich as the owner of Chelsea Football Club, it has become home (or one of them, anyway) to numerous Russian oligarchs and to billionaires from all over the world, living in palaces for the twenty-first century. Before venturing to this manor, a glance through Peter York's *Cooler, Faster, More Expensive*, an updated version of his *Sloane Ranger's Handbook*, will provide entertaining insights into the psychology and behaviour patterns of this most distinctive of all social groupings.

Highlights of the area today include the Saatchi Gallery, housed in the former Duke of York's Headquarters. There is a small food market immediately outside the gallery on Saturdays, and the nearby Pimlico Farmers' Market is also good. The V&A remains a huge draw, as does the Serpentine Gallery Pavilion every summer in Kensington Gardens. Recently, controversy has surrounded the proposed redevelopment of the former Chelsea Barracks on Chelsea Bridge Road, in the shadow of Sir Christopher Wren's Royal Hospital. It will be interesting to see how the area matures over the coming years.

The South Kensington hub that is Brompton Cross has become a destination for chic fashion emporiums – think Chanel, Ralph Lauren and Joseph – plus designer furniture retailers, with the Conran Shop and Bibendum at its heart.

Bibendum Restaurant and Oyster Bar

Michelin House, 81 Fulham Road, SW3 6RD
020 7581 5817 www.bibendum.co.uk

With its handsome architecture (the main headquarters of the Michelin Tyre Company from 1911) and its excellent location, Bibendum is one of the most sophisticated places to dine in the capital. (TC) Since 1987, when Paul Hamlyn and I created its new format and reopened the building, Bibendum has offered a sense of *joie de vivre* that is still hard to equal.

The Coffee Bar on the ground floor opens early to serve freshly baked viennoiserie and milky bridge rolls, the house speciality. A small counter selling wet fish and a variety of crustacea, plus a working florist and the Conran Shop next door, help establish the forecourt as a hub of activity.

Lunch at the Oyster Bar is an essential for anybody visiting London. The original tiled floors and walls depict motor-racing scenes from the Art Nouveau and Deco periods, while the French overtones add a touch of pure class. The sight of plateaux de fruits de mer served by well-trained staff in their indispensable black-and-whites are irresistible.

The menu also includes salads, smoked fish, and a house terrine, with decadence in the form of Sevruga caviar and a good selection of Champagnes.

Upstairs the atmosphere is elegant, but without any pretentiousness. The armchairs are comfortable and change their colour every season. Diners are bathed in natural light, and the space between the white linen-covered tables is conducive to a sociable ambience. Colourful stained glass images of Monsieur Bibendum, the iconic Michelin man, keep an eye on things, and his distinctive figure is immortalized in the decanters, flower vases, table legs, bar, graphic art, coat stands and the butter dishes.

Simon Hopkinson, the founding chef who has inspired so many other top chefs, and his successor Matthew Harris have consistently delivered classic dishes with a French bias and the occasional contemporary twist. The portions are always generous and the flavours more so.

Bibendum (not to be confused with the wine company of the same name, with which has no connection) has an award-winning wine list. It also won *Tatler*'s 'Most Consistently Excellent Restaurant' award. ❍

Above left
The corpulent form of Monsieur Bibendum.
Above right
Plateau de fruits de mer at Bibendum oyster bar.

Left and right
Monsieur Bibendum in stained glass form oversees the restaurant.

Left and right
Mosaic floor, exquisite glazed tiles and ornate ceiling details in the oyster bar.

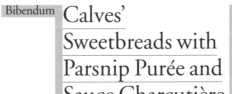

Calves' Sweetbreads with Parsnip Purée and Sauce Charcutière

Serves 4

1 kg (2 lb) calves' sweetbreads
vegetable oil
salt and freshly ground black pepper

For the parsnip puree
750 g (1 1/2 lb) parsnips, cut into chunks
1.2 litres (2 pints) milk
4 garlic cloves
1 sprig of thyme
75 g (3 oz) unsalted butter

For the sauce charcutiere
50 g (2 oz) unsalted butter
1 shallot, finely chopped
1/2 teaspoon mustard powder
1/2 teaspoon redcurrant jelly
250 ml (8 fl oz) white wine
125 ml (4 fl oz) strong veal or chicken stock
25 g (1 oz) cornichons, thinly sliced
1 tablespoon Dijon mustard

To prepare the sweetbreads, bring a large pan of salted water to the boil. Drop the sweetbreads in and simmer for 6 minutes. Take off the heat, remove them from the pan and leave until they are cool enough to handle. Now peel off the outer membrane; be sure to get it all off as it is rubbery and unpleasant to eat. Divide into 4 equal portions and season with salt and pepper.

To make the parsnip purée, place the parsnips in a saucepan with the milk, garlic and thyme. Bring to the boil and reduce to a simmer until cooked, about 12 minutes. Remove the parsnips, garlic and thyme from the milk and place in a blender. Discard the milk. Add the butter and blend until smooth. Season with salt and pepper then pass through a fine sieve. Warm through.

Meanwhile, make the sauce: melt 25 g (1 oz) of the butter in a saucepan and sweat the shallot until soft and golden brown. Add the mustard powder, redcurrant jelly and wine. Simmer until the liquid is reduced by two-thirds. Add the stock and bring back to the boil, add the cornichons and whisk in the Dijon mustard. Now add the remaining butter, whisking constantly. Season and set aside, but keep warm.

Heat a little oil in a large frying pan and sauté the sweetbreads for 5 minutes each side or until golden brown and crusty.

To serve, spoon a portion of the parsnip purée on each plate and put the sweetbreads on top, then spoon the sauce around the edge like a moat.

Watermelon and Mint Granita

Serves 6–8

1 medium-sized watermelon
juice of 1/2 lemon
50 g (2 oz) icing sugar
leaves of 1/2 bunch of mint, finely chopped

Mint crème chantilly (optional)
250 ml (8 fl oz) double cream
1 teaspoon vanilla essence
2 tablespoons crème de menthe
50 g (2 oz) icing sugar

Cut the melon into wedges and scoop out the flesh. Pop it in the food processor or blender and pulse until you have a slush. Place this in a fine sieve and push through to create the juice. Measure 1 litre (1 3/4 pints) watermelon juice and add the lemon juice. Whisk in the sugar and then stir in the mint leaves.

Pour the liquid into a shallow metal tray and place in the freezer. Then every 20 minutes or so open the freezer and stir the liquid. As crystals start to form scrape them away from the edge. This process will need to be repeated until you have a tray full of pink crystals, which can take 3–4 hours.

If making the mint crème chantilly, place all the ingredients in a large bowl and whisk until thick. Chill before serving.

Serve the granita in tumblers or other suitable glasses, embellished by a spoonful of the mint crème chantilly.

Recipes featured in *The Bibendum Cookbook* by Terence Conran, Simon Hopkinson and Matthew Harris, Conran Octopus.

Mussels in Gewürztraminer with Chives and Cream

Serves 4

2 kg (4 lb) mussels
100 g (3¹/2 oz) unsalted butter
50 g (2 oz) diced carrot (2–3 mm/about ¹/8 inch square)
50 g (2 oz) diced leek (2–3mm/about ¹/8 inch square)
50 g (2 oz) diced celery (2–3mm/about ¹/8 inch square)
50 g (2 oz) shallot, finely chopped
2 garlic cloves, finely chopped
375 ml (13 fl oz) Gewürztraminer
125 ml (4 fl oz) double cream
¹/2 lemon
1 bunch of chives, finely chopped
salt and freshly ground black pepper

First make sure the mussels are clean by rinsing them in cold water and going through them one at a time, discarding any open mussels, and removing the beard that is a stringy bit that can stick out the side of the shells; if you just pinch it with your fingers and pull hard, it will come away.

In a large saucepan with a lid, melt the butter and gently fry the vegetables and garlic without colouring them, stirring frequently. After 5 minutes add the wine and boil until it has reduced by half. Now add the mussels and cover the pan with a lid. Gently shake the pan to and fro keeping the lid on with one hand and holding on to the pan handle with the other. After 3 minutes lift the lid and peek at the mussels; if they are not yet all open return to the heat and shake for another minute or two until open. Discard any that remain closed.

Now add the cream and stir it in. Taste the liquid in the bottom of the pan and season with salt and pepper and a squeeze of lemon juice. You are now ready to serve so stir in the chopped chives and serve in deep bowls, making sure to pour in plenty of sauce.

Recipes featured in *The Bibendum Cookbook* by Terence Conran, Simon Hopkinson and Matthew Harris, Conran Octopus.

Chelsea / Fulham / South Kensington

143

Right **Abel Lusa at Capote Y Toros.** Below **A beautiful lemon dessert from Cambio de Tercio.**

Cambio de Tercio 163 Old Brompton Road, SW5 0LJ
020 7244 8970 www.cambiodetercio.co.uk

The Spanish government awarded the founders, Abel Lusa and David Rivero, the 'Premios Alimentos de Espana 2003' for being the best Spanish restaurant anywhere outside Spain. This is the flagship of Abel Lusa's mini-group of four restaurants, and it certainly deserves recognition as one of the finest exponents of modern Spanish food and culture in London. As with all Lusa's restaurants, the interior is awash with colour, with vivid yellow and pink walls and bullfighter art and references.

You could immerse yourself in Spanish food and drink by trying all three of Abel's restaurants on the Old Brompton Road in one evening, as they are all just a short step away from each other. Start with a glass of fino and cured ham at Capote Y Toros, then cross the road to Tendido (see page 151) for some hot tapas or maybe a gourmet paella, before crossing back to Cambio to enjoy one of the chef's specialities of oxtail or suckling pig, finishing with a caramelized torrija (Spanish bread pudding) with crema Catalana ice cream or maybe some Manchego. What a night that would be.

The fourth tapas bar and grill in the stable, Tendido Cuarto, is on the New King's Road. **○**

Capote Y Toros 157 Old Brompton Road, SW5 0LJ
020 7373 0567

The latest offering from Abel Lusa is simply fantastic. With just eight tables and some bar stools with dining shelves, it is small but perfectly formed. The offer is principally based on Iberico hams, Andalucian tapas and over 40 different sherries, though there is also a decent wine list. The shelves are lined with bottles of sherry, from the salty dry Finos and Manzanilla to sweet Pedro Ximenez, while hams hang from the ceiling and collages of bullfighting scenes and posters cover the walls. **○**

Mousse Oloroso

Serves 10

9 leaves of fine leaf gelatine
400 ml (13 fl oz) milk
1.5 litres (2½ pints) double cream
400 ml (13 fl oz) Oloroso sherry, plus extra for serving
125 g (4 oz) egg yolks
125 g (4 oz) caster sugar
caramelized figs (optional)

Mix the milk with the sherry and 400 ml (13 fl oz) of the double cream, then set aside.

In a separate bowl, whisk together the egg yolks and caster sugar with 100 ml (3½ fl oz) of the double cream and set aside.

Place the gelatine leaves in a shallow bowl of iced water for about 10 minutes, just to soften.

Meanwhile in a large bowl whip the remaining 1 litre (1¾ pints) double cream until it reaches thick ribbon stage, then whisk in the egg and sugar mixture.

Remove the softened gelatine from the water and whisk it into the milk and sherry mixture until dissolved. Finally, very gently mix the milk, sherry and gelatine mixture into the cream mixture until everything is combined.

Divide into attractive tall glasses and chill in the refrigerator for 3 hours before serving. Serve with halved caramelized figs if liked, and drizzle over a few drops of sherry.

Chelsea / Fulham / South Kensington

145

Left **Julian Opie art hangs on the walls at Cassis.** Right **The bar at Cassis.**

Cassis 232–6 Brompton Road, SW3 2BB

020 7581 1101 www.cassisbistro.co.uk

Much thought and attention to detail have been devoted to this *very* upscale Provençal bistro. The interior design, menu, staffing and pricing all nod towards the young affluent crowd that it serves. As an example, the wine list includes over 700 bins – way over the top, but as the proprietor Marlon Abela is a wine fanatic, perhaps understandable.

The choice of art is also interesting. While the Julian Opie works are appealing and display his unique style of portraiture, if money were no object the quintessential artists of the light and colour of the French Riviera – Picasso, Matisse, Chagall, Cézanne et al – perhaps would be more relevant.

The cooking is very technique-driven, and you can enjoy some really lovely food. The perfect meal here has to be pissaladière with a pastis, followed by bouillabaisse served with rouille, croûtons and Gruyère. The bouillabaisse at Cassis is very refined, with whole fillets of sea bass, red mullet and excellent clams. The service of this great dish is also noteworthy, and the front-of-house team, led by the genial manager Jean-Marie, is highly poised, especially when making steak tartare at the table.

Concertina doors opening on to the pavement, a long bar with cosy booths, and some carefully considered table positions (each with a fragrant pot of rosemary), all make this place a pleasant eating experience in the heart of a rarefied shopping district. ◐

Oli
Barker

La Famiglia in Chelsea is my favourite Italian restaurant – the wild boar ragu hits the spot. My other Italian favourite is Franco Manca – the pizzas are just delicious.

Head chef, Terroirs

Right **A very upmarket bouillabaisse at Cassis served with rouille, croutons and Gruyère.**

Pissaladière

Serves 8

12 g ($\frac{1}{3}$ oz) salt
500 g (1 lb) plain flour
20 g ($\frac{3}{4}$ oz) fresh yeast
250 ml (8 fl oz) water
50 ml (2 fl oz) olive oil
100 g ($3\frac{1}{2}$ oz) butter
4 sprigs of thyme
500 g (1 lb) onions, thinly sliced
anchovies
black olives

First prepare the dough: add 10 g of the salt to the flour. In a large bowl, stir the yeast into the water and add the olive oil. Whisk it thoroughly until the yeast has dissolved. Then tip the flour into the water mixture and mix together by hand until it forms a soft ball of dough. Leave it in the bowl to rest for 2 hours at room temperature.

Knead the dough again by hand, then wrap in clingfilm and leave to rest in the refrigerator while you prepare the onions.

Put a large saucepan over a low heat and add the butter, thyme sprigs and remaining salt. Add the onions, stir, then cover with a lid and sweat slowly for about 1 hour. Stir from time to time to stop them sticking to the bottom of the pan.

Take the dough and spread it with your hands thinly over a large baking sheet (or 2 if necessary). Bake in a preheated oven, 180°C (350°F), Gas Mark 4, for 10 minutes. Once the dough is cooked, spoon over the cooked onions and arrange anchovies and black olives on top.

The pissaladière is now ready to warm through in the oven whenever your guests are at the table!

Le Cercle 1 Wilbraham Place, SW1X 9AE
020 7901 9999 www.lecercle.co.uk

The food comes from the Club Gascon team with Pascal Aussignac, the chef-proprietor. The difference is that they have created a 'grazing' menu that allows diners to order several smaller portions of traditional French favourites. For us, the overall effect is better than Club Gascon. The bar is also a good place to meet friends, share a bottle of wine and order a few small plates of smartly presented but rustic-flavoured foods. ○

Daylesford 44b Pimlico Road, SW1W 8LP
020 7881 8060 www.daylesfordorganic.com

This farmshop and café close to Sloane Square is an offshoot of the very impressive farmshop in the village of Daylesford in Gloucestershire. Both are definitely worthy of a visit.

The Daylesford brand was set up by Lady Bamford many years ago – well before organic produce was popular in the UK. Now the Daylesford operation comprises its own organic cattle farms, a creamery making its own cheeses, a bakery producing bread, cakes and pastries, a market garden and kitchens that create an extensive range of own-brand soups and prepared meals. All of these products, plus much more, are available at this shop.

The produce comes directly from the farm, although the elegant shop – very easy on the eye with masses of beautiful marble – scarcely brings to mind the concept of farm-to-fork. All of the produce is not only of an exceptionally high standard but also very stylishly presented and packaged. ○

Far left **Pissaladière and pastis at Cassis.** This page **The quality of the food and displays at Daylesford is excellent.**

Eight Over Eight 392 King's Road, SW3 5UZ
020 7349 9934 www.rickerrestaurants.com/eightovereight/

Will Ricker seems to own a pan-Asian eatery on every corner of every cool neighbourhood in London. Eight Over Eight, a sister of the celebrity-lined E&O in Notting Hill (see page 48), serves good dim sum, sushi, sashimi and tempura as well as pad Thai and steamed sea bass specials. Its success is down to the quality of the food, stylish interior design and killer cocktails. ○

The Harwood Arms 27 Walham Grove, SW6 1QP
020 7386 1847 www.harwoodarms.com

The Harwood Arms was the first pub to secure a Michelin star for its seasonal and resolutely British food. As we're not great fans of either gastropubs or the Michelin star system, it follows that we shouldn't be too keen on the Harwood Arms. But in fact the opposite is true.

One of the reasons why we enjoy this particular offering is the amount of game peppered across the menus. On a recent visit outside the main game seasons, bar snacks included a venison Scotch egg, rabbit rissole with Oxford sauce, and roe deer and walnut terrine. The triumvirate who manage the pub include chef Mike Robinson, who is equally well known for his shooting and hunting activities in rural Berkshire, and who apparently personally shoots much of the game in season. Mike is also the proprietor of the Pot Kiln in Frilsham near Newbury. The other partners are Brett Graham from the Ledbury in Notting Hill and Edwin Vaux of Vaux Brewery, who looks after the pub side. While it cannot be said that the Harwood Arms is a true boozer, it hasn't lost all of its pub charm, with Edwin contributing his fair share of character in the form of some great beers.

Some of the table details are little over the top, arguably, and the plates are a bit fancy, but the service is very professional without being too starchy which the makes the overall experience very enjoyable.

If you are planning a visit to the Harwood Arms, we suggest you also call in at the nearby Vagabond Wines, one of the new wave of wine retailers that are popping up all over London. They have over 100 wines available to taste in small measures and at very reasonable prices. ●

The Pig's Ear 35 Old Church Street, SW3 5BS
020 7352 2908 www.thepigsear.info

This is fine example of a London pub: the food is good, the atmosphere welcoming and the interior has been furbished with sensitivity and respect. Though it may have been said before, they have made a silk purse out of a sow's ear. ●

Right **The bar at The Pig's Ear is another pub that welcomes dogs.** Far right **Jamón at Tendido Cero.**

Rasoi Vineet Bhatia 10 Lincoln Street, SW3 2TS
020 7225 1881 www.rasoi-uk.com

Progressive, visionary, innovative with contemporary twists – all are epithets one associates with Rasoi (meaning kitchen) Vineet Bhatia. Having grown up in Bombay, as it was then known, Vineet gained a classical training. But he has now formed his own style of new-wave Indian food. After making a name for himself in at South Kensington's Star of India in the 1990s, he launched Zaika, where he became the first Indian chef-restaurateur to gain a Michelin star. His new restaurant has also been granted the same accolade, which – given Vineet's use of luxury ingredients and his nine-course tasting menu, as well as his amazing creativity – is hardly surprising. ◉

Restaurant Gordon Ramsay 68 Royal Hospital Road, SW3 4HP
020 7352 4441 www.gordonramsay.com

The Gordon Ramsay brand has suffered recently, but the flagship restaurant has retained its three coveted Michelin stars since 2000. Key people who have moved on from Gordon's empire, some acrimoniously, have attracted much attention, but Mark Askew, the executive head chef, and Jean-Claude Breton, the maitre d', have both been with Gordon since the early days. The head chef here is now Clare Smyth. The restaurant is next door to the Chelsea Physic Garden, which is also well worth a visit. ◉

Tendido Cero 174 Old Brompton Road, SW5 0BA
020 7370 3685 www.cambiodetercio.co.uk

If we had to choose one from Abel Lusa's three restaurants in this corner of South Kensington, it would be Tendido Cero. Everything, from the passionate, gesticulating staff to the atmosphere and lighting, is pitched at just the right level. The menu is simply presented in two categories, cold and hot tapas, with all the usual suspects: jamón, quesos, toasted tomato breads, boquerones, calamares, piquillo peppers, croquetas, tortilla, chorizo, gambas and much more. And of course every meal must end with either chocolate churros or crema Catalana. ◉

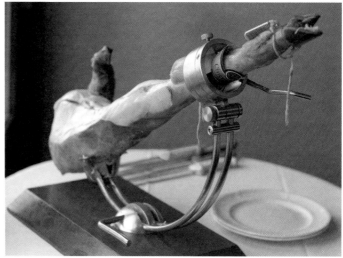

Tinello 87 Pimlico Road, SW1W 8PH
020 7730 3663 www.tinello.co.uk

After plying their trade at Locanda Locatelli (see page 249), brothers Massimiliano and Federico Sali have been rewarded with a restaurant of their own. They certainly deserve it. This is an impressive partnership and a very assured restaurant. Federico is the chef and Massimiliano runs the front of house, while also overseeing the wine list.

The intriguing lighting has evidently been given considerable thought, with each table having its own bronze pendant light that can be adjusted via a Heath Robinson-style contraption of cord and ball. This produces a bronze glow on the white table linen and a very flattering light on diners. Some might argue that the dining room is little too dark, but to us it seems just about right for lunch and very chic in the evening. The many local gallerists may find it conducive to confidential discussions and off-the-record advice.

The menu is presented in four main categories – antipasti, small eats, pasta and second piatti – with the usual contorni (side dishes) and desserts. The 'small eats' category seems to be sweeping London as an essential component of all new restaurant menus. While some think it merely a wheeze by restaurateurs to induce their patrons to inadvertently order too much food, others think it a great way to enjoy many different flavours and ingredients for relatively little money. At Tinello, the zucchine fritte (fried courgettes) from the small eats section are a must – though don't expect something *piccolo*, as servings are generous.

(PP) The service at high-end Italian restaurants can sometimes fall behind the standard of food. This is not the case at Tinello. I recently dined with an acquaintance who insisted on ordering off-menu and requested dishes that he had enjoyed at the restaurant several months earlier. The service staff were accommodating and handled these requests perfectly front of house, and I do wonder how they manage to pull it off with the kitchen team. Anyway, full marks for dealing consummately well with such a difficult customer. ◉

Federico Sali

For a romantic meal, I would choose Galvin at Windows, or The Wolesley for its atmosphere and ambience. Franco Manca in Chiswick is my favourite neighbourhood restaurant.

Co-owner, Tinello

Above left
Massimiliano Sali, co-owner of Tinello.
Above **The chic Tinello interior.**

Roast Monkfish, Stewed Red Onion, Black Olives and Pine Kernels

Serves 4

6 tablespoons extra-virgin olive oil
3 red onions, finely sliced
5 tablespoons white wine vinegar
2 tablespoons vegetable or sunflower oil
4 monkfish tails, each weighing about 220 g (7^{1}/2 oz)
^{1}/2 wine glass white wine
150 ml (^{1}/4 pint) fish stock
2 tablespoons tomato passata
2 tablespoons toasted pine kernels
2 tablespoons pitted black olives
10 basil leaves
salt

Put 2 tablespoons of the olive oil in a pan, add the onions and a pinch of salt, cover and cook gently for about 10 minutes or until the onions are translucent but not coloured. Add the vinegar, cook for another 2–3 minutes and set aside.

Put a non-stick pan (or 2 if necessary) on to heat. Add the vegetable or sunflower oil. Season the fish with salt, put in the pans and cook quickly for 2–3 minutes, then reduce the heat and add the wine to the pan. Allow the alcohol to cook out, then add the fish stock and the tomato passata and cook for 1 more minute.

Add the pine kernels, black olives and basil leaves and cook for 2 minutes more, then turn off the heat and toss the monkfish tails in the sauce.

Divide the onions between 4 plates, place a monkfish tail on each, spoon the sauce on top and drizzle with the rest of the olive oil.

Fig Tart

Serves 8

125 g (4 oz) butter, at room temperature
125 g (4 oz) caster sugar
60 g (2 ^{1}/2 oz) egg yolks
3 teaspoons baking powder
175 g (6 oz) plain flour
pinch of salt
150 g (5 oz) dried figs, chopped

Put the butter into a food processor with a paddle attachment and mix until soft. Add the sugar and continue to mix until the mixture turns pale, then add the egg yolks gradually until all are incorporated.

Reduce the speed and add the baking powder, flour, salt and dried figs. Mix well, then turn the speed up to maximum for 1–2 minutes (no more) to incorporate some air, which will make the mixture a little lighter and fluffier in texture.

Pour the mixture into a buttered 28-cm (11-inch) tart tin or 8 individual buttered 10-cm (4-inch) fluted tart tins and bake in a preheated oven, 170°C (340°F), Gas Mark 3^{1}/2, for about 15–20 minutes (check after 10 minutes if making individual tarts) or until golden.

Let the tarts cool in the tins before serving at room temperature with vanilla ice cream.

Nettle Pappardelle and Duck Ragù

Serves 4

For the pasta (makes about 600 g/1¼ lb)

2 handfuls of young nettle leaves

500 g (1 lb) '00' flour

pinch of salt

3 large eggs

25 ml (1 fl oz) olive oil

For the duck ragù

2 kg (4 lb) minced duck legs, without the fat

5 tablespoons olive oil

2 carrots, finely chopped

2 celery stalks, finely chopped

2 onions, finely chopped

sprig of rosemary and sprig of sage, tied together

2 garlic cloves, peeled

250 ml (8 fl oz) white wine

2 litres (3½ pints) duck stock

salt and freshly ground black pepper

To make the pasta

Blanch the nettles in boiling salted water for 30 seconds, drain and put into a food processor. Pulse to a purée adding a little water if the mixture is too dry.

Sift the flour on to a clean work surface and make a well in the middle. Sprinkle the salt into the well, then crack in the eggs, add the olive oil and the nettle purée.

Break the yolks with the fingertips of one hand and begin to move your fingers in a circular motion, gradually incorporating the flour until you have worked in enough to start bringing it together in a ball. Then you can start to knead the dough by pushing it with the heel of your hand, folding the top back on itself, turning it a little clockwise and repeating, again and again, for about 10 minutes. Divide the dough into 2 balls, wrap each in a clean damp cloth and rest for about an hour before using.

Roll out the first ball of dough with a rolling pin (keep the rest covered in the damp cloth) until it is about 1 cm (½ inch) thick and will go through the pasta machine comfortably.

Put the machine on the first (thickest) setting to start with, then feed the piece of pasta through the machine, turning the handle with one hand and supporting the dough as it comes through with the other. Then change to the second, thinner setting and put it through again. Repeat another 2–3 times, taking the setting down one each time.

Next, fold the strip of pasta back on itself, put the machine back on to the first setting and put the pasta through again. Repeat 3–4 more times, again taking the setting down one each time, and you will see that the pasta begins to take on a sheen. As it begins to get longer you will find that you have to pull it very gently so that it doesn't begin to concertina. You shouldn't need to dust it with flour unless you feel it is too soft and likely to stick and stretch too much.

Now cut your strip in half. Keep one half covered in a damp cloth, then fold the length of the other strip into three, bringing one end in and the other over the top of that, so that the pasta is the same width as the machine. Roll it with a rolling pin, so it is no more than 5 mm (¼ inch) thick, then put the machine back on to the first setting and feed the pasta through the opposite way, i.e. widthways, not lengthways. Keep feeding it through this way, taking it down two or three settings as you go until it is about 1.5 mm (¹/₁₆ inch) thick.

Using your rolling pin as a straight edge, cut the pasta across into strips 2–2.5 cm (about 1 inch) wide.

Dust a tray with flour. With a spatula, lift up the strips, 3 or 4 at a time, and lay them on the tray. Dust again with flour and cover. Repeat all steps with the second ball of dough.

To make the duck ragù

Lay the minced duck on a tray, press it down and let it come to room temperature, so that it will sear, rather than boil, in the pan.

Heat the oil in a wide-bottomed saucepan, add the vegetables, herbs and whole garlic cloves, and sweat over a high heat for 5–8 minutes without allowing it to colour (you will need to keep stirring).

Season the meat with salt and pepper and add to the pan of vegetables, making sure that the meat covers the base of the pan. Leave for about 5–6 minutes, so that the meat seals underneath and heats through completely before you start stirring. Take care though, that the vegetables don't burn – add a little more oil if necessary.

Stir the meat and vegetables occasionally for about 10–12 minutes until the meat starts to stick to the bottom of the pan. At this point add the white wine, allow the alcohol to cook out, then add the stock.

Bring to the boil, then lower the heat to a simmer and cook for about 1½ hours.

When you are ready to serve the ragú, put it back into a pan and heat through. Cook the pasta for 3 minutes in boiling water, then drain, reserving the cooking water. Add the pasta to the ragú and toss well, if necessary adding some of the cooking water to loosen the sauce. Serve immediately.

Tom
Aikens

" My favourite London food shop is my local fishmongers, Rex on Chelsea Green, who are never open on a Monday (which is a good sign). They serve the freshest and best fish.

Tom Aikens and Tom's Kitchen

Tom Aikens 43 Elystan Street, SW3 3NT
020 7584 2003 www.tomaikens.co.uk

Tom has achieved a certain notoriety as an unruly taskmaster, but more importantly has garnered numerous awards, not least among them two Michelin stars when he was at Pied à Terre in the 1990s. He has spent his career in some of the world's finest kitchens, as well as in what might be called 'private service', as personal chef to the Lloyd Webber and Bamford families. His eponymous Chelsea restaurant currently has one star, and has been tipped to secure a second in the near future.

Anouska Hempel has designed the restaurant, with tableware that seems to be particularly desirable (judging by the amount of it that disappears from the tables!).

Though a rather basic way to view the food, one of the enjoyable aspects of Tom's dishes is that you always get plenty of sauce on your plate: it's particularly annoying when other chefs provide a mere drizzle to accompany a large piece of protein, but that's just a personal view.

The restaurant has recently secured investment from a Turkish restaurant group based in Istanbul to help expand his brand. ◉

Tom's Kitchen 27 Cale Street, SW3 3QP
0207 349 0202 www.tomskitchen.co.uk

Open for breakfast, brunch at the weekends, lunch and dinner, Tom Aikens' other restaurant is a multi-layered operation, with a ground-floor dining room (they call it a brasserie, though it isn't really), a first-floor bar and private dining rooms on the upper floors. Tom uses fine British produce, adding a touch of French luxury with foie gras here and there. The ground-floor dining room is fitted-out with refectory tables and glazed wall tiles, and the pleasing menu ranges from the signature seven-hour confit of lamb for two to simple delights such as fish and chips, shepherd's pie, pork belly and (very fine) sausages and mash with onion gravy.

There is also a Tom's Kitchen at the magnificent Somerset House on the Strand, with a terrace overlooking the Thames and the South Bank. ◉

Left **Tom Aikens in his kitchen.**
Above **Tom's Kitchen is spread across several floors with different eating options at each level.**

Troubadour 263–7 Old Brompton Road, SW5 9JA

020 7370 1434 www.troubadour.co.uk

The first coffee-and-café-culture revolution hit London in the late 17th century and continued into the 18th. Dr Johnson and his *Dictionary of the English Language* and Edward Lloyd's insurance empire were just two of the great enterprises that grew out of coffee house discussions.

The second revolution came in the 1950s. It was in 1954 that the Troubadour opened as a destination for the intelligentsia, the cultured and the bohemian. It now stands as the antithesis of what must be viewed as the third coffee revolution, in the form of Starbucks, Caffè Nero, Prêt à Manger and their ilk.

The highly atmospheric Troubadour houses a café, delicatessen, art gallery and cellar-club, where it continues its strong links with emerging musical talents. Its impressive list of past performers includes Jimi Hendrix, Paul Simon, Bob Dylan and Joni Mitchell. **◉**

Whole Foods 63–97 Kensington High Street, W8 5SE

020 7368 4500 www.wholefoodsmarket.com

Whole Foods Market is huge in America, but its arrival in London has been less successful than might have been hoped. Newspaper stories about the project's massive investment and ambitious aims soon gave way to reports of unimaginable financial losses.

But what is Whole Foods really like? There is much to be impressed by, and some elements that are still disappointing – though much less so now than when it first opened. On balance, it's worth a visit. The hot foods and salads on the ground floor still need attention, and it would be nice to see more genuine experts on the shop floor. On a recent visit to the cheese room, we encountered little enthusiasm from the person behind the counter; there was none of the information or opportunities to sample that are second nature at Neal's Yard Dairy or La Fromagerie.

The positives are certainly the large selection of products and ingredients (the butchery counter is 23 metres long, or some 75 feet), plus the huge displays of seasonal treats. The prices also seem to have come down. You could spend a good hour or two touring the store and marvelling at the range of foods and drinks on display. Or maybe just call in for a few veggies. Either is sure to be a good experience. Upstairs, there are a few restaurants including Shabu Shabu and a branch of Saf (see page 110).

It was reported that this branch of Whole Foods is now breaking even. Whether this is true or not, we wish Whole Foods the best of luck. **◉**

Zaika 1 Kensington High Street, W8 5SF

020 7795 6533 www.zaika-restaurant.co.uk

In its original site on Fulham Road, this was one of the first top-flight new-style Indian restaurants. Its present site was once a rather grand bank, and much of the internal architecture has been retained and fused with a rich colour palette.

Zaika translates as 'sophisticated flavours', which sums up the ethos behind the menu. **◉**

More places to visit in the area

L'Art du Fromage
1a Langton Street, SW10 0JL
020 7352 2759
www.artdufromage.co.uk
A small restaurant that specializes in recipes with cheese either at their heart, such as tartiflette or raclette, or in a major supporting role.

Aubaine
260–2 Brompton Road, SW3 2AS
020 7052 0100   www.aubaine.co.uk
A boulangerie, pâtisserie and French café with an atmosphere tailor-made for the area.

Le Colombier
145 Dovehouse Street, SW3 6LB
020 7351 1155
www.le-colombier-restaurant.co.uk
The embodiment of French charm, with brasserie dishes that have stood the test of time.

Hunan
51 Pimlico Road, SW1W 8NE
020 7730 5712
www.hunanlondon.com
Known as the restaurant without a menu, this is a great place if you enjoy a broad range of ingredients and spicy Chinese dishes.

La Poule au Pot
231 Ebury Street, SW1W 8UT
020 7730 7763 www.pouleaupot.co.uk
Another step back in time courtesy of the French: a very old-school romantic interior and a small outside terrace for balmy summer evenings.

Santini
29 Ebury Street, SW1W 0NZ
020 7730 4094
www.santini-restaurant.com
If the nearby Tinello (see page 152) attracts a younger crowd, the long-established Santini restaurant with a Venetian accent is known for its more mature clientele and its discreet location.

Union Market
472 Fulham Road, SW6 1BY
020 73862470
www.unionmarket.co.uk
A large specialist food store in the former Fulham Broadway tube station.

Above **Battered fish and chips – Tom's Kitchen style.**

The City
Spitalfields

The dining and drinking options in the City continue to evolve and improve. Fifteen years ago decent restaurants simply didn't exist in the Square Mile. All this has since changed, and it is now alive with high-quality eating establishments. More hotels are opening, shopping malls and high-quality retailers are vying for trade, and the latest trend is restaurants located at the top of the city's new skyscrapers. The Gherkin, the Heron Tower (one of the few new skyscrapers without a sobriquet), the Helter-Skelter, the Cheese Grater, the Walkie-Talkie – all allow for extensive in-house dining options.

While the City's core financial activities might be in the doldrums, the food and leisure scene is not – except at the weekends. Despite efforts to bring some life to the City on Saturdays and Sundays it is still a place best experienced during midweek, especially on Thursday evenings.

Over the same period the City has also changed its personality in many other ways. The trading floor culture is disappearing, the venture capitalists have realized it isn't vital to be located in the City, and new overseas finance houses are making London their global headquarters. The Corporation of London, the authority that governs the City, has overseen this change by encouraging the new in the form of world-beating architecture, but, thankfully, they have also retained a sense of tradition. Most lampposts and public buildings carry the heraldic shield of St. George with the dragon to indicate the Corporation's existence. The Lord Mayor's Parade and the annual banquet with all their frills, are good examples of the pomp and circumstance that continue to permeate.

1 Lombard Street EC3V 9AA
020 7929 6611   www.1lombardstreet.com

With changes in the banking world over recent years, many restaurants and bars have sprung up in former banking halls or local branch buildings. Many such conversions are to be found in the City: one of the grandest of all must be 1 Lombard Street, located opposite the ultimate bank, the Bank of England. The neoclassical Grade II listed building features an internal domed ceiling by Pietro Agostini. Soren Jessen, himself a former banker, and evergreen chef Herbert Berger have together created a buzzing brasserie, with a central bar under the dome and an adjoining fine dining restaurant. The brasserie serves old-fashioned classics with confidence, while the dining room serves more Michelin-focused European dishes. ○

28°–50° 140 Fetter Lane, EC4A 1BT
020 7242 8877   www.2850.co.uk

The name refers to the degrees of latitude within which virtually all the world's wine is grown. The owners, Xavier Rousset and Agnar Sverisson, also describe this subterranean restaurant as a 'wine workshop', where every month they showcase a different winemaker. While not massive – unlike in other wine-related bars and restaurants – the wine list here is certainly sufficient. It offers some 15 whites and 15 reds, plus a 'collectors' list' that gives customers the opportunity to sell their own wines via 28°–50°, while the restaurant owners undertake to sell them at very attractive prices. An interesting idea.

Xavier and Agnar are rapidly building quite a reputation for themselves. Agnar, the Icelandic chef, is very talented and comes across as quite cerebral; Xavier, meanwhile, is a master sommelier who contributes regularly to industry journals.

Head chef Paul Walsh is also very talented, and has spent five years as sous chef at the three-star Gordon Ramsay restaurant. He has certainly applied the precision cooking that he must have learned there to the small but attractive menu at 28°–50°. ○

Helena Puolakka

L'Anima is my favourite Italian restaurant in London.
Executive chef, Skylon

Above left **The domed ceiling at 1 Lombard Street.** Above right **Wine displays set the tone at 28°–50°.**

L'Anima 1 Snowden Street, Broadgate West, EC2A 2DQ
020 7422 7000 www.lanima.co.uk

There is much to admire about this restaurant, but from a restaurateur's perspective it is the kitchen that we admire the most. Chef patron Francesco Mazzei appears to have been given carte blanche: the space is huge, and the range of heavy-duty expensive equipment and chefs' toys – including the now mandatory Josper grill – leaves us green with envy.

The bar and dining room are also very fine, with their array of natural materials – from porphyry and travertine, marble and limestone to white leather upholstery – and natural light floods the restaurant. The Mies van der Rohe dining chairs, meanwhile, call to mind the great Four Seasons restaurant in the Seagram Building in New York.

The food more than lives up to the quality of the kitchen and the overall design. This is some of the finest contemporary Italian food in London, let alone the Square Mile. (PP) L'Anima (meaning 'soul' in Italian) is quite close to my office, and I have visited it quite often over the last year or so, dining there with various chefs and as well as with Terence Conran. We have always found the food to be expressive and delicious. Francesco delivers an enjoyable and apparently effortless combination of rustic flavours with all the refinement you would expect in such a classy place. His signature dish is a tagliata of beef with marrowbone, presented in the form of a mushroom.

Francesco now hosts cookery classes in his state-of-the-art kitchen – a glimpse of the stainless steel hardware alone would justify the cost. ◉

Below **The bar at L'Anima.**

Above **The L'Anima dining room.**

Right
The impressive private dining room in the wine cellar at L'Anima.
Left and above
Francesco Mazzei (far left) and his chefs preparing food in the kitchen.

Above **The communal Barber Osgerby furniture at Canteen, and a Canteen breakfast sandwich.**
Left **The fun graphics and identity at Chilango.**

Bar Battu 48 Gresham Street, EC2V 7AY
020 7036 6100 www.barbattu.com

This simple wine-focused bistro has been overlooked by many key publications and journalists, and overshadowed by other operators who have contrived to hog the limelight and sing the 'natural' wine song to a wider audience. The Bar Battu approach is very similar to that of Brawn (see page 100) and Terroirs (see page 220), combining simple wines made with nothing but grape juice (possibly with the addition of a dash of sulphur) with earthy recipes in which the finished whole is always greater than its constituent parts. The chef here is the very capable and reliable Sydney Aldridge, who has filled his menu with well-known and desirable French bistro fare. The saucisson, terrines and rillettes hit the spot, while the coq au vin, boudin noir and veal chop with anchovy butter are all sublime. The menu also includes the now ubiquitous 'small plates' option.

Staff are enthusiastic and informed about the wines, and the small interior features charming French poster art and a clutch of flea market finds. If every street in London had a place like this, then maybe England too would be the home of *liberté*, *égalité* and *fraternité*. ●

Canteen 2 Crispin Place, Spitalfields Market, E1 6DW
0845 686 1122 www.canteen.co.uk

Canteen is a very welcome addition to the Spitalfields scene. Located at the heart of the new Foster and Partners extension to the market and overlooking the traders' trestle tables, the restaurant's interior features simple, communal and democratic blond wood bench seats and long tables by Barber Osgerby, as well as angular booths with individual anglepoise lights.

The menu respects the British culinary heritage while also delivering modern and stylish cooking, a deft touch and well-judged portions (a rare virtue in restaurants serving 'British' cuisine). The chef is committed to providing honest food that is nationally sourced, skilfully prepared and reasonably priced. Provenance is paramount.

The kitchen bakes daily-changing pies to order, serving them with good gravy, mash and greens. The choice of fried fish changes, according to the best catch of the day. Canteen boasts an enticing range of roast meats and serves an all-day breakfast menu: think Welsh rarebit, crumpets, black pudding and the best Cumberland sausages. ●

Chilango 142 Fleet Street, EC4A 2BP
020 7353 6761 www.chilango.co.uk

Chilango is a bit of Mexican fun on Fleet Street. Everything – from the graphics to the staff – is bright and bubbly. It's also one of a small chain of eateries. We wouldn't normally recommend this type of fast, casual style of food, but the management continue to deliver something that remains very popular. The queues at lunch are quite something.

(PP) The soft flour tortilla burrito with beef, spicy salsa and avocado is my personal favourite. ●

Cigalon 115 Chancery Lane, WC2A 1PP
020 7242 8373 www.cigalon.co.uk

Named after Marcel Pagnol's 1935 film about a renowned chef who opens a restaurant in a small Provençal village, Cigalon is an *hommage* to the life and food of Provence – think lavender, pine trees, cicadas, pastis on the terrace, azure skies, terracotta walls and captivating food markets… The menu includes all the treats you'd expect from the south of France, with well executed regional specialities including salade niçoise, soupe au pistou, anchoïade, aïoli, Camargue rice and beef, plus – a very rare treat for London – pieds et paquets, a stew of lambs' tripe and trotters.

The exclusively French wine list specializes in wines from Provence and Corsica that perfectly match the food. (PP) I dined here with two eminent chefs and we loved the food. We also indulged in some of the regional aperitifs, and savoured wine with that lovely taste and aroma of the *garrigue*. ○

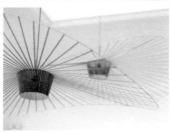

Peter Weeden

London's best wine list is at Coq d'Argent. Sommelier Olivier Marie has spent over a decade building this list to its current glorious position and the continuity shows.

Head chef, Boundary Restaurant

Left **Yann Osouf at Cigalon with the open kitchen and Robata grill in the background.**

Cinnamon Kitchen 9 Devonshire Square, EC2M 4YL
020 7626 5000 www.cinnamon-kitchen.com

The City now has a modern Indian restaurant to be proud of: Vivek Singh's innovative and creative cooking is a delight. Anyone with concerns about the suitability of spices and curries for lunch can rest assured: though it may be a better fit for a fun and relaxed supper, this is certainly not an inappropriate choice for a business lunch. (PP) I recently visited for lunch and the outside terrace was very busy with 'suits'. The different breads, dips and chutneys were irresistible. The interior spaces are very glitzy, with dining and drinking options ranging from the tandoor bar and grill to the sexy Anise bar. A great place for a first date or perhaps a secret assignation. ○

Coq d'Argent 1 Poultry, EC2R 8EJ
020 7395 5000 www.coqdargent.co.uk

If you work in the Square Mile then you must have been to Coq d'Argent. If you haven't, you're certainly missing out.

Set on the top floor of James Stirling's bold post-modern building at the heart of the City, with spacious gardens designed by Arabella Lennox-Boyd and a Conran-designed restaurant, it was destined to be a success. Since opening in 1998 it has proved to be a perennial favourite with City dealers and big shots. Superstar chef and all-round good guy Mickael Weiss has been the chef at Coq d'Argent since 2001, and somehow manages to cope with a 150-cover formal dining room with an outside terrace, a large grill restaurant and barbecue terraces, a busy bar and a buoyant party and events business. Le Coq, as it is known, is a stunning destination for a celebration.

Mickael's deftly prepared regional French menu is huge, as you would expect, with coq au vin as his signature dish, frogs' legs and snails, oysters, crustaceans, Châteaubriand, great fish, delicious desserts and a well-stocked cheese trolley. Needless to say, the wine list is primed for bonus day.

The restaurant interior is modern, like the menu, with black-and-white photographs of French artisans, plus a rampant *coq* by Anthony Caro. ○

Above **The bar at Cinnamon Kitchen.** Above right **The Devonshire Square atrium.** Left **Mickael Weiss on the rooftop lawn at Coq d'Argent.**

Coq au Vin

Serves 4

4 corn-fed chicken legs and 2 breasts on the bone
1 each of carrot, onion and celery stick, diced
1 spring onion
1 sprig of thyme
1 garlic clove
1 bay leaf
1 litre (1³/4 pints) red wine
plain flour, for dusting
2 tablespoons olive oil
500 ml (17 fl oz) chicken stock
salt and freshly ground black pepper

For the garnish

100 g (3½ oz) unsmoked streaky bacon, cut into lardons
200 g (7 oz) button mushrooms
12 baby onions, peeled
2 slices white bread, crust removed
2–3 tablespoons olive oil or clarified butter
1 garlic clove, peeled and finely chopped
1 handful of flat-leaf parsley, finely chopped

Cut the chicken legs in two through the joint, separating the drumstick from the thigh. Cut the breast through the bones in four pieces.

Place the diced vegetables, herbs, garlic and wine in a bowl and add the chicken making sure they are well covered in the marinade.

Cover the bowl with cling film and set it in the refrigerator overnight. Or, leave it to marinate at room temperature for 6 hours.

After marinating, preheat the oven to 170°C (340°F) Gas Mark 4. Remove the chicken from the bowl and dry it with kitchen paper. Dust the chicken with flour, shaking off any excess. Place a casserole dish over a medium heat and add the olive oil. Brown the chicken pieces until they are golden all over. Pour the marinade with the vegetables into the casserole over the chicken. Turn up the heat and bring to the boil. Once boiling add the stock.

Place the casserole in the oven. After 55–60 minutes, remove the chicken and strain the sauce into a bowl. Pour the sauce back in to the casserole and then reduce the liquid to your desired consistency. Put the chicken back into the sauce and bring it to a slow simmer before serving.

Meanwhile, place the lardons in a frying pan over a medium heat. Fry until they colour and release their fat. Add the mushrooms and baby onions and stir to coat them in the fat. Cook them until they gain a bit of colour.

To make the croutons, add the oil or clarified butter to frying pan over a medium heat. Cut the bread slices into 4 triangles each and add them with the garlic to the pan and fry until they are crispy and brown. Remove the croutons from the oil and drain on kitchen paper.

To serve, place the coq in a serving dish. Top it with the bacon and mushroom garnish, and place the croutons on top. Sprinkle with the chopped parsley and serve.

Passion Fruit Tart

Serves 8

200 g (7 oz) sweet shortcrust pastry
12 passion fruit
9 eggs
400 g (13 oz) caster sugar
250 ml (8 fl oz) double cream

To serve

icing sugar, for dusting
crème fraîche, to serve
4 passion fruit, quartered

You will need a 25 x 4 cm (10 x 1½ in) tart tin.

Preheat the oven to 180°C (350°F) Gas Mark 3½. Roll out the sweet pastry on a floured work surface to a thickness of about 3 mm (just less than ¼ inches). Lay the pastry into tart tin and blind bake.

While the tart case is baking, remove the flesh from the passion fruit by cutting them in half and scooping the flesh out with a spoon. Place the passion fruit flesh in a blender and blitz, pulsing it a couple of times to make a pulp. Pass the passion fruit purée through a sieve in to a bowl, and discard the pulp.

Whisk the eggs and sugar together in a large bowl and set them aside. Place a saucepan over a medium heat, add the cream and heat it until it is nearly boiling. Remove the cream from the heat and whisk it in to the egg and sugar mixture, then whisk in the passion purée.

Turn the oven down to 110°C (225°F) Gas Mark ¼. Fill the tart case with the filling and place it in the oven. Bake for 50 minutes or until the filling has nearly set.

When it is done, remove it from the oven and leave it to cool for a couple of hours. To serve, cut it into servings and place on a heatproof surface. Sprinkle each piece individually with icing sugar and then burn with a blowtorch (if you don't have a blowtorch, flash each slice under a very hot grill) just until the sugar caramelizes. Set the pieces of tart aside.

Keep 8 of the passion fruit quarters to the side. Remove the pulp from the rest, and place it in a bowl. Whisk it lightly to separate the seeds. Place a slice of passion fruit tart on a serving plate. Top each slice with a teaspoon of crème fraîche. Drizzle some of the pulp around the slice and finish with one of the reserved passion fruit quarters.

Galvin La Chapelle 35 Spital Square, E1 6DY
020 7299 0400 www.galvinrestaurants.com

Chris and Jeff Galvin's City restaurant is named after the celebrated
Hermitage La Chapelle wine, itself named after the chapel that overlooks
the vineyards in the Rhône valley. As you would expect, the wine list includes
many different vintages of this prized wine, including the 1961, one of
the most mythical wines of the 20th century, at an eye-watering £19,500.

Set in the stunning 19th century St. Botolph's Hall, the restaurant
has been described by reviewers as the kind of place you see in movies.
Dining in the Gallery on the mezzanine level gives you sweeping views of
the room below and brings you closer to the impressively vaulted ceiling.

Many of their dishes are quite elaborate and decorative, with distinct
flavours. You need to clear your diary and set aside the afternoon so that
you can truly enjoy the experience at this restaurant: try the seven-course
menu gourmand, with a different wine to accompany each course. The
head sommelier has prepared a highly informative wine list that should
perhaps be read online in advance.

(PP) I found the service to be very intuitive – something that is hard
to find. But if I'm honest – and this is just my personal view – I find the
brothers' more informal Café à Vin in the adjoining building more
enjoyable. Here you can enjoy simple French food cooked by a Michelin-
standard kitchen: perfect charcuterie with celeriac remoulade, confit de
canard, seared bavette and baba au rhum, all coming from such a highly
qualified brigade, and all at a fraction of the price of the main dining room. ◗

Above **The main
dining room at
Galvin La Chapelle.**
Left **A warm
welcome awaits.**

Lasagne of Dorset Crab with Beurre Nantaise

Serves 10

For the pasta
140 g (scant 5 oz) strong plain flour
1 egg
1½ egg yolks
½ tablespoon olive oil
pinch of salt

For the crab mousse
200 g (7 oz) scallops (white flesh only)
250 ml (8 fl oz) double cream
pinch of salt
cayenne pepper
400 g (13 oz) white Dorset crab meat, cooked and picked

For the beurre Nantaise
1 shallot, finely diced
200 g (7 oz) cold unsalted butter, diced
50 ml (2 fl oz) white wine
25 ml (1 fl oz) white wine vinegar
a few sprigs of thyme
1 star anise
50 ml (2 fl oz) water
100 ml (3½ fl oz) chicken stock
25 ml (1 fl oz) double cream
juice of ½ lemon
1 tablespoon finely chopped chives
salt and freshly ground black pepper

You will need 10 metal cooking rings, 7cm (3 inches) in diameter

For the pasta
Place all the pasta ingredients into a food processor and blitz until the mixture resembles breadcrumbs. Tip out on to a floured work surface and knead for 5 minutes until it forms a dough. Wrap in clingfilm and place in the refrigerator for at least 1 hour.

When rested, roll out the dough using a pasta machine until very thin. Blanch in boiling salted water for 1 minute, then plunge into a bowl of iced water. When cold, drain and cut out 30 circles with a 7-cm (3-inch) metal cooking ring. Lay the pasta circles in trays lined with clingfilm and set aside.

For the scallop mousse
Place the bowl of a food processor in the freezer for 1 hour to chill.

In the chilled bowl, blitz the scallop flesh for 3 or 4 minutes until nicely puréed. With the machine running, slowly add half the double cream, then season with salt and cayenne pepper. Add the remainder of the cream a little faster. Pour into a bowl and gently fold in the white crab meat. Taste and adjust the seasoning.

For the beurre Nantaise
In a large saucepan, cook the diced shallot in 10 g (scant ½ oz) of the butter over a low heat until soft but not coloured.

Add the white wine, vinegar, thyme, star anise and water. Reduce to a thick syrup, then add the chicken stock.

Boil down to a syrup again, then add the double cream. Boil for 1 minute, then gradually whisk in the remaining cold butter, maintaining the heat in the sauce as you go.

Remove the thyme and the star anise from the sauce, then season with salt, pepper and a small squeeze of lemon juice. Set aside and keep warm.

To assemble
Place a pasta circle in the bottom of each metal cooking ring. Put a thick layer of crab mix on top, followed by another pasta circle, another layer of crab mousse and a final layer of pasta. Steam the lasagne in a double stack steamer, or in the oven if you have a steam setting for 12 minutes.

Place in warm serving bowls. Run a small knife around the inside of each lasagne to remove the ring. Finish the beurre Nantaise by stirring in the chives, then spoon over each lasagne and serve.

Left **The impressive 19th century St. Botolph's Hall now houses Galvin La Chapelle.**

Leadenhall Cheese 4–5 Leadenhall Market, EC3V 1LR
020 7929 1697 www.cheeseatleadenhall.co.uk

If you work in the City of London this place must be a blessing. You can call in and choose from over 100 different cheeses, plus chutneys, biscuits, ports and a few carefully selected wines. You could buy your chilled cheese at lunchtime and store it in your briefcase until after the train home, by which time it should be perfectly ripe for supper.

The best time to visit the market is Friday morning, when a few extra stalls sell charcuterie, olives, antipasti and other snacks. The architecture isn't bad either. The spectacular market building by Sir Horace Jones (Victorian architect *du jour*) dates back to 1881. The site's long connection with British cheese, meanwhile, goes back as far as 1397, when cheesemongers from across the land were bound by law to bring all their cheeses to Leadenhall Market. ●

Above **Patriotic bunting adorns the Sir Horace Jones Leadenhall Market.** Right **Antipasti and charcuterie on sale at Leadenhall.**

David Burke

The Momouth Coffee Company at Borough Market serves the best coffee in London, but my favourite London café is the Cat and Cucumber at Tower Bridge.

Head chef, Lutyens

Above **Maurice, Fleet Street's legendary doorman, at Lutyens.**

Lutyens 85 Fleet Street, EC4Y 1AE
020 7583 8385 www.lutyens-restaurant.com

In the summer of 2009, we opened Lutyens in the former Press Association and Reuters building at 85 Fleet Street – the same address where Samuel Pepys was born on 23 February 1633. Designed by Sir Edwin Lutyens in 1939, and for half a century to come the area was renowned as the home of journalism and newspapers in London. Over the last 20 years all this has changed, and the denizens of Fleet Street are now high-flying bankers and lawyers.

Irishman David Burke is the head chef, and all of the menus follow his distinctive Franco-Irish style. David says that his cooking is based on classic ingredients and recipes with robust flavours, simply presented and generously served. The menus include real treats such cèpes bordelaise, a delicious soupe de poisson, rognons de veau, rabbit with bacon and mustard sauce, French pigeons with foie gras, or a simple entrecôte béarnaise, and you can also be assured of a fine selection of fruits de mer. In the game season, grouse are always in demand, and David likes to roast little woodcock and snipe when they are available. Dover sole has been a popular feature on the lunch menu since day one and we never intend to remove it, despite the high prices. The spectacular battered fish and chips also prove popular in the bar. Also on the menu is a crêpe parmentier with smoked salmon and caviar – very decadent. Simple Irish delights such as champ, Irish stew and crubeens also deserve a mention, and David insists – as you may imagine – on the best-quality Galway Bay oysters.

(PP) It is also worth mentioning that David Burke has worked with Terence for over 20 years, from the early days at Bibendum to the opening of Le Pont de la Tour. We appointed him before we had officially signed the lease for Lutyens and he hasn't let us down: his food quality and drive for success are inspiring. He's a great restaurateur.

The wine cellar is well stocked, as in all our restaurants, though here we find that our clients are very precise in their requirements. White and red burgundy wines are particular popular, Bordeaux less so, and thanks to the head sommelier's puzzling (to us) predilection there is also an extensive collection of German wines.

Lutyens offers a range of dining and drinking options, from breakfast served in the bar and the private members' club to four private meeting and dining rooms, a charcuterie bar and a small outside dining terrace in the shadow of the church garden. Of course we are also very proud of the restaurant design and of its many different details, from the mosaic floor that references Reuters ticker-tape to the black lacquer furniture that evokes the period of the building's heyday. The club area houses a collection of Lutyens books, we have acquired a few original Lutyens chairs, and the walls of the private dining rooms feature the great architect's drawings for buildings from private houses in Surrey to the Viceroy's House in New Delhi.

It is our aim to provide a grown-up and sophisticated City restaurant that is ideal both for clinching that global deal and for simple suppers with friends and a romantic glass of Champagne. We hope you enjoy it. ○

Above
All the furniture at Lutyens is designed by Terence Conran and was made in the UK by his company, Benchmark.
Middle left **Lutyens Bar with a mosaic floor that references the Reuters' ticker tape.**
Above right **A triple tier plateau de fruits de mer at Lutyens.**
Left **A pre-service briefing at Lutyens.**

Roast Chicken

Serves 4–6

1.8 kg (3 ½ lb) Landaise chicken
(or other good free-range chicken)
5 garlic cloves, crushed
½ lemon
small bunch of thyme
unsalted butter, at room temperature
1 onion, roughly chopped
1 leek, white part only, roughly chopped
1 celery stick, roughly chopped
1 teaspoon plain flour
250–300 ml (8–10 fl oz) chicken stock
salt and freshly ground black pepper

Preheat the oven to 200°C (400°F) Gas Mark 6.

Check the bird's cavity is empty, then place the garlic, lemon half and thyme inside. Smear a thin layer of butter over the chicken and apply a generous amount of salt.

Scatter the onion, leek and celery over the base of a roasting tin and place the chicken on top. Place in the oven and roast for 15 minutes, then baste with the cooking juices. Lower the heat to 180°C (350°F) Gas Mark 4 and cook for a further 45 minutes, basting every 10 minutes or so. Check that the bird is cooked by piercing the thickest part of the thigh with a skewer: the juices should run clear. Turn off the oven and move the roasting tin to the bottom shelf to rest for 10–15 minutes.

Remove from the oven and scrape the garlic, lemon and thyme out of the cavity of the bird into the roasting tin. Transfer the bird to a warm plate to rest for another 10–15 minutes. Put the roasting tin on the hob over a low heat and stir in the flour. Gradually stir in the stock, bring to the boil and boil rapidly for 3–4 minutes to make the gravy. Taste and adjust the seasoning, then strain and serve with the chicken.

Left **The charcuterie counter at Lutyens.**

Dover Sole with Beurre Mâitre d'Hôtel

Dover sole is one of our best sellers at lunch – there would be a riot if it was removed from the menu. Mâitre d'hôtel butter is an ideal partner for most grilled fish and is also rather good with an entrecote steak. It also works with a little garlic and other herbs including tarragon, chives or mint.

1 Dover sole per person, approximately 600–700g (1lb 3oz–1lb 5oz), head, fins and back skin removed, and trimmed (ask your fishmonger to do this)

1 lemon, sliced

For the beurre mâitre d'hôtel (serves 10–12)

250 g (8 oz) unsalted butter, at room temperature

25 g (1 oz) chopped parsley

juice of one lemon

pinch of salt and finely ground black pepper

olive oil

Make the butter in advance so it can be chilled: place the butter in a medium bowl and cream with a spatula or wooden spoon. Add the remaining ingredients and mix well. Place the mix on a sheet of greaseproof paper and roll into a sausage shape about 5 cm (2 inches) in diameter. Store in the refrigerator until you are ready to use for up to a week, or in the freezer for longer.

Brush the sole with a small amount of olive oil. We bar-mark the top fillet to create the criss-cross pattern by heating metal skewers over a gas flame and pressing to the flesh. Cook on a baking tray under a hot preheated grill on just one side (white skin on the underside) for 8–10 minutes. Alternatively, you can cook the sole in a ridged grill pan to achieve the bar marks, although you must ensure that the pan is very hot before adding the fish and do not touch it for a couple of minutes to avoid it sticking to the pan.

The cooking time will obviously depend on the size of the fish and the intensity of your grill. Try to avoid putting the fillet too close to the heat. Once the fish flesh is cooked and flakes easily or cooked to your liking, place a disk of the butter about 1 cm (1/2 inch) thick on the fillet and place under the grill for another 30–60 seconds until the butter just begins to melt. If you are cooking for a few people or your grill isn't that large you could use the oven for this final stage.

Season with salt and pepper, and serve with a slice of lemon, steamed new potatoes and spinach.

Tartes Fines aux Pommes with Caramel Ice Cream

Serves 4

For the caramel ice cream

300 g (10 oz) caster sugar
60 g (generous 2 oz) salted butter, chilled and cut into small dice
5 egg yolks
500 ml (17 fl oz) milk
250 ml (8 fl oz) double cream
1 teaspoon vanilla extract

For the tartes fines

800 g (1 lb 10 oz) readymade puff pastry
4 large Golden Delicious or Granny Smith apples
melted unsalted butter, for brushing
icing sugar, for dusting

First make the ice cream. Put the sugar in a large, heavy-based pan, place on a high heat and cook until it turns a deep, dark caramel colour. You need to be bold with this and take it as far as you dare, otherwise the caramel will not have the requisite bitter edge and the ice cream will taste too sweet. Don't be tempted to move the pan about too much or stir the sugar while it is melting, or it will cook unevenly; if a patch of sugar isn't cooking as fast as the rest, just gently tilt the pan so it shifts slightly.

When the caramel is ready, remove from the heat, add the diced butter and whisk gently to incorporate. In a large bowl, whisk together the egg yolks, milk, cream and vanilla extract. Return the caramel to a low heat, pour in the cream mixture and cook, stirring with a wooden spoon, until the mixture is thick enough to coat the back of the spoon; if you have a thermometer handy, it should register 85°C (185°F). (Be careful not to have the heat too high or you will end up with brown scrambled eggs.)

Remove from the heat, pour the mixture through a fine sieve into a bowl and leave to cool. Chill, then churn in an ice cream machine according to the manufacturer's instructions.

For the tartes, roll out the puff pastry on a lightly floured surface to about 5 mm (¼ inch) thick. Prick it all over with a fork and cut out 4 discs about 18 cm (7 inches) in diameter. Place each one on a piece of baking parchment and put in the refrigerator to chill.

Peel, quarter and core the apples and slice thinly. Take the pastry from the refrigerator and arrange the apples on top in overlapping concentric circles. Use any small pieces of apple to fill the centre of the tarts. Brush with melted butter to stop the apple oxidizing and return the tarts to the refrigerator to rest for 20–30 minutes.

Heat the oven to 200°C (400°F), Gas Mark 6, and put 2 large baking sheets in to heat. Sift a generous dusting of icing sugar over the top of each tarte and transfer them to the hot baking sheets, still on the parchment paper – it's important to have the baking sheets good and hot, as this kick-starts the cooking process, ensuring a crisp base. Bake for 12–15 minutes or until the apples are tender and slightly caramelized and the pastry is crisp. Carefully transfer the tartes to serving plates, put a ball of caramel ice cream in the centre of each, dust with more icing sugar and serve immediately.

You can store the uncooked tartes in the freezer (where they will keep for months), and bake from frozen – just add a few minutes to the cooking time if necessary.

Below **David Burke, Lutyens head chef.**

Now 22–3 Liverpool Street, EC2M 7PD
020 7042 9191 www.nowstreetfood.com

If China is now the country with the greatest global influence, then we should pay attention to the launch of this fast-food concept based on Chinese street food: steamed dumplings, spring rolls with hoi sin sauce and wonton soup, to go. Not the dream lunch, perhaps, but none the less very popular – there's a good chance that this brand will soon have branches popping up all over London. ◉

Chris Galvin

London is the greatest melting pot of ethnic cuisine in the world today and finally, we are blessed with lots of 'young guns' cooking and serving daring dishes and concepts.

Owner, Galvin La Chapelle

Above **Steaming baskets in the window at Now.**

Above left **Sir Christopher Wren's Dome of St. Paul's cathedral (top) and Paternoster Square (below).**
Above right **Well-marbled beef at Paternoster Chop House.**

Paternoster Chop House

Warwick Court, Paternoster Square, EC4M 7DX
020 7029 9400 www.paternosterchophouse.co.uk

Paternoster Square is a historic location, and before it was rebuilt at the turn of the millennium the development received much flak, especially from royal quarters. Today it hosts a bustling office community, and the venerable London Stock Exchange has found its new home on the square. St. Paul's is just a short walk through the rebuilt Temple Bar, where the dining chamber is a popular venue for receptions and business meetings, and the Millennium Bridge across to Tate Modern lies just a few hundred yards beyond Sir Christopher Wren's masterpiece.

It was only fitting that Conran Restaurants should launch (in 2004) a chop house with a gutsy British menu featuring a beast of the day, a fine selection of meats from the spit roast and grill, line- and diver-caught fish and shellfish. There is also a back-to-basics Sunday lunch menu, along with much more of the best from the farms and fields of Britain.

Far left **The view from Coq d'Argent towards The Royal Exchange at Bank.** Left **The REX central courtyard.**

Royal Exchange Grand Café The Courtyard, Bank, EC3V 3LR
020 7618 2480 www.theroyalexchange.com

This impressive all-day upmarket café and oyster bar is laid out in the airy courtyard that was once the trading floor of this truly grand Grade I listed building. It was a great trading centre and stock exchange for London in its day, but the original building and a second one on the same site were both destroyed by fire. The current building first opened for trading on 1 January 1845, and now houses a galaxy of luxury shops and offices, cafés, restaurants and bars. The logo of Sauterelle features the grasshopper (*sauterelle* in French) of the Gresham family crest, a motif echoed by the weathervane on the roof.

We recommend lunch in the courtyard with a plate of charcuterie, some langoustines and a crab tartine, and a glass of chilled Chablis. ◉

Sweetings 39 Queen Victoria Street, EC4N 4SF 020 7248 3062
The term 'institution' is applied to restaurants all too often and too easily, but in the case of Sweetings – which has been trading since 1889, with few apparent changes, and is still full most days – the accolade is fully justified.

The devastating damage suffered by Queen Victoria Street during the Blitz reputedly destroyed the wet fish counter, which was replaced by a large window. In the 1980s, when the City started to become the global financial centre it is today, word went around that a compensation cheque for £10,000 had been delivered by a recently relocated German bank. Apocryphal, perhaps, but a nice addition to the legend that is Sweetings.

The food is pure nursery fare with a fishy emphasis, so you can gorge on potted shrimps, cods' roe, skate wings with brown butter, crab and smoked salmon. In recent years many chefs have taken to featuring traditional English puddings on their menus, though in a lighter and less liberal manner. Not at Sweetings. Here the steamed syrup pudding and baked jam roll are vast.

Above **A Dave Bray line-drawing at REX.**

Sweetings is open only for lunch, Monday to Friday, you can't make a reservation, and they don't serve coffee, but it's definitely worth a visit. Take your godson to show him how things used to be done. ◉

More places to visit in the area

Barbecoa
20 New Change Passage, EC4M 9AG
020 3005 8555 www.barbecoa.com
A joint venture by Jamie Oliver and barbecue expert Adam Perry Lang from America, this striking Tom Dixon-designed restaurant specializes in cooking meat and seafood using different forms of fire – Robata grills, tandoors, wood pits etc. The view of St. Paul's is stunning, especially at night.

The Don Restaurant and Bistro
The Courtyard, 20 St. Swithins Lane, EC4N 8AD 020 7626 2606
www.thedonrestaurant.com
Here, on the site of the old Sandeman port cellars, you can enjoy high-quality Gallic fare and a far-reaching wine list. The atmospheric rooms and friendly staff make this a preferred destination for City dining.

Goodman
11 Old Jewry, EC2R 8DU
020 7600 8220
www.goodmanrestaurants.com
A New York-style steakhouse that serves both USDA corn-fed beef and grass-fed beef from Scotland and Ireland.

Konditor & Cook
30 St. Mary Axe, EC3A 8BF
0844 854 93 69
www.konditorandcook.com
A fantastic bakery and cake shop in the City, though in an awkward location at the base of the Gherkin.

Soseki
20 Bury Street 1F, EC3A 5AX
020 7621 9211 www.soseki.co.uk
Superior sushi, and you can also rest assured that all the fish comes from sustainable stocks. The owners are at the forefront of a campaign to conserve the marine environment.

Above **The REX charcuterie board.**

Clerkenwell Farringdon Smithfield

Only hardened foodies should chart a course to Clerkenwell and Farringdon, an area that has Smithfield meat market as its focal point, but those who do venture to this 'bloody cool and offaly good' corner of London won't be disappointed. The UK's biggest meat market and some of the coolest bars, clubs and restaurants in the capital coexist in a relationship of perfect symbiosis. As the nightclubs empty at four in the morning, goggle-eyed clubbers are greeted by the sight of colliding guts, flesh and bones, steered by an army of men in white coats – incomprehensible if you don't know the area; disconcerting if you do. By breakfast time, a fleet of white vans will be discharging their bovine, porcine, ovine and avian consignments. Soon after this, the market porters will slip away for a pint of ale and a slap-up English breakfast, before heading home for a hard day's sleep. Then butchers' shops open and chefs take their deliveries, and by lunchtime meaty treats will have started to appear. At dinner your favourite slab of beef will arrive on the plate, and overnight the whole process begins all over again. While New York's Meatpacking District has gained similar notoriety for its hip bars and eateries, somehow the sight of a few carcasses in the open warehouses between Gansevoort Street and West 15th doesn't deliver the same concentrated carnivorous hit. And Sir Horace Jones's Victorian temple to the meat trade is a sight in its own right. St. John with its offal, Smith's with its rare breeds and Club Gascon with its foie gras all contribute to the area's new heritage. Even Saki, a Japanese offering, steps up to the plate with its monkfish liver sushi. So best not go to Smithfield and ask for the vegetarian option.

Med Pepper
za 3⁰⁰

Meal Deal 5⁵⁰

Pizza or Quiche
with
Salad

on & Smac 4²⁵

n fed chicken

Sweetcorn & Tomato
Quiche 3¹⁰

Tomato

& Yuzu 2⁹⁵
Soup

Roast 3⁵⁰
Salmon

NEWBY NEWBY
NEWBY NEWBY
NEWBY NEWBY

Bistrot Bruno Loubet

The Zetter Hotel, St. John's Square, 86–8 Clerkenwell Road, EC1M 5RJ
020 7324 4455 www.bistrotbrunoloubet.com

Bruno's return to London has had the food critics fawning and drooling. After arriving in the UK in 1982 to work for Pierre Koffmann at the three Michelin-starred La Tante Claire, he set up a couple of restaurants of his own and made his mark in the 1990s, before disappearing to Australia in 2001. The decade (almost) that he was away was punctuated by regular reports that we might see his return, and in early 2010 the inevitable happened. In The Zetter Hotel, with the support of the hotel's experienced patrons, Bruno has now found an excellent home for his distinctive style.

This is a chef with traditional values who has created a *modern* (our emphasis) French bistro. (PP) I was intrigued by Bruno's pigs' trotter dish. Given his past experience with Pierre Koffmann, a chef synonymous with one of the best pigs' trotter dishes, I expected something quite different. Instead of the unctuous brown reduction sauce, however, this was served with a peanut and chilli salsa plus a pickled cucumber salad. His reinvented salade Lyonnaise is another example of Bruno's modern approach.

The press appear to have been right about Bruno's appeal, and the restaurant is buzzing. If you go in the evening we recommend a pre-dinner cocktail (a stiff martini is always good) at The Zetter Townhouse Cocktail Lounge (see page 194), just across the square behind the restaurant. ◗

Above left
Bruno Loubet.
Above right **The Russell Sage-designed restaurant at The Zetter Hotel.**
Right **Beetroot ravioli with rocket salad from the menu at Bistrot Bruno Loubet.**

Grilled Quail with Broad Bean and Herb Risotto

Serves 6

6 quails

For the marinade

4 garlic cloves, chopped
2 tablespoons picked fresh thyme leaves
6 tablespoons pomegranate molasses
4 tablespoons olive oil

For the risotto

600 ml (1 pint) chicken stock
180 g (6 oz) small frozen peas (defrosted)
500 g (1 lb) broad beans
75 g (3 oz) butter
1 onion, finely diced
1 garlic clove, chopped
160 g (5 1/2 oz) risotto rice
100 ml (3 1/2 fl oz) white wine
6 spring onions, finely chopped
1 tablespoon chopped mint
1 tablespoon chopped flat leaf parsley
juice of 1/2 lemon
50 g (2 oz) grated Parmesan
salt and freshly ground black pepper

To serve

olive oil
micro herbs or small salad leaves

About 4 hours before cooking, bone out the quails, starting from the side of the breastbone going down to the back of each quail, to give two half quails (alternatively, ask your butcher to do this for you).

In a large bowl, mix together all the ingredients for the marinade, then add the quails and gently coat them with the mixture. Lay the quails on a baking tray, cover with clingfilm and place in the refrigerator to marinate while you prepare the risotto.

In a saucepan add half the chicken stock and bring to the boil. Add the peas with a pinch of salt, and bring back to the boil. Cook for 2 minutes then liquidize in a blender to a smooth consistency, the set aside.

Put the broad beans in a bowl, pour boiling water over them, then when cool enough to handle pop them out of their skins and set aside.

In a heavy-based pan, melt 30 g (1 1/2 oz) of the butter over a medium heat and add the onion. Stir and cook until translucent, but without colouring. Add the garlic, stir for a further minute, then add the rice. Stir for 2 minutes, increase the heat then add the white wine. Stir until the alcohol has cooked out, then turn the heat to medium and start adding the rest of the chicken stock, one small ladleful at a time. It is important to stir well between each ladleful and to make sure the stock has been completely absorbed by the rice before adding the next. Finish this operation by addiing the liquidized peas. Check the rice is cooked before adding the broad beans and the spring onions. Stir well for 30 seconds, set aside and keep warm.

Grill the quails on a barbecue skin-side down (or in batches in a griddle pan over a high heat) and carefully lift the quails to check good markings on the skin have formed before turning them 45 degrees to achieve a nice cross marking. Turn the quails over and repeat. When cooked, set the quails on a metal tray or in a warm place to rest.

Add the mint, parsley, lemon juice, Parmesan and remainder of the butter to the risotto and stir well. Taste and adjust the seasoning if necessary.

To serve, spoon the risotto on to serving plates and top with the quails. Pour any juices from the quails over, and finish with a drizzle of good olive oil. Garnish the top with micro herbs or small salad leaves.

Club Gascon 57 West Smithfield, EC1A 9DS
020 7796 0600 www.clubgascon.com

Pascal Aussignac has created a multiple award-winning and Michelin-starred eatery devoted to the food of south-west France. The dining room seats about 60 people and has a City boy atmosphere, with dark woods, marble and linen napery. Cellar Gascon next door is a busy wine bar with a peerless list of wines from Gascony. Serious bar snacks follow the same robust duck, foie gras and porcine direction. ◑

Comptoir Gascon 63 Charterhouse Street, EC1M 6HJ
020 7680 0851 www.comptoirgascon.com

The Club Gascon team offers more duck, goose, pork and other meats in this small, rustic 30-seat bistro, with a few bakery and deli items also available. (PP) While most people prefer the original Club Gascon site, this more humble offer is more to my taste.

The French fries cooked in duck fat are (as Michael Winner might say) historic. ◑

The Eagle 159 Farringdon Road, EC1R 3AL
020 7837 1353

Having opened in 1991, The Eagle is reputedly the first gastropub in London. During years of both metamorphosis and proliferation in the world of gastropubs, The Eagle has thankfully remained unchanged and true to its original idea. This is probably the best format for a business of this type: let pubs remain pubs, with good inexpensive grub, and let restaurants be restaurants.

The ground-floor open kitchen sets the tone, and everything is stripped back. The Eagle puts on no airs and graces, and it is perhaps a little too scruffy for some tastes, yet the place is packed with integrity, and is robust in every sense, with a generally faultless kitchen.

The original chef, David Eyre, has now set up a new restaurant with his brother at 70 Leonard Street, EC2 www.eyrebrothers.co.uk. ◑

Bruno Loubet

My favourite neighbourhood restaurant is The Ship in Wandsworth. It's hidden between a cement factory and a bus depot, which doesn't seem promising but the convivial atmosphere is infectious and the food is equally good.

Chef patron, Bistrot Bruno Loubet

Above left **Pascal Aussignac.**
Above **The different cuts and grades of meat that are presented at Hix.**

Above and right **The Hix dining room.** Left **Blackcurrant and white chocolate cheesecake at Hix.**

This page **Inside Hix.** Right **Mark Hix is an art enthusiast and is well-loved by the art community.**

Left **Beef flank and oyster pie from Hix.**

Hix Oyster & Chop House

36–7 Greenhill Rents, Cowcross Street, EC1M 6BN
020 7017 1930 www.hixoysterandchophouse.co.uk

This no-fuss eating house is Mark Hix's first solo project. In his illustrious career he has worked with Anton Edelman and Anton Mosimann at the grand hotels along Park Lane, and even more impressively chalked up a commendable 17 years with Caprice Holdings. Mark was the head chef at Le Caprice, The Ivy and J Sheekey, before becoming Chef Director for a much larger group of restaurants encompassing everything from Vietnamese to Italian menus. Mark was also the key figure responsible for devising and establishing the magnificent Scott's in Mayfair. Having been responsible for the food at London's most fashionable restaurants, he certainly knows a thing or two about how to run such places.

The kitchen here serves up hearty and gutsy British food without any frills. Just how we like it. Everything is well sourced and proudly British. From wild herbs, sea vegetables and English garden vegetables to a Barnsley chop or rib steak and excellent flank and oyster pies, there is much to relish here. The fruit puddings and fools are excellent, and the British cheeses live up to their well-deserved international reputation.

Try the De Beauvoir smoked salmon 'Hix Cure', smoked over oak and apple chips using salt and molasses at Mark's home in east London.

The style and layout of the restaurant, formerly a sausage factory, complement the stripped-down food perfectly, while evidence of Mark's design awareness and knowledge of art are all around.

Left **Inside the shop at The Modern Pantry.** Right **English breakfast served in The Modern Pantry style.** Below **Convivial dining at the ground floor communal table.**

Right **Anna Hansen is highly regarded and has secured critical acclaim for her restaurant.**

The Modern Pantry 47–8 St. John's Square, EC1V 4JJ
020 7553 9210 www.themodernpantry.co.uk

Before 2008, when Anna Hansen opened The Modern Pantry, fusion food (sometimes known disparagingly as 'confusion food') seemed, like nouvelle cuisine, to be dead and buried in London. With the exception of The Providores, Peter Gordon's excellent restaurant in Marylebone (see page 254), Londoners had abandoned this sometimes misunderstood style of food just as quickly as they had embraced it in the 1990s. While we might not rush to visit The Modern Pantry, there can be no doubt that the city benefits from diversity and creativity. This is an interesting project that brings together global recipes and ingredients in a pleasingly simple setting. From east meets west to wacky flavour combinations, the menus can be challenging, and seem to be characterized chiefly by a riot of textures, flavours and aromas. On the whole the combinations seem to work, and occasionally you will find nuggets of brilliance. Given the different components in each dish the kitchen certainly deserves credit for championing this style of food. We can't imagine anything further removed from Escoffier's great dictum, '*Faîtes simple*', or Elizabeth David's advocacy of 'the avoidance of all unnecessary complication and elaboration'.

Set in a handsome Georgian townhouse overlooking St. John's Square are three dining spaces. The ground-floor café, with its communal table and large windows, is a delight, even if it feels a little like a goldfish bowl as pedestrians pass by. Upstairs is more suitable for intimate suppers, and on a sunny day the outside seating is best. ◐

Above **St. John's Square with The Modern Pantry in the background.**

Christoffer Hruskova

North Road 69–73 St. John Street, EC1M 4AN
020 3217 0033 www.northroadrestaurant.co.uk

This corner of London is endowed with many restaurants that might be described as robust and distilled. Blessed with a strong character, they jettison frills and fawning details. When we first heard about this new restaurant we feared the worst, assuming that it would be too fancy and not what the area wants or needs. We were in part prejudiced by the recent closure of a nearby restaurant whose rather overweening chef promised to bring Michelin stars to the area. The restaurant flopped. The opposite is more likely to be the case for North Road, and given the current direction adopted by Michelin inspectors, the area may get its first star. (Just as we went to press North Road were awarded a Michelin star.)

Danish chef and owner Christoffer Hruskova blends the best British ingredients with Nordic methods and cooking styles. It's a combination that works quite well. He puts pickles and wild herbs with Gloucester Old Spot pork, for example; Dorset lobster with redcurrant wine and rose petals; and sea trout with wild garlic bulbs, salad roots, salad stems and leaves. The venison, meanwhile, is presented in (intentionally) burned hay and garnished with beetroot in different forms plus wild sorrel. Even the humble and delicious Jersey Royal is presented with lovage plus caramelized and burned onions. One of the desserts, called 'flavours of nature', includes birch, nettles, oak shoots and green strawberries. This smörgåsbord of foraged and wild ingredients is on-message at the moment. With Rene Redzepi of Noma in Copenhagen currently the hottest chef in the world, it isn't surprising that this modern northern European style of cooking is in demand. The Scandinavian-influenced interior at North Road, meanwhile, is subtle and stylish.

(PP) I don't normally order the tasting menu at restaurants, but did so at North Road, together with the sommelier's suggestions at each course. It was a very interesting way to sample the chef's skills and appreciate this new style of cooking, which might not be so evident with just a starter, main and dessert. I recommend it. ◉

Left **Danish chef Christoffer Hruskova, owner of North Road.** Right **Scandinavian food and interiors at North Road.**

Asparagus with Nettle Emulsion, Yogurt and Hop Shoots

Serves 4

For the nettle emulsion

200 g (7 oz) nettle leaves
1/2 banana shallot, chopped
1/2 teaspoon English mustard
1 slice white bread, crusts removed, torn into pieces
75–100 ml (3–3 1/2 fl oz) virgin rapeseed oil
1 tablespoon cider vinegar or white wine vinegar
salt and freshly ground black pepper

For the asparagus and hop shoots

16 green asparagus spears
16–20 hop shoots
virgin rapeseed oil

To serve

40 ml (1 1/2 fl oz) natural yogurt
16 chickweed shoots (optional)

Wash the nettle leaves and blanch by pouring boiling water over, then draining and placing in a bowl of iced water. Transfer them to a blender with the chopped shallot, mustard and bread. Blend, gradually adding the oil until the mixture emulsifies and thickens. Season with vinegar, salt and pepper to taste.

Using a vegetable peeler, shave 4 of the asparagus spears into long strips and put the shavings in a bowl of iced water for 4–5 minutes until they curl up.

Pan-fry the remaining 12 asparagus in rapeseed oil until golden, then add the hop shoots and fry for another minute.

Divide the fried asparagus between 4 plates and top with the nettle emulsion and yogurt; drain the asparagus shavings and serve, along with the hops and chickweed, if using.

Jersey Potatoes, Burnt Onion and Lovage

Serves 4

small bunch of lovage
1 onion
16 small Jersey Royal potatoes
12 button onions, peeled
oil, for frying

For the potato spuma

2 baking potatoes
1/2 white onion, finely chopped
25 g (1 oz) butter
100 ml (3 1/2 fl oz) double cream
100 ml (3 1/2 fl oz) milk
salt and freshly ground black pepper

Pick the lovage leaves off the stems and dry the stems in a very low oven for 1 hour.

Heat the oven to 200°C (400°F), Gas Mark 6, and cook the whole onion for about 1 hour until it is black and dry. Blend and sift the burnt onion until you have a fine powder.

For the potato spuma, bake the baking potatoes in the oven at 180°C (350°F), Gas Mark 4, for 1 hour, then scrape the flesh out of the skins and set aside to keep warm. Cut the skins into strips.

Sauté the white onion in a little oil over a medium heat until soft but not coloured. Then add the baked potato flesh, butter, cream and milk, and mix to a glossy mash (you can serve it at this stage as normal mash if you prefer).

Put the mash into a spuma bottle and add 2 CO_2 capsules to the spuma, keep it at 65°C (150°F).

Cook the Jersey Royal potatoes in a saucepan of boiling salted water until tender and pan-fry the button onions in a little oil over a medium heat – keep both warm until ready to serve.

Deep-fry the lovage stems and baked potato skin strips in oil at 150°C (300°F) until crisp, drain on kitchen paper and season with salt.

To serve, roll the fried button onions in the burnt onion powder. Divide between 4 plates with the Jersey Royal potatoes. Add the warm potato spuma or mash, crispy lovage stems and potato skins. Finally, dust with burnt onion powder and serve.

Left **Trevor Gulliver and Fergus Henderson in the bar at St. John.** Right **St. John chutney is the perfect accompaniment for any meat.** Below right **Roast bone marrow and parsley salad.**

St. John Bar & Restaurant 26 St. John Street, EC1M 4AY

020 7251 0848 www.stjohnrestaurant.com

It's now over fifteen years since Trevor Gulliver tempted Fergus Henderson and Jon Spiteri to set up a new restaurant close to Smithfield Meat Market. Jon was indispensable in the early years and has subsequently moved on. Fergus's Nose to Tail menu, has meanwhile gained a worldwide reputation.

When Trevor found the building it had been used – among other functions – as a smokehouse. He simply painted the walls white, put in a skylight, installed a kitchen and dropped in some tables and chairs. This no-fuss approach is a major factor in the success of the place.

The food is beyond reproach, naturally. Laconic and to the point best describes not only the style of the menu, but also what appears on the plate. Nobody else cooks to this standard and uses the range of ingredients pioneered by Fergus. His parents have a lot to answer for, it should be said. Brian Henderson has always enjoyed the best food and wine in generous quantities. Elizabeth is a fine cook, in the Henderson tradition. Fergus learned at her stove, though he originally trained as an architect.

We thoroughly recommend calling in as often as possible, whether for a morning fillip, a long lunch or a simple supper. Or why not just collect a few Eccles cakes or a seed cake from the bakery?

(PP) As well as going to the restaurant as much as possible, I also celebrate my birthdays here. For my thirty-fifth we had a raucous party for 18 and shared a whole suckling pig; for my fortieth things were slightly more sedate with an unimpeachable grouse. It's just a wonderful place to be. ⊙

Doug Wregg

"

The best bakery in London is St. John, where the smell of baking bread causes you to faint with hunger when you go in.

Co-owner, Brawn, Terroirs and Les Caves de Pyrène

Left **The unique St. John bread.**

St. John's Eccles Cakes

**Should easily make a dozen cakes.
Any left-over pastry freezes very well.**

I stress the St. John in our Eccles cake, as I am sure Eccles cake bakers in Eccles will not recognize them as an Eccles cake they know.

Oddly enough, for a restaurant with a certain carnivorous reputation, we serve a vegetarian Eccles cake, omitting to use the traditional lard in the pastry. Instead, we use puff pastry, so apologies to Eccles, but this recipe's results are delicious and particularly fine when consumed with Lancashire cheese.

For the pastry

125 g (4 oz) unsalted butter (butter A), cold from the fridge
500 g (1 lb) strong white flour
a pinch of sea salt
250 ml (8 fl oz) water
375g (12 oz) unsalted butter (butter B), cold from the fridge

For the filling

50 g (2 oz) unsalted butter
110 g (4 oz) dark brown sugar
220 g (7³/₄ oz) currants
1 teaspoon ground allspice
1 teaspoon ground nutmeg

For the glaze

3 egg whites, beaten with a fork
a shallow bowl of caster sugar

To make the puff pastry, mix butter A with the flour and salt using your fingers until the mixture resembles breadcrumbs. Then cautiously add the water and mix until you have a firm paste. Pat the pastry into a square and wrap it in clingfilm. Leave it to rest in the fridge for at least one hour before using.

To make the filling, melt the butter and sugar together, Place all the dry ingredients into a bowl and then add the butter and sugar mixture. Mix them well. Leave the mixture to cool and rest before using it. Once rested, roll the pastry dough into a rectangle about 8 mm (¹/₃ inch) thick, then beat butter B between greaseproof paper into a rectangle a wee bit smaller than half the dough rectangle. Lay the butter on the dough, leaving a space at the end. Fold the unbuttered half over the butter and fold the edges over, so you now have butter-in-dough package. Pat it square, wrap it in cling film, and allow to rest in the fridge.

After the pastry has been in the fridge for at least 15 minutes, roll it out into a rectangle in the opposite direction to your initial major fold. (Each time you roll out the pastry to fold, turn your pastry and roll across the previous direction you rolled. You will have to sprinkle flour on the surface of your rolling pin, however, it is very important to dust the flour off the pastry before folding it at every turn in the process.)

Once the pastry is approximately 1–1.5 cm (about ¹/₂ inch) thick, fold it like a traditional letter, with one end of the rectangle to the halfway mark, and the other end over this. Pat it square and place it in the fridge for at least 15 minutes to rest again. Repeat this process twice more, but no more than that! This is essential for successful puff. Return it to the fridge to rest for 1 hour or more. Do not be deterred. In writing this, it seems like a more complicated process than it is in practice.

To make the Eccles cakes, preheat the oven to 220°C (425°F) Gas Mark 7. Roll the puff pastry out to 8 mm (¹/₃ inch) thick and cut circles approximately 9 cm (3¹/₂ inch) in diameter. On half of these spoon a blob of your filling mixture in the centre of the circle, then place the other pastry circles on top. Pinch the edges together, gently press to flatten the cakes, then slash the top three times. (I'm told it is very significant how many times an Eccles cake is slashed.)

Paint the top with the egg white, then dip it into the sugar. They are now ready to bake for 15–20 minutes in the oven. Keep an eye on them so that they don't burn.

They can be eaten either hot or cold and, as I mentioned earlier, are particularly marvellous with Lancashire cheese.

Recipe featured in *Nose to Tail Eating*, Bloomsbury

Saki Bar and Food Emporium 4 West Smithfield, EC1A 9JX
020 7489 7033 www.saki-food.com

Saki (not to be confused with sake, the Japanese rice wine) means 'happiness' in Japanese. Saki Bar and Food Emporium is a modern and innovative concept that is bursting with technology and redolent of a healthy, balanced diet.

On the ground floor they have an advanced noodle-making machine and takeaway sushi and sashimi. The shelves at the rear of the food boutique are stocked with wasabi, nori, miso, soy sauce, pickled things, sake, shochu, Japanese cookery books, tableware and even rice cookers.

In the basement is a lively bar serving creative cocktails and a Kobachi menu – the Japanese equivalent of tapas. Wi-Fi access is available throughout, and the Japanese paperless toilets have heated seats.

The basement restaurant has a small sushi bar and about 70 seats, with an extensive menu including sea urchin and (in season) monkfish liver, a rarity sometimes known as the 'foie gras of the sea'. ⊙

Above top left
Making sushi in the basement restaurant of Saki.
Above left and right
Japanese products for sale in Saki's Food Emporium.

Right **Smithfield Market porters and butchers.** Left **The breakfast and sandwiches at Smith's.**

Smithfield Meat and Poultry Market

Charterhouse Street, EC1A 9PQ 020 7236 8734

One of the oldest markets in London, Smithfield has been supplying meat and poultry to the populace for over 800 years. The building, designed by Sir Horace Jones, suffered a fire in 1958 and was replaced in 1962, though much of its original Victorian splendour survives, and it is Grade II listed.

The market still influences the cost of meat and poultry in the UK today, with hundreds of butchers and suppliers visiting it on a weekly basis. Anyone can visit the market and shop there, but access to certain areas is restricted to those wearing clean protective clothing, in accordance with hygiene standards. ●

Smith's of Smithfield 67–77 Charterhouse Street, EC1M 6HJ

020 7251 7950 www.smithsofsmithfield.co.uk

John Torode, the personality behind Smith's, is a distinguished Australian chef, television personality and restaurateur. He possesses a relaxed style absolutely at one with the Smithfield vibe, and this former warehouse opposite the meat market offers a multitude of dining and drinking options. The common thread that connects the five floors, each with its own distinctive character, is a passion for unpretentious food that tastes great.

On the ground floor the décor is simple, with bench seats, leather sofas and a long bar. An open kitchen serves up an excellent all-day breakfast, along with club sandwiches, meat pies, sausage and mash, brunch and freshly squeezed juices. Good beer is the order of the day.

The first floor houses a smart wine bar and a private dining and events space. Above, on the second floor, is a 130-seat dining room and a semi-open kitchen that offers food prepared according to a range of cooking methods, from the wok to clay ovens and charcoal grills. The menu here crosses several continents and includes a grill section and a 10-oz beef burger with mature cheddar and Old Spot bacon.

On the top floor you reach the summit in culinary terms: the menu is dedicated to the best of British meat, organic foods and seasonal vegetables. ●

Left **The ground floor bar at Smith's.**

Right **The Zetter Townhouse interiors are eccentric but comfortable.**

194 **Vinoteca** 7 St. John Street, EC1M 4AA

020 7253 8786 www.vinoteca.co.uk

This is one of London's modern wine bars inspired (as the name suggests) by the popular Italian and Spanish models. There are about 275 wines on offer, with some 25 available by the glass, each listed with eloquent tasting notes. Without ignoring the popular varietals, the lists also include many less well-known grapes, such as furmint from Hungary and garganega from Italy. With its décor of heavy oak furniture, blackboards and a little poster art, the place is invariably buzzing. While the emphasis is intended to be on the wine, the food is also jolly good and highly appropriate. If you've enjoyed a particular wine, you can also buy a case to take home: an interesting concept thought up by three independent wine merchants. ○

The Zetter Townhouse Cocktail Lounge

49–50 St. John's Square EC1V 4JJ

020 7324 4545 www.thezettertownhouse.com

This 13-bedroom sister to the main Zetter Hotel, just across the square, houses an eccentrically-decorated cocktail lounge. The main attraction is clearly the cocktails, but don't overlook the food by Bruno Loubet.

Tony Conigliaro, widely acknowledged as one of the country's top drink creators, and Camille Hobby-Limon have devised a drinks list simultaneously respectful of the past and ultra-contemporary. The service is pitch perfect, and the attention to details, especially the range of glassware, makes this place a must for any barfly. ○

Right **The range of glassware and cocktails at The Zetter Townhouse are to be admired and enjoyed.**

More places to visit in the area

Above **Although only recently opened, The Zetter Townhouse interiors have been cleverly designed to look like a long-established townhouse.**

Le Café du Marché
22 Charterhouse Square,
Charterhouse Mews, Smithfield,
EC1M 6DX 020 7608 1609
www.cafedumarche.co.uk
Hidden away at the end of a cobbled mews, this charming French eating house is very atmospheric and ideal for discreet assignations.

Look Mum No Hands
49 Old Street, EC1V 9HX
020 7253 1025
www.lookmumnohands.com
Combining a café with a bicycle workshop.

St Ali
27 Clerkenwell Road, EC1M 5RN
020 7253 5754 www.stali.co.uk
Australians are serious about coffee, and this London outpost of a highly praised Melbourne-based coffee roastery and café is studious about its subject. Go for a coffee-fuelled brunch.

Covent Garden
Soho
The Strand

With the exception of the august Royal Opera House (also known as Covent Garden, confusingly), the Covent Garden piazza and quadrangle are today little more than a children's tourist attraction, with street-performance artists, novelty shops and stalls selling tourist paraphernalia. But this belies its long history as a major source of fruit and vegetables for London. In the Middle Ages it was a thriving kitchen garden supplying the Convent of St. Peter of Westminster (hence its name), which as it grew was managed by grants from the Abbot of Westminster.

In the early 17th century, the area was redesigned by Inigo Jones, one of the great English Renaissance architects. The market became more commercial, and when its competitors were wiped out by the Great Fire of London in 1666, Covent Garden became London's pre-eminent fruit and vegetable market. So it remained until its demise in the 1970s.

Harking back to its history, Covent Garden now hosts occasional farmers' markets, food fairs and a very good French market. Unless you have tickets for the opera or ballet, it's only worthwhile visiting the piazza on these special days – although the major land and property owners in the area are trying hard to rectify this tarnished image. Restaurant entrepreneur Richard Caring has done a deal to bring the very fine New York brasserie Balthazar to the impressive former home of the Theatre Museum, which should add some much-needed class to the piazza area. Theatreland and the excitement of Soho have long supported the restaurant business: one cannot survive without the other, and it makes for a relationship of happy coexistence.

Arbutus 63–4 Frith Street, W1D 3JN

020 7734 4545   www.arbutusrestaurant.co.uk

While the food at Arbutus (named after the plant genus that includes the strawberry tree) is very good and modestly priced, the major attraction for us has to be the wine list – or more specifically the wine pricing, and the fact that you can order almost all of the wines in 250 ml carafes. This means that you can enjoy a third of a bottle of Meursault or Pouilly-Fuissé followed by a 1er Cru Santenay or Nuits-Saint-Georges for less than the cost of a full bottle. It is rare to find this calibre of wines available by the glass, and even rarer in 250 ml carafes. The list is an ideal size for this location, with about 25 white, 25 red, a few rosé and sweet wines and about five Champagnes.

On all of our visits the food has been faultless. Rooted in a regional French style but not strictly limited to it, the menus are seasonal and great value for money. The *prix fixe* menu is now famed, and all of the à la carte items are very kindly priced. This is probably because Anthony Demetre, the chef patron, has become expert in seeking out the best deals from his suppliers, as well as in using secondary and tertiary cuts of meat and undervalued fish to create harmonious flavours. It seems that this sensible and long-term approach to pricing is paying off, as Arbutus is always busy. ◗

Bar Shu 28 Frith Street, W1D 5LF

020 7287 6688   www.bar-shu.co.uk

We urge you to call seven or eight friends and arrange to meet for dinner at Bar Shu as soon as possible. We suggest a large table so that you can taste and enjoy as many of the varied dishes as possible. The menu descriptions are great, including 'numbing and hot eel strips', 'pock-marked Old Woman's bean curd', 'ants climbing tree' and 'the legendary Dan Dan noodles'.

Bar Shu specializes in food from the Chinese province of Sichuan, with Fuchsia Dunlop, the highly rated author of *Sichuan Cookery*, as their consultant. In nearby Chinatown you can find a glut of Cantonese dining options, but with only a few exceptions these have all become homogeneous in a sea of MSG. The Bar Shu team has recently opened Ba Shan, just across the road, which we hear is equally good and probably better suited to smaller groups.

(PP) Bar Shu is a chilli-fuelled alternative that for me is more of a cultural experience, with a menu including traditional Chengdu street snacks with noodles and dumplings, plus a large selection of fragrant appetizers. You can also sample banquet delicacies. ◗

Above right **Chicken sot l'y laisse at Arbutus.** Above left **Sichuan dining at Bar Shu.** Left **Peking duck in the windows in China Town.**

Oli
Barker

"

Where do I go for a romantic
meal? Mrs Barker and I go for
steak and kidney pie at Julie's.
Is that romantic? Otherwise
Barrafina is my favourite
restaurant for Spanish food.

Head chef, Terroirs and Brawn

Barrafina 54 Frith Street, W1D 4SL
020 7813 8016 www.barrafina.co.uk

Modelled on Cal Pep in the El Born district of Barcelona, this proper
tapas bar by Sam and Eddie Hart has just 23 seats, all of which are at the
bar counter, overlooking the chefs at work. While staunchly British,
Sam and Eddie have a mother who is half Spanish and they regularly
holidayed on Mallorca when they were young, as well as spending some
formative time in Spain, Eddie in Madrid and Sam in Barcelona. They
are supported in this venture by Basque-born head chef Nieves Barragán
Mohacho. The menu has a strong but not exclusively Basque influence.

Para picar – meaning 'for picking at' – heads the menu with a range
of lovely fried things that are ideal for eating with your hands, such as
croquetas, chiperones and pimentos de padrón. Then comes a selection
of cold meats, tortilla, seafood and meat, and you can finish with either
a crema Catalana or a Santiago tart.

We really like the restaurant's motto, 'Sourcing Not Saucing':
very appropriate for this simple operation where the condition of the
raw ingredients is so very important.

You might need to queue to get a seat, but it will be worth the wait.
If you want something more comfortable, head to sister restaurant Fino
(see page 244). ◉

Below **Expect
queues to secure
a counter dining
position at
Barrafina.**

Above **Haidee Becker art in the dining room at Bocca di Lupo.** Right **Dining at the bar allows guest to watch the chefs at work.**

Bocca di Lupo 12 Archer Street, W1D 7BB
020 7734 2223 www.boccadilupo.com
&
Gelupo 7 Archer Street, W1D 7AU
020 7287 5555 www.gelupo.com

Bocca di Lupo ('mouth of the wolf') is all about authentic regional Italian food, not from one specific part of Italy, but from each of its 20 dialects and regions. Most people who are familiar with Italy will know that before they were unified some 150 years ago, each of the country's 20 independent states had its own food culture. The menu lists the source of each recipe and its inspiration, whether it be buristo (blood salame) from Toscano, octopus and celery salad from Sicilia, broad bean tortelloni with ricotta from Puglia, or dishes from Lazio, Calabria, Veneto, Campania, etc. It's all a big geography lesson with delicious food to boot. The wine list is also pure Italian and offers a Grand Tour of the key wine producing regions.

Chef patron Jacob Kenedy gleaned his knowledge of Italian regional food from a sabbatical spent touring the country. With partner Victor Hugo he has created one of the most interesting Italian restaurants in London, demonstrating a full appreciation of the credo less is more, and of the essential truth that good Italian food is inherently simple.

Dining at the bar counter is a great treat for anyone who enjoys watching skilled chefs at work.

(PP) I first visited Bocca di Lupo some time after it opened, when business was booming for Jacob and Victor. As soon as we sat down, it became apparent that at least three of the surrounding tables were dissatisfied with elements of their meal. Not a promising start, reminding me of other restaurants in the past that have been inundated by demand after a hugely successful launch period. But on reflection I think the tables around us were being a little over-picky, and maybe there was a bit of the snowball effect in operation. Our meal was absolutely fantastic – everything from the charming and efficient service to the scrummy food. And I loved the captivating wall art by Haidee Becker, especially as our table was directly under one of the canvases. Perhaps these differing experiences merely serve to illustrate the vagaries of the restaurant business.

During the course of our 'research' for this edition of *Eat London*, we have made a special point of visiting a few ice cream parlours, as they used to be known. We can confirm that Gelupo, the gelato offshoot of Bocca located across the road from it, is by far the best and the ice cream is supreme. ●

Above **Archer Street looking quiet and clean, don't expect the same if you go late evening.** Left **Gelupo is located directly opposite Bocca di Lupo on Archer Street.**

Shaved Radish and Celeriac Salad with Pomegranate, Pecorino and Truffle Oil

Serves 4 as a starter

1 bunch of breakfast radishes (about 8)
1/2 black radish or 5cm (1/4 inch) green mooli (Chinese greengrocers) or mooli – about 150 g (5 oz) in any case
a chunk of celeriac, about 1/4 of a very small bulb, peeled (50–60 g/2 oz)
a little chunk of Pecorino Romano cheese (about 50 g/2 oz)
1/4 pomegranate, seeds picked out or 6 tablespoons seeds
a few sprigs of flat leaf parsley, leaves picked

For the dressing

1 tablespoon white truffle oil
5 tablespoons extra virgin olive oil
1 tablespoon white balsamic vinegar
juice of 1/4 lemon (or 2 more teaspoons white balsamic)

Make a dressing with the oils, vinegar, lemon and a little salt and pepper. Taste for seasoning.

Prepare the vegetables just before you serve, as radishes dry out and celeriac blackens with time. Wash the radishes (unpeeled) and shave thinly, using a mandolin ideally. Use a potato peeler to shave the celeriac and Pecorino. Toss the vegetables in a bowl with the pomegranate seeds and parsley, and dress lightly. Serve in haphazard but tall piles on individual plates or bowls to share from.

Roast Suckling Pig with Grapes

A simply roasted suckling pig is one of the finer things in life. It requires a capacious oven but little else.

600–800 g (1 lb 3 oz–1 lb 10 oz) of pig per person
oil, for rubbing
1 bottle white wine
1 large bunch of white or flame grapes
as many bay leaves as guests
salt

In a domestic oven, you might have to settle for half a pig (I prefer the fore end – fattier and juicier) or a tiny piglet.

Season the pig inside and out with fine salt and lightly oil the skin, then set aside skin-side up on a wide tray. With your oven on maximum heat, roast the pig until the skin bubbles and crisps – around 40 minutes – and then reduce the temperature to 150°C (300°F) Gas Mark 2 and bake until the meat is meltingly tender, approximately another 2–2½ hours. For very small pigs (6 kg/12 lb or less) this might be 20 minutes less – test by poking the bottom with your finger, if the meat feels soft and giving beneath then it's ready.

Remove the pig from its tray and let it rest for 20 minutes in a warm place – both to allow it to rest and to release some of its juices, which make the best bread moppings known to man, and to let it cool a little.

Meanwhile, take the tray and pour off the fat, leaving the juices. Add the bottle of white wine and cook it over the hob until the alcoholic smell is gone and the pan deglazed, then add the grapes cut into small bunches (8–10 grapes per person) and the bay leaves. Return the tray to the oven for 5 minutes while portioning the pig into large chunks on the bone, to be served with nothing but its sauce, bay leaves and grapes.

Recipes featured in *Bocca Cookbook* by Jacob Kenedy, Bloomsbury

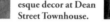

Left and right **The 1980s-style chintz and Laura Ashley-esque decor at Dean Street Townhouse.**

Dean Street Townhouse 69–71 Dean Street, W1D 3SE

020 7434 1775 www.deanstreettownhouse.com

Many of the Soho House group of clubs, bars and restaurants – of which Dean Street Townhouse is one – tend to under-deliver on the food and service, while over-supplying in terms of the clientele and the sexiness of the atmosphere. This seems to be the first establishment to deliver on all fronts, while the restaurant floor and kitchen also seem to be managed in a professional manner. A blissful fusion.

The look of the hotel is very interesting, in that it promotes a style that has otherwise generally been banished to the annals of design history. The look has been lent a few cool credentials in the form of 60 unique pieces of modern art by respected names.

The hotel bedrooms are quite small (the smallest are modestly described as 'tiny'), but if it's location that counts you can't be more central than the middle of Soho. The slender outside terrace is one of the hottest locations in town – good for everything from breakfast to late night drinks. ◐

Right and below **The art in the dining room at Dean Street Townhouse is by emerging British artists.**

Left **The bar at Dean Street Townhouse is an ideal people-watching location.**

Smoked Haddock Soufflé with Chive Butter Sauce

Serves 4

For the soufflé

150 g (5 oz) skinless smoked haddock
175 ml (6 fl oz) milk
25 g (1 oz) butter, plus extra to coat the moulds
25 g (1 oz) flour
35 g (1 1/2 oz) Keen's Cheddar, grated
35 g (1 1/2 oz) Parmesan cheese, grated
1/4 teaspoon salt
nutmeg, to taste
5 g (1/4 oz) anchovy sauce
1/4 teaspoon Tabasco
1 teaspooon Worcestershire sauce
8 g (generous 1/4 oz) English mustard
2 egg yolks
4 egg whites

For the chive butter sauce

600 ml (1 pint) white wine
75 g (3 oz) shallots, finely sliced
75 g (3 oz) leeks, chopped
1/2 garlic clove
1/4 bay leaf
small pinch thyme leaves, picked
small pinch white peppercorns
250 ml (8 fl oz) double cream
400 g (13 oz) butter, diced
English mustard, to taste
finely chopped chives, to taste
salt and pepper

To make the soufflé, place the smoked haddock in a baking dish, pour over the milk and and simmer over a gentle heat for 30 minutes. Strain, keep the haddock to one side and chill the milk.

In a saucepan, melt the butter over a medium heat, add the flour and cook, stirring, for 2–3 minutes. Gradually add the milk to the flour mixture to form a smooth, thick sauce. Pour the sauce into a large bowl and add the salt and nutmeg to taste. Flake the haddock into large pieces and add to the mixture. Add the Cheddar and mix, then add the condiments and egg yolks, mixing well again.

In a clean bowl, whisk the egg whites until they form medium peaks, then gently fold them into the fish mixture.

Brush 4 individual 150 ml (1/4-pint) plastic pudding moulds with soft butter, then line with the grated Parmesan and tap out any excess. Fill the moulds three-quarters full with the soufflé mixture (to the line of the mould), place in a deep tray and fill it with water to come three-quarters of the way up the sides of the moulds. Bake in a preheated oven, 180°C (350°F), Gas Mark 4, for 13 minutes.

Serve straight away, or chill and store in the moulds in the refrigerator. If chilled, serve by turning out the moulds on to a baking tray lined with a sheet of greaseproof paper and reheat in the oven at 180°C (350°F), Gas Mark 4, for 13 minutes. Check the soufflés are hot in the middle before serving.

To make the chive butter sauce, reduce the white wine with the shallots, leek, garlic, bay leaf, thyme and peppercorns. Add the cream and reduce for 10 minutes. Remove from the heat and slowly whisk in the butter. The sauce should be of a light coating consistency. Leave off the heat to infuse for 20 minutes, then pass through a fine sieve. Keep warm, and when ready to serve add the English mustard to taste and chopped chives.

To serve the soufflés, turn each on to a warm plate and spoon over generous amounts of the chive butter sauce.

Four Seasons 12 Gerrard Street, W1D 5PR

020 7494 0870 www.fs-restaurants.co.uk

In the past we have been dismissive of the innumerable restaurants in Chinatown because of their overuse of MSG. Four Seasons is an exception, however. The staff may not be very welcoming (this is standard in Chinatown), nor should you be deterred by the plastic laminated menus with photographs of the food. The house speciality is roast duck, which is good, but we recommend something that isn't on the menu. As soon as you are seated, simply ask for the three meats (duck, chicken and barbecued pork) on rice, plus the Chinese broccoli with garlic sauce. The attitude of the staff will change, and they will bring you some delicious food. Look around and you will notice that everybody is eating the same.

(PP) I recently visited this restaurant after a cocktail reception also attended by HM The Queen. The food at Four Seasons was certainly equal to the fancy canapés and Champagne served at the palace.

If you are feeling particularly ambitious after the Four Seasons and up for a late night we also recommend the Experimental Cocktail Club at 13a Gerrard Street, open until 3am and very plush. ○

Gauthier Soho 21 Romilly Street, W1D 5AF

020 7494 3111 www.gauthiersoho.co.uk

When Richard Corrigan decamped to upmarket premises in Mayfair, we feared that Alexis Gauthier would struggle to come close to the excellent reputation of his predecessor on this site. But if a recent visit is anything to go by, this new offering is even more popular – and deservedly so. Completely different from the gutsy Irish flavours that Richard delivered, it is more refined and delicate. Everything has been lightened up, from the decor to the waiters' white tunic jackets. The food, also much lighter, is now (as they put it) 'vegecentric'. Alexis Gauthier is very earnest when it comes to making vegetables the centre of attention. The level of technique and skill in this kitchen is very high: Alexis has previously worked with Alain Ducasse, and it shows in his food.

Recently, Alexis has started to list the calorie count for each item on the menu. While we think this is a little crazy, we can appreciate why he wants to do it. The radish, fennel and crab salad is 242 calories, for instance, a summer truffle risotto is 557 calories, and if you go for the *goût du jour d'eté* the total count is 1,852 calories. The vegetarian tasting menu is 1,600 calories, surprising only a little less than the meat version. Precise as the cooking at Gauthier is, we struggle to comprehend how they can be quite so punctilious with the calorie count. But we are full of praise for Alexis nevertheless.

(PP) Given that this style of food isn't my normal fare, I was impressed by the cooking at Gauthier. In fact, I would go so far as to say that it is the restaurant of the star-chasing variety that has most impressed me over recent years. They are usually so infuriating, whereas I really think that Alexis is doing something interesting here, and that he has an admirable respect for classic French technique and the key ingredients that should be associated with this level of dining. The service was also exceptional. ○

Right **Alexis Gauthier's food is often more healthy and lighter than other Michelin star style restaurants.**

Right **One of the small dining rooms on the ground floor at Gauthier Soho.**

Great Queen Street 32 Great Queen Street, WC2B 5AA
020 7242 0622

This place is all about great, no-nonsense cooking and nothing else. For this reason alone it is very lovable. To describe the interior as utilitarian would be flattering. Don't go to Great Queen Street for physical comfort: go for the reassuring comfort that a slow-roasted joint of meat can bring. No gimmicks, no fuss, just great seasonal ingredients prepared by rightly self-confident cooks. You can make a reservation here, unlike at its sister establishment the Anchor & Hope (see page 284). ○

Hawksmoor 11 Langley Street, WC2H 9JG
020 7856 2154 www.thehawksmoor.co.uk

This excellent steak house uses only British beef, supplied by The Ginger Pig butcher and cooked on a real charcoal grill. The range of cuts and the different weights of meat – you can order a 600 g sirloin or maybe a 400 g rump steak – is impressive in trencherman style.

The adjoining bar will always fix fantastic cocktails and the subterranean interior is very clubby. The designers have managed to make it look as though it has been around for a very long time, when in fact it is very new.

(PP) I dined here with a foodie friend and we went overboard with the different extras and sauces that you can choose to accompany your steaks. We had grilled bone marrow, anchovy butter, Stilton hollandaise, béarnaise and a range of side dishes, including beef dripping and triple-cooked chips. I think we also had vegetables, but they didn't seem to register in our post-prandial reflections. Add a pre-lunch bloody Mary, a very retro prawn cocktail for a first course, a decent bottle of full-bodied red, plus a steamed pudding and some chocolate, and you quickly see how the bill can escalate. Good and lovingly-reared British beef is expensive. ○

Les Deux Salons 40– 2 William IV Street, WC2N 4DD
020 7420 2050 www.lesdeuxsalons.co.uk

This third restaurant from Anthony Demetre and Will Smith (after Arbutus and Wild Honey in Mayfair) is modelled on a Parisian brasserie, with all the key signifiers, including aged mirrors, brass rails, globe lights and a beautiful mosaic floor. Much larger than their other operations, it is all the better for it (although some have voiced reservations about the service), with a menu focused on the French classics that we all know and love.

(PP) My petit salé was mesmerizing and the bavette steak cooked in the Josper was exactly as it should be (and much better than the tired and poor versions you sometimes get in France).

As with the other restaurants in the mini-group, the enlightened approach to wine pricing means that all of the wines on the list are available by the glass and in 250 ml carafes.

This is also a good place for afternoon tea with cakes – and without all the fuss and pretentiousness that accompany tea at most of the central London hotels. ○

Top **The impressive Josper grill (a coal fired internal barbecue) at Hawksmoor.**

Cornflake Ice Cream

Makes 600 ml (1 pint)

250 ml (8 fl oz) milk

150–175 g (5–6 oz) cornflakes

250 ml (8 fl oz) double cream

6 free-range egg yolks

100 g (3½ oz) caster sugar

Pour the milk over the cornflakes, leave overnight, then strain and discard the soggy cornflakes. Place the milk and cream in a small heavy saucepan and bring to the boil.

Whisk the egg yolks and sugar together in a heatproof bowl, then pour the milk and cream mixture over and whisk again. Place the bowl over a saucepan of barely simmering water and heat gently until the mixture becomes thick enough to coat the back of a spoon.

Leave to cool, then pass through a sieve. Chill well in the refrigerator before churning in an ice cream maker according to the manufacturers instructions.

To make a cornflake ice cream milkshake, blend 3 scoops of cornflake ice cream with 200 ml (7 fl oz) milk and an ice cube, and garnish with cornflakes.

209

Above **The subterranean dining room at Hawksmoor is new but looks long-established thanks in part to the use of a reclaimed parquet floor.**

Hix 66–70 Brewer Street, W1F 9UP
020 7292 3518 www.hixsoho.co.uk

Compared with Mark Hix's first restaurant near Smithfield (see page 185), this is a slightly smarter version of his trademark British cooking. The range of ingredients is broader and the menu boasts several seldom-seen British dishes. Mark is very good at resurrecting long-forgotten foods: when was the last time you had River Exe sand eels, Bridgewater Bay silver mullet, Kentish air-dried lamb or sea buckthorn and berry posset?

This restaurant is also known for its art, and particularly for the mobiles that hang from the ceiling. The roll-call of British artists who show their work at Mark's restaurant is testimony to his many friendships with members of the art community. Mark's Bar, below the restaurant, is also renowned for its late-night partying. ◑

Above left **Ceiling mobiles in the ground floor dining room at Hix.**
Above right **A neon sign, that is also art, indicates the route to Mark's Bar at Hix.**

Gary Lee

"

My favourite neighbourhood restaurant in London is Eat 17 in Walthamstow. It's around the corner from my house, they have their own deli and make their own bread. They also source locally and are reasonably priced. I also like Polpo for the atmosphere and ambiance. I like their no fuss attitude and there's always a great buzz.

Head chef, The Ivy

The Ivy 1–5 West Street, WC2H 9NQ
020 7836 4751   www.the-ivy.co.uk

Everybody talks about the celebrity clientele and how difficult it is to get a table at this legendary restaurant, but underneath all the glitz lies an extremely well-managed business serving good, honest brasserie-style food. The menu is comprehensive, with hors d'oeuvres including everything from steak tartare to Beluga caviar. The shellfish ranges from oysters to lobster and chips, while the eggs, pasta and rice section offers brunch classics such as eggs Benedict and salt beef hash, or – better still – kedgeree. The fish, roasts and grills and the entrées section also offer wide choices from far-flung cuisines: it is not unusual to find Thai baked sea bass with soy sauce or achari lamb masala on the menu. (PP) Simple grilled calf's liver or rib steaks are my favourites. Then there's always The Ivy hamburger or maybe fish cakes, and the eternally popular shepherd's pie. And you usually get a choice of at least a dozen side dishes. In addition, The Ivy is one of the few restaurants still serving great savouries such as Welsh rarebit. It isn't haute cuisine, but it most certainly is a long-established great menu that's seasonal, classic and also modern.

Despite the change of ownership over recent years and the frequent prophecies of doom, the main players are still there, and this surely contributes to the success of the service. The calibre of the managers and waiting staff eclipses that of most other restaurants: the staff seem to communicate with each other at some telepathic level, and their skill at the table is undeniable. ◉

Right **A rare glimpse beyond the harlequin-style stained glass to the dining room at The Ivy.**

Seared Scallops with Pickled Daikon and Chilli Jam

Serves 4

For the pickled daikon

200 ml (7 fl oz) water
150 ml (1/4 pint) rice wine vinegar
1 teaspoon fine salt
2 tablespoons sugar
2 teaspoons pink peppercorns
3 whole cloves, crushed
1 red chilli, finely chopped
1 daikon (about 300g in weight), peeled and cut into julienne strips using a mandolin or food processor

For the chilli jam

1 1/2 tablespoons sunflower oil
3 garlic cloves, crushed
2 red chillies, finely chopped
1 teaspoon cumin seeds
1 teaspoon black mustard seeds
400 g can chopped tomatoes
1/2 teaspoon salt
40 g (1 1/2 oz) palm sugar
1/2 teaspoon ground turmeric
2 1/2 tablespoons red wine vinegar
15 g (1/2 oz) fresh coriander, chopped

For the scallops

1 green apple, cored, thinly sliced and stored in water with 1 teaspoon of lemon juice to prevent discoloration
6 red radishes (about 40 g/1 1/2 oz), thinly sliced
30 g (just over 1 oz) blood chard leaves
about 2 tablespoons olive oil
400 g (13 oz) king scallops, cleaned
salt and black pepper

Start with the daikon. Warm the water and rice wine vinegar in a medium-sized saucepan over a medium heat. Add the salt, sugar, pink peppercorns, cloves and chilli. Once the sugar and salt have dissolved, remove from the heat and leave to cool, before adding the daikon. Leave in the refrigerator for at least a few hours and preferably overnight.

For the chilli jam, heat the sunflower oil in a medium-sized pan and fry the garlic, chilli, cumin seeds and mustard seeds for a couple of minutes, taking care not to burn the spices. Add the tomatoes, salt, palm sugar, turmeric and red wine vinegar and bring to the boil. Reduce the heat and leave to simmer gently for 35 minutes or until thick. Remove from the heat, stir in the coriander and leave to cool. This an be stored in a sterilized container in the refrigerator for up to 2 weeks.

When you are ready to serve, drain the apple slices and pat them dry. Place them in a mixing bowl with the radish, blood chard leaves, 1 tablespoon of olive oil and 75 g (3 oz) of the pickled daikon. Toss and season with salt and pepper to taste. Heat up another tablespoon of olive oil in a large frying pan. Lightly season each scallop with salt and pepper and cook for 2–3 minutes on each side until golden and caramelized round the edges. Remove from the pan and add to the salad. Gently mix to combine all the ingredients, add more olive oil if needed and divide between four plates. Top each salad with 1 teaspoon of chilli jam and serve.

Above **A table setting with a brass napkin ring at Nopi.**

J. Sheekey 28–32 St. Martin's Court, WC2N 4AL
020 7240 2565 www.j-sheekey.co.uk

The service at this fish and seafood restaurant is really very good – grown up and perceptive in manner, with seasoned waiting staff practising non-verbal communication with an 'I've seen it all before' confidence. Sometimes service is about more than just delivering food and drink to diners' tables – an important point fully appreciated by the front-of-house team at J. Sheekey. You can also be sure that the kitchen will do a great job for you. The menu is a delight, with all manner of piscine pleasures, from a small selection of caviar (for absolute decadence, showing off or just the flavour) to a full array of fresh fish, crustaceans and bivalves from British shores and seas, plus a few from more distant waters. The fish pie is a perennial favourite, together with serious Dover sole, lobster thermidor and dressed crab.

J. Sheekey has recently expanded next door to include a proper horseshoe-shaped oyster bar. Enjoying a plateau de fruits de mer while seated at the bar and watching the chefs at work is one of the most pleasurable dining experiences in London. ○

Nopi 21–2 Warwick Street, W1B 5NE
020 7494 9584 www.nopi-restaurant.com

A soft blend of strong flavours from the sunny Mediterranean, Middle East and Asia has been carefully and eruditely brought together at Nopi. The menu is divided into four key sections, Veg, Fish, Meat and Sweets, and has been designed for sharing with friends (although it does work equally well when not sharing). Each section includes a choice of about six items, and they recommend three savoury dishes per person. It all works rather well.

Nopi (an acronym of 'north of Piccadilly') is the brainchild of Yotam Ottolenghi. Don't expect the trademark meringues in the window and the beautifully presented food displays that you find in his mini-chain of delis and cafés, however. This is an all-day brasserie, but not in the traditional sense. There is a fresh and modern approach to everything here. The interior is a happy and unusual combination of white and brass that feels fresh and uplifting, with great attention to detail and some charming elements such as the mirrors in the toilets, the large brass flower vases with pretty blooms, and the brass 1920s-style doors that originally graced the portals of Harvey Nichols.

(PP) I was a little concerned about being allocated a table downstairs, as opposed to the light and airy ground floor. I shouldn't have been. Sitting at the large communal tables in the basement is great fun: you can watch the kitchen toil away and admire the shelves of ingredients. The space doubles up as a dry store for the kitchen, and given the style of food they serve there is lots to see and admire. We had a lot of food, probably around 20 small plates, and without exception all of the ingredient combinations worked brilliantly. It was all both delicious and creative. I want to say that the vegetables were the highlight, but in fact the whole ensemble was equally good. I can't wait to go again. ○

Top right **The clean white and brass colour scheme at Nopi.**
Left **In the kitchen at Nopi.**

Polpetto Upstairs at The French House, 49 Dean Street, W1D 5BG
020 7734 1969 www.polpetto.co.uk

The little sister to Polpo, with just 28 seats, Polpetto is located above
The French House, Soho's most iconic pub. Russell Norman continues
to feed Soho nighthawks here with his version of Venetian osteria dishes.
Everything is small, from the plates to the prices.

Polpo 41 Beak Street, W1F 9SB
020 7734 4479 www.polpo.co.uk

Russell Norman is the new king of Soho. He boasts an unimpeachable
CV, having managed a range of impressive restaurants, including Zuma,
and also held the top front-of-house job in the capital when he was
operations director for Caprice Holdings. But all that is behind him,
and he is now Soho's leading restaurateur. Russell and his business partner
have launched a completely new style of eatery for London: a bacaro, a
type of wine bar on the Venetian model, specializing in *cicheti*, or easy-to-eat snacks. At Polpo this means anchovy and chickpea
crostino, artichoke and prosciutto, chopped chicken liver crostino,
arancini or potato and Parmesan crocheta. All are great, and ideal with
either a Bellini or an Aperol or Campari spritz. You can follow them
with a range of pizzetta, paidina and panino, then cheese, fritto misto,
prawn and monk's beard risotto, calamari, then cotechino sausage, calf's
liver or maybe a simple plate of cold meats. Finish with an affogato or
maybe tiramisu.

(PP) My first visit was on a Saturday lunchtime, that eternally
difficult time for any restaurateur to crack, and the place was rocking.
It couldn't have been busier, with queues everywhere. Despite this,
the staff could not have been calmer or more accommodating. While
perched at a shelf just inside the entrance, we enjoyed an assortment
of dishes, plate after plate in perfect condition. It proved a perfect
location for watching everybody arrive with high hopes and leaving
with sated pleasure.

One of Russell's original touches is in the style and look of his
restaurants. They are all stripped back to basics, with exposed walls
and beams, with tiled ceilings and no fuss or bother: he has mastered
the blessed speakeasy style that so many try and so few get right.

There is now a small Campari bar under Polpo that is equally
good for meeting friends and enjoying your *cicheti*.

This 18th century building was once home to Giovanni Antonio
Canal (1697–1768), better known as the painter Canaletto, celebrated
for his vedute of Venice. You couldn't make it up. ○

Princi 135 Wardour Street, London, W1F 0UT
020 7478 8888 www.princi.co.uk

This truly impressive Italian bakery and café is a joint venture by a famous
Milanese bakery and Alan Yau. This in itself promises great things, and
we can assure you that you won't be disappointed. The vast food displays
set the pulse racing and the wood oven-cooked pizza and endless other
baked delights are perfect at any time of the day. Unmissable. ○

Above **Bread
making at Princi
is to be admired.**

Spinach, Chickpea and Chilli Bruschetta

Serves 4

350 g (11 1/2 oz) dried chickpeas
2 sprigs of rosemary
1/2 garlic head, cut in two, plus 2 extra garlic cloves
1 onion, chopped into wedges
1 large ladleful of tomato sauce or passata
1 punnet of cherry tomatoes
extra virgin olive oil
100 ml (3 1/2 fl oz) red wine vinegar
25 g (1 oz) caster sugar
4 long red chillies, deseeded and diced
4 red onions, cut into medium to large wedges, cores removed
large pinch of salt
50–100 ml (2–3 1/2 fl oz) water
salt and freshly ground black pepper
4 slices of ciabatta, to serve
bag of baby spinach

Soak the chickpeas overnight. The following morning rinse them well, put in a saucepan with the rosemary, 1/2 garlic head, onion wedges and tomato sauce, then add water to cover by 2.5 cm (1 inch). Bring to the boil, reduce the heat to a simmer and cover with lid. Cook the chickpeas until tender, season with salt and pepper while still warm and add a generous splash of olive oil. Set aside and keep warm.

Put the cherry tomatoes in a very hot (nearly smoking) pan. Allow them to blacken a little and their skins to pop, turning them occasionally. Crush 1 of the garlic cloves and add to the pan with salt, olive oil, a splash of the red wine vinegar and a pinch of sugar. It's likely to flame, but just combine the ingredients. Remove from the heat and allow to cool. Set aside.

Put the chilli and red onion wedges into a large pan with a generous pinch of salt and a splash of olive oil. Put a lid on the pan and soften the chillies and onions over a low heat, without allowing them to colour. Once they are soft, add the rest of the red wine vinegar and water and turn up the heat to reduce; finally add the rest of the sugar.

To serve, griddle the slices of ciabatta and rub one side with the cut side of the remaining garlic clove. Divide the chickpeas between the ciabatta, spoon over the tomatoes and red onion mixture and scatter with baby spinach leaves.

Swordfish with Pink Peppercorns and Lime Dressing

Swordfish is no longer served at Polpo, but this recipe works well with any smoked white fish.

Serves 4

3–4 very fine slices smoked swordfish per person, or any smoked white fish
large handful of pink peppercorns
fronds from the top of 1 fennel

For the dressing

zest and juice of 4 limes
2 teaspoons caster sugar
350 ml (12 fl oz) extra virgin olive oil
1 red chilli, deseeded and finely sliced
3 garlic cloves, finely sliced
3 fennel tops, finely sliced
salt and freshly ground black pepper

Mix all the dressing ingredients together in a bowl and add salt and pepper to taste.

Arrange the smoked fish on a large serving platter and spoon over the dressing. Scatter over the peppercorns and fennel leaves to serve.

Quo Vadis 26–9 Dean Street, W1D 3LL

020 7437 9585 www.quovadissoho.co.uk

Amid a sea of informal and buzzy eateries patronized by the cool young denizens of Soho, Quo Vadis presents a more grown-up option with an eloquent British grill menu. ○

St. John Hotel 1 Leicester Street, WC2H 7BL

020 3301 8020 www.stjohnhotellondon.com

Trevor Gulliver and Fergus Henderson are endeavouring, with Westminster Council, to improve the reputation of this difficult site just off Leicester Square (one of the most horrible places in London in our opinion), and the presence of the peerless St. John lineage in the form of this new restaurant and hotel will certainly help. The question is, what can Leicester Square do for St. John? The restaurant feels slightly smaller and more compact than the other St. John dining rooms, but with the usual white walls and highly visible stainless steel-clad open kitchen. This smaller scale enables the staff, in their trademark white jackets, to keep a close on your every move, delivering efficiency and promptness with each course.

Head chef Tom Harris oversees everything from breakfast buns (something the team take very seriously) to late, late supper (food is served until 2am). Call in for elevenses or a little bun moment in the afternoon. Then there is also room service for those who have taken a 'post-supper room', as the management call their bedrooms. With the addition of the hotel, their famous strap line of 'nose-to-tail' eating has become 'from table to bed'.

(PP) On my first visit I went with a very ambitious young chef and was bemused to note his slightly negative reaction to the pared back approach: some people, it seems, still don't get the true brilliance of the St. John way. Personally I thought every flavour jumped off the plate. Their sultana and marc ice cream is unsurpassed – there must have been a measure of marc in every spoonful. ○

Above left **Outside the St. John Hotel. The signs indicate its former use as a fish and shellfish restaurant.**

Above **The open
kitchen and
pleasingly austere
and simple dining
room at St. John.**

Savoy Grill Strand, WC2R 0EU

020 7592 1600   www.gordonramsay.com/thesavoygrill

The Savoy Grill was launched by the Gordon Ramsay team at a time when the chef's public profile must have been at its nadir. His father-in-law had been sacked as CEO of the company and senior employees were leaving to start their own ventures. In addition to all this, the grill was opening after the fanfare of the hotel launch and the cringeworthy behind-the-scenes television documentary that accompanied it.

Despite all this, the Ramsay team had the good judgement to return the menu to something quite sensible, a 'proper' grill menu – going back to the good old days, as many might say. It includes an extensive selection of meats, with over a dozen options – everything from rib-eye to lamb cutlets, and pork chop to a mixed grill – simply grilled and offered with a choice of sauces. Equally attractive is the prospect of a good steak-and-onion pudding or a Lancashire hotpot. The fancy Ramsay hallmarks have been dropped in favour of some good hearty food, with all the ingredients displaying exceptional provenance and conditioning.

> My favourite specialist food shop experience in London is I Camisa in Soho for all my Italian deli treats. A trip here always ends with a fridge full of charcuterie, mozzarellas and Sicilian olives – not forgetting every obscure pasta shape there is, from tiny *orzo* and *ditalini* to big *candele*.
>
> Chef de Cuisine, The Langham

We went for a martini in the American bar before dinner in the Grill. The martinis were pretty good and the piano bar atmosphere pleasant, but the sight of people queuing to get into the bar seemed all wrong for this type of establishment. Overall the evening was satisfactory, with no particular highlights and equally nothing to be critical about – which is a shame, because this could and should be a unique experience for Londoners to be proud of. It has to be said that our expectations of this once patrician location are very high. Go and judge for yourself if you get the chance. ◉

Spuntino 61 Rupert Street, W1D 7PW

No telephone, no reservations

Moving away from the Venetian theme of Polpo and Polpetto, Spuntino is all about New York's Lower East Side diner culture. While the food is different from that at Russell's other joints, the speakeasy style is not. The entrance would be easy to miss if it weren't for the queues, and the inside is all about exposed tiles and bare filament lights without shades. The louche character of the surroundings all adds to the drama.

The menu includes 'sliders' – of-the-moment tiny burgers, mac and cheese, fried soft shell crab, grits, a peanut butter sandwich, and the much-talked-about truffled egg toast. Not exactly gourmet treats, but that's not the point: this den-like space is all about great cocktails, with food to soak up the booze.

There's no telephone and you can't make a reservation, but don't be deterred. Go off peak: it's great fun. ◉

Left **The discreet and almost hidden entrance to Spuntino.**
Right **Russell Norman, owner at Spuntino.**

One of the first and finest of the new-style wine bars (with great food, unlike their predecessors) that have become very popular in London over recent years, Terroirs is all about wine and food produced by artisans. All the key buzz words and beliefs are high on the agenda, with everything sustainably produced, organic, biodynamic, with minimal intervention and low or no sulphur dioxide, and many of the wines are unfiltered or unrefined.

There are two bars and two dining rooms to choose from, upstairs and downstairs, both pleasant in their own way. The menus are dominated by delicious French and Italian ingredients and recipes of renown. There is always a desirable selection of charcuterie, from the cured hams of the Pyrenees and Tuscany, via Lyon, to terrines and rillettes made in the Terroirs kitchens. The small plates selection offers a range of dishes from steak tartare to globe artichoke vinaigrette, salads, snails, smoked eel and much more. The main course *plats du jour* all complement the extensive wine list perfectly: try a bavette steak, confit de canard or maybe just a simple roast Landais chicken. The winter cassoulet is a full-on treat, and the boudin noir with a fried duck egg ambrosial. Cheese is taken very seriously, naturally, with perfectly conditioned specimens provided by Androuet of Spitalfields.

As you would expect, the wine list – particularly the selection by the glass – is extensive and engaging. Doug Wregg, one of the directors of Les Caves de Pyrène, the wine merchants behind Terroirs, is an excellent writer, and his synopsis for each of the wines is a joy to read, offering insights into everything from the character of the winemaker to little history lessons and some humour, with a huge serving of savoir-faire. ◉

Doug Wregg

My favourite restaurants in London are J. Sheekey for a romantic meal – you are made to feel like a millionaire even when you've only got a few quid in your pocket. For atmosphere, Chez Bruce has many virtues: friendly, buzzy, not too formal and always delivers – a local restaurant that's worth trekking across town for. The Lansdowne is a family favourite because my kids are going through a pizza phase. The wood-fired oven receive the full thumbs-up from my 3- and 6-year-old food critics. Co-owner, Brawn, Terroirs and Les Caves de Pyrène

Above, left and right
**Inside Terroirs
with its reclaimed
French poster art
and street signs.**

Pork Rillons

Serves 6–8

1 kg (2¼ lb) pork belly (preferably from the thick end, with skin left on and bones removed)
50 g (2 oz) sea salt
250 g (8 oz) lard
250 ml (9 fl oz) dry white wine
125 ml (4 fl oz) water
3 bay leaves
large sprig of thyme
4 garlic cloves (split in two)
freshly ground black pepper

The day before, dice the pork belly into 5 cm (2 inch) cubes with the skin left on. Toss the cubes in the sea salt, cover and leave in the refrigerator for 12 hours.

The next day, wash the salt from the cubed belly and dry thoroughly. Melt a little of the lard in a large hot pan, add the pork belly cubes and brown them on all sides until nicely caramelized all over. Transfer the belly pieces to an ovenproof dish, making sure they sit together snugly in one layer and not on top of each other. Add the wine, water, bay leaves, thyme, garlic and the rest of the lard (when melted the liquid should come up to half the depth of the pork), and place in a preheated oven, 140°C (275°F), Gas Mark 1, for about 1½ hours or until tender, and if necessary cook for a further 30 minutes. If the lard is becoming too hot and burning the pork, very carefully add a little more water to lower its cooking temperature.

When the rillons are cooked, leave them to cool in the fat. To serve, remove them from the fat and place them in a really hot oven, 200°C (400°F), Gas Mark 6, for 5–6 minutes until they are sizzling and crispy on the outside. Serve with a simple green salad dressed with a good, punchy mustard vinaigrette, a lively glass of Sancerre and some bread.

Covent Garden / Soho / The Strand

221

Whole Foods 69–75 Brewer Street, W1F 9US

020 7434 3179 www.wholefoodsmarket.com/stores/soho/

A useful resource for those (unlike us) who are devoted to healthy foods and a carefully controlled diet. The fact that it is adjacent to a huge gym comes as no surprise. But this is nevertheless an excellent source for a full range of essential ingredients, whatever the dietary persuasions for which you may be catering. ●

Wright Brothers Soho Oyster House

13 Kingly Street and G7/G8 Kingly Court, W1B 5PW

020 7434 3611 www.thewrightbrothers.co.uk

Sister to the acclaimed oyster bar opposite Borough Market, this place is much larger and laid out over several floors. It may be slightly less atmospheric, but still offers the full range of shellfish and oysters, plus excellent fresh fish from Cornish day-boats. ●

Yauatcha 15–17 Broadwick Street, W1F 0DL

020 7494 8888 www.yauatcha.com

Another masterpiece, created by Alan Yau and now sold to the international Hakkasan group: an all-day contemporary Chinese teahouse and restaurant that has been a success since day one back in 2004. All manner of rumours circulated at the time about how the client had asked designer Christian Liaigre to change and adjust everything after it was already completed, but now this hardly matters, as the whole operation is such a complete and utter success in a very sexy setting. Upstairs is delightful, and the staff must surely wear the best uniforms in London, designed by Tom Yip, art director on the film *Crouching Tiger, Hidden Dragon*. ●

Right **Plateau de fruits de mer is essential at Wright Brothers.**

Left **The ground floor pâtisserie at Yauatcha where the cakes are all excellent.**

More places to visit in the area

Arigato Japanese Supermarket
48–50 Brewer Street, W1F 9TG
020 7287 1722
A great source for all manner of Japanese and Asian ingredients, from wasabi to special rice and vinegars, plus a decent range of sake. They also have a small in-store sushi bar.

Cây Tre
42–3 Dean Street, W1D 4QA
020 7317 9118 www.caytresoho.co.uk
The best pho in Soho, plus the design of this French-Vietnamese cafe and cocktail bar is very cool.

Cox Cookies & Cake
13 Brewer Street, W1F 0RH
020 7434 0242
www.coxcookiesandcake.com
Not really our sort of place, but perfect for the area and great for camp and slightly risqué cupcakes.

Fernandez & Wells
43 Lexington Street, W1F 9AL;
73 Beak Street, W1F 9SR;
16a St. Anne's Court, W1F 0BG
www.fernandezandwells.com
A mini-chain of three premises dotted around Soho, including an espresso bar and a simple café. Ultra-cool, great coffee.

Hummus Bros
88 Wardour Street, W1F 0TJ
020 7734 1311 www.hbros.co.uk
We like Hummus Bros because Christian and Ronen, the two friends (not brothers) who set up the business, are devoted to fresh ingredients, flavour and simplicity. With an added dash of humour, the whole concept is slightly eccentric. 'Hummusychology' (their terminology) proffers interesting observations on ways of scooping your hummus with a choice of pitta and various toppings.

Imli
167–8 Wardour Street, W1F 8WR
020 7287 4243 www.imli.co.uk
From the people behind Tamarind (see page 297), another really excellent new-wave Indian restaurant in Mayfair, Imli is a more informal and casual offering. The menu is delightfully small and includes simple Indian street food at great value-for-money prices. The service is slick and the environment modern, without any elaborate nonsense. This is a great place to go after the theatre or for a quick lunch.

Lina Stores
18 Brewer Street, W1F 0SH
020 7437 6482 www.linastores.co.uk
It's been around for decades and is still one of the best traditional Italian delis in the heart of Soho, much loved by the community and foodies alike. They don't come much better than this.

Massimo Restaurant and Oyster Bar
10 Northumberland Avenue,
WC2N 5AE 020 7998 0555
www.massimo-restaurant.co.uk
A very impressive and glamorous space designed by designer *du jour* David Collins in a huge hotel that also offers several other very expensive-looking restaurant and bar spaces. Massimo is an Italian restaurant that specializes in fish and crustacea. The staff are slightly over-enthusiastic and the food slightly underwhelming. Somewhere to take posh grown-up family friends, perhaps.

Paramount Centre Point
101–3 New Oxford Street,
WC1A 1DD 020 7420 2900
www.paramount.uk.net/#/restaurant/
Located at the top of the iconic Centre Point Tower, this bar and restaurant offers one of the best views in London. Tom Dixon designed the space and some of the furniture, and the bar is accessorized by a string of Karuselli armchairs (one of Terence's favourites) by Yrjö Kukkapuro. It's hard for the food to compete with the view, so go for an early evening cocktail before moving on to somewhere more grounded like Arbutus for a lovely supper.

Randall & Aubin
16 Brewer Street, W1F 0SQ
020 7287 4447
www.randallandaubin.com
Housed in a former butcher's shop and surrounded by sex shops and peep shows, this atmospheric Champagne and oyster bar serves great lobster and chips.

Rules
35 Maiden Lane, WC2E 7LB
020 7836 5314 www.rules.co.uk
Opened in 1798, Rules is the oldest restaurant in London. They serve traditional British food, with great game, hand-raised pigs, aged beef and a hearty steak-and-kidney pudding. The ornate interiors are worth a visit, too.

Yalla Yalla
1 Green's Court, W1F 0HA
020 7287 7663 www.yalla-yalla.co.uk
Beirut street food may not sound that appealing, but trust us: there are some very big flavours and delicious morsels to be found at this tiny restaurant.

Finsbury
Islington
King's Cross
St. Pancras

At last the St. Pancras project is complete. The high Gothic-revival treasure that Sir John Betjeman feared was 'too beautiful and too romantic to survive' has achieved the almost impossible. Originally designed by Sir George Gilbert Scott, the building opened as the Midland Grand Hotel on 5 May 1873. Now, 138 years later, it reopened as the St. Pancras Renaissance Hotel, together with some extremely desirable apartments developed by the Manhattan Loft Corporation. The corporation's head, Harry Handelsman, has been a major player in bringing this great building back to life: without his determination, it is said that the building would still be in a derelict state. Incidentally, the new hotel is just about okay, however, those interested in something different might find Rough Luxe on nearby Birkenhead Street a more agreeable abode.

With the hotel and apartment project, the restored St. Pancras Station and new Eurostar Terminal brought vigour and life to the area, plus a small dash (well, it's a start) of French chic and sophistication. Since they were opened by the Queen in 2007, the neighbourhood has never needed to look back. In just a fraction over two hours, Parisians can bid *au revoir* to the Gare du Nord and *bonjour* to London. Or (more likely) Londoners can do the reverse. We're convinced that the French on the whole still concur with President Jacques Chirac's quip about British food when he said: 'One cannot trust people whose cuisine is so bad.' True, our traditional cooking may not match up to that of other nations, but the London restaurant and food scene certainly does. Many would argue that it now eclipses its equivalents in Paris, New York, Barcelona, or indeed anywhere else.

ENGLISH
RHUBARB
£3·99 e/1kg

Suffolk
ORGANIC
WHITE MUSHROOMS
79p p/100g

Almeida 30 Almeida Street, N1 1AD
020 7354 4777 www.almeida-restaurant.co.uk

The Almeida restaurant lies directly opposite the Almeida Theatre, and in our view the two complement each other perfectly. Favoured by distinguished thespians, the Almeida Theatre stages a diverse programme of new and contemporary drama, Shakespeare and mini-operas. It's hard to imagine a more sophisticated urban night out than an evening at the theatre partnered with a pre- or post-performance meal at the Almeida restaurant. Bustling Upper Street, at the end of Almeida Street, offers a plethora of dining and drinking destinations (most of which come and go within a few years), which creates challenging competition for the Almeida. Yet this neighbourhood restaurant has now been around for some 10 years. ◐

Camino 3 Varnishers Yard, The Regent Quarter, N1 9FD
020 7841 7331 www.camino.uk.com

If you find yourself in the King's Cross area with time to spare – maybe you've missed a train or arrived too early for a departure – then call in at this nearby excellent and very authentic Spanish tapas bar. With a whiff of fiesta and glass or three of Cava, you might want to stay for more than you originally intended. ◐

Doug Wregg

Caravan is my favourite place for breakfast, jazzing up the traditional format with some easy fusion and washing it down with the best coffee in London.

Co-owner, Brawn, Terroirs and Les Caves de Pyrène

Above left **Copper pans hanging in the kitchen at Almeida.** Above **Caravan in Exmouth Market is perfect for brunch dining with great eggs and bacon.**

Above right **Caravan also includes a coffee roastery in the basement.**

Caravan 11–13 Exmouth Market, EC1R 4QD
020 7833 8115 www.caravanonexmouth.co.uk

Pitch perfect, in every sense. The corner location of this Kiwi-managed café-cum-restaurant on the edge of desirable Exmouth Market is hugely appealing: the tables both inside and on the pavement are a pure delight, especially when you catch the aroma of the coffee roasting in the basement. The relaxation of the setting is matched by the exacting commitment and skill displayed in the presentation of the food, wine and coffee. It is hardly surprising, therefore, that since its opening in early 2010 Caravan has been a runaway success. Miles Kirby, head chef and head roaster (and not many people can claim that joint title) is an alumnus of The Providores, so you can expect a global rollcall of ingredients. Could fusion food be making a comeback, dare we ask? In the right hands it can work, and Miles is certainly one of the few people who can make it enjoyable. The small coffee roastery in the basement has also captured the attention of many other restaurateurs, and now has its emulators around town. ◐

Left **At work in Euphorium Bakery.**

Euphorium Bakery 202 Upper Street, N1 1RQ
020 7704 6905 www.euphoriumbakery.com

This is an emphatically French bakery and pâtisserie, with top-quality breads, viennoiserie, savouries and cakes. The pain de campagne and pain paysan are classics. They also bake hard-to-find pure rye bread, made with 100 per cent rye flour from Germany, plus fougasse provençale, Scandinavian bread, focaccia and the classic baguette.

The Euphorium ovens also bake excellent pizza with French-inspired toppings sold by the slice, choux pastry éclairs, quiche, chocolate delights and much more. Other branches have opened, but this is the best location. ⊙

Frederick's Camden Passage, N1 8EG
020 7359 2888 www.fredericks.co.uk

In well over 20 years of trading, Frederick's has seen Islington boom while at the same time managing to retain its excellent reputation as a location for business entertaining, social gatherings and special occasions. The restaurant is family-run and you can tell. The main dining room lies in a glass-vaulted conservatory and there is also a small space for al fresco dining. The wine list is seriously attractive. This is the ideal restaurant for a sedate supper after seeing a performance at nearby Sadler's Wells. ⊙

La Fromagerie 30 Highbury Park, N5 2AA
020 7359 7440 www.lafromagerie.co.uk

(PP) On a Saturday morning I can leave home on my beloved Vespa and scoot to La Fromagerie, one of my favourite places, in (my fastest time) 10 minutes and 15 seconds. The Marylebone La Fromagerie is larger and includes a greater range of delicious foods, but I save that for a special occasion. The Highbury branch is my regular treat. Patricia Michelson is definitely one of my food heroes, and I just adore everything in this shop, from the cheese maps and the pork pies to the tinned cassoulet and confit de canard, not forgetting the all-important cheese room. Absolute heaven. If only it could be just a little closer. ⊙

Right **The displays and the quality of the cheese at La Fromagerie in Highbury and Marylebone are the most impressive in London.**

The Gilbert Scott St. Pancras Renaissance Hotel

Euston Road, NW1 2AR 020 7278 3888 www.thegilbertscott.co.uk

This is a reasonably good restaurant, and we suspect it will get better as time passes; at the moment, however, we can't help thinking that it's a great shame it isn't better. The building has an illustrious history and pedigree, and the internal and external architecture are both hugely impressive. The scale of the public spaces is enormously generous, and the potential is tremendous. Expectations are correspondingly high, and the current offering falls slightly short.

Marcus Wareing, the restaurateur chosen for this grand stage, has devised a brasserie based on British foods from the past – mostly from the Victorian era, which makes eminently good sense. His team have done a great deal of research, and they score high for effort. The menu is full of names that are redolent of British culinary heritage and regional dishes, such as Harrogate loaf, Kentish pigeon pot, Suffolk stew, Manchester tart, soles in coffins, Mrs Beeton's snow eggs and Lord Mayor's trifle. It just seems that the idea is outstripping the execution, for the moment at least. There is some good food to be had, and the service is eager and willing, but it doesn't seem to gel fully. Perhaps it will bed down and improve with time.

The interior design is a great success, especially the bar with its magnificent bell chandeliers. But when all the excitment of the opening has died down, we do wonder who, apart from hotel residents, will dine here. **○**

James Elliott Master Butcher 96 Essex Road, N1 8LU

020 7726 3658

Rosy-cheeked butchers are always on hand here to offer a friendly greeting and expert advice. They seem to know a large number of their customers personally, which is surely a good sign. James Elliott specializes in free-range, dry-plucked ducks and chicken, Suffolk pork, aged foreribs of beef and Lincolnshire lamb, accompanied by a thoughtful selection of condiments, a few cheeses, butter, quails' eggs and a small collection of black puddings. **○**

Right **A butcher at James Elliott breaking down a whole beast.**

Bruno Loubet

Medcalf 40 Exmouth Market, EC1R 4QE

020 7833 3533 www.medcalfbar.co.uk

Occupying the former premises of an esteemed butcher's shop, Medcalf serves distinctly British food from a daily-changing menu, in a long, narrow room with stylishly appointed, mostly reclaimed, furniture. Their art and creative music policy add interest to Friday evenings. ○

Morgan M 50 Long Lane, EC1A 9EJ

020 7609 3560 www.morganm.com

Morgan Meunier is a chef with a vision and high ambitions for his food, which he describes as 'a modern approach to cooking rooted in classical French cuisine'. His meticulous artistry on the plate is embodied in his signature dessert, dark chocolate moelleux. This is the type of serious cooking that sets out to attract the attentions of the Michelin inspector. The intimate dining room, seating 48, is subtly decorated with cream walls, oak floors and comfortable green upholstered armchairs. A shelf reverentially stocked with past editions of Michelin guides might also catch any inspector's attention.

The residents in this area are very lucky to have Morgan M on their doorstep, as this is the standard of food more usually found in Mayfair or St. James's. For the moment, however, this is without doubt the best French restaurant in Islington. ○

Morito 32 Exmouth Market, EC1R 4QL 020 7278 7007

Little Morito is a baby offshoot of the main restaurant (see opposite), located immediately next door in what was formerly the Brindisa Spanish produce store. It is both small and very straightforward. The sign on the door says it all: Mezze, Tapas, Raciones. ○

Left **The dining room at Morgan M.**

Moro 34–6 Exmouth Market, EC1R 4QE
020 7833 8336 www.moro.co.uk

According to the first Moro cookbook, the menu was born of a desire to cook within the wonderful traditions of the Mediterranean, while still exploring new and exciting flavours. From its inception in 1997, Moro has been cooking excellent Spanish food with more than a hint of North African flavours and ingredients. The kitchen team manage to capture the influence of the Moorish occupation of Spain from the 8th to the 15th centuries and at the same time present everything in a modern and modest manner. As an exponent of this culinary direction Moro stands alone: nothing similar or close to this standard of cooking exists in London today. Some chefs might introduce an occasional dish linking saffron and cinnamon, paprika and cumin, but at Moro the link between these two great culinary traditions imbues the entire menu, and it's a delight.

Before opening the restaurant on Exmouth Market, the recently married proprietors Sam and Sam Clark set off in a camper van to explore the food and culture of Spain and Morocco as far as the Sahara. Clearly the journey was worthwhile. The food the Clarks serve shows their previous experience at the seminal River Café (see page 20), and they adopt the same relaxed idiom, yet have created a lively dining room and an impressive open kitchen. Charcoal-grilled meat, poultry and fish, together with dishes such as wood-oven roasted pork with green mojo sauce and wrinkled potatoes, form the heart of the menu. Along with the River Café, Moro is one of the few restaurants that really understands excellent wood-oven cooking. The long zinc bar is a lively spot from which to enjoy various tapas, cured hams and a glass of sherry. As well as its excellent food and ambience, Moro also offers great value for money. Given its popularity, the temptation to increase the prices on the menu must have been strong; fortunately for us, the passion and belief in running a sustainable, popular restaurant appears to be even stronger. ◐

Above **Sweet and sour poached spring vegetables with labneh on toast.**
Left **Samuel Clark in the kitchen at Moro.**
Right **Chargrilled sardines with beetroot pilaf from the menu at Moro.**

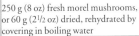

Morels with Butter Beans, Tomatoes and Sweet Herbs

Serves 6–8 as a mezze, or 4 as a starter or light meal

250 g (8 oz) fresh morel mushrooms, or 60 g (2½ oz) dried, rehydrated by covering in boiling water
12–16 sweet cherry tomatoes, quartered
2 tablespoons roughly chopped flat leaf parsley
1 tablespoon roughly torn basil leaves
1 tablespoon each of roughly chopped tarragon and dill
½ red onion, chopped
300 g (10 oz) cooked butter beans, such as Spanish *judión* beans, or white beans
3–4 teaspoons olive oil

For the dressing
½ garlic clove, crushed
1 tablespoon lemon juice
4 tablespoons extra virgin olive oil
sea salt and freshly ground black pepper

Trim the ends of the morels, then fill a sink with cold water, add the morels and toss for a minute to remove any grit. If they are still dirty, rinse again. Leave to drain thoroughly in a colander. If using dried morels, lift them out of the soaking liquid so as not to disturb any grit that might have settled at the bottom of the bowl. Put them into a small saucepan, then pour in the soaking liquid through a fine-mesh sieve to remove any grit. Heat the pan over a high heat until you are left with roughly 1 tablespoon of liquid. Season with a little salt.

Meanwhile, make the dressing. Combine the garlic, lemon juice and olive oil with some salt and pepper and whisk together. Now mix the tomatoes, herbs and onion with the dressing and set aside to let the flavours mingle.

When you are ready to eat, warm up the beans in their cooking liquid and season with salt. Place a large frying pan over a medium-to-high heat and add the olive oil. When it is hot, add the morels and their liquid and fry for 2–3 minutes, stirring occasionally, until the mushrooms are soft and have a tiny bit of colour. Remove from the heat and taste. Now toss together the warm drained beans, half the morels and any juice with the dressed tomatoes. Taste for seasoning and serve immediately with the remaining mushrooms scattered on top.

Cuttlefish with Broad Beans and Mint

Serves 6–8 as a tapa, or 4 as a starter or light meal

3 small cuttlefish or 3 medium squid (roughly the size of your hand), cleaned
4 tablespoons olive oil
½ large onion, roughly chopped
2 garlic cloves, thinly sliced
½ teaspoon fennel seeds (optional)
1 bay leaf (preferably fresh)
½ teaspoon sweet paprika
150 ml (¼ pint) white wine or fino sherry
200 ml (7 fl oz) water
1 kg (2 lb) small young broad beans in the pods, shelled, or 275 g (9 oz) fresh (or frozen) shelled broad beans
3 level tablespoons roughly chopped mint
2 tablespoons extra virgin olive oil
sea salt and freshly ground black pepper

Cut the bodies and wings of the cuttlefish or squid into small strips (no wider than 1 cm/½ inch or longer than 4 cm/1½ inches), and the tentacles in halves or quarters, depending on size.

In a medium pan with a lid, heat the olive oil over a medium heat. Add the onion and a pinch of salt and fry gently for 5–10 minutes, stirring occasionally. When the onion begins to turn golden and caramelize, add the garlic, fennel seeds (if using) and bay leaf and fry for a further 2 minutes. Add the cuttlefish or squid and paprika, stir well, then pour on the wine and water. Cover, bring to a simmer and turn the heat down low. Depending on the thickness of the cuttlefish or squid pieces, cook for 30–50 minutes, stirring occasionally, or until they start to become tender. Add the broad beans and cook uncovered over a higher heat for 10–15 minutes more, or until the beans are tender and the juices run thick. Stir in the mint and extra virgin olive oil and serve straight away with a glass of chilled sherry.

234 **Ottolenghi** 287 Upper Street, N1 2TZ
020 7288 1454 www.ottolenghi.co.uk

Following the success of the Notting Hill branch, Ottolenghi opened
in Islington. This not-inexpensive delicatessen and restaurant serves
Mediterranean foods with an occasional North African influence, all
made with the very best ingredients. All the food is made on site in the
kitchen below the shop.

The all-white room is dominated by a long, central all-white dining
table, surrounded by iconic white 1968 Verner Panton chairs. Flanking
this long thin space are beautiful displays of salads, prepared *traiteur* foods
and bakery items, all looking as though they are straight out of the pages
of *Vogue Entertaining*. The epic display of meringues in the window
ensures the patronage of elegant Islington ladies who lunch. ◉

Right **The
Ottolenghi
food displays are
jaw-dropping.**

Paul A. Young – Chocolaterie 33 Camden Passage, N1 8EA
020 7424 5750 www.paulayoung.co.uk

Yorkshireman Paul Young – a regular on television, former head pastry chef for Marco Pierre White, and winner of a gold medal at the World Chocolate Awards – now boasts not only this boutique chocolaterie on beguiling Camden Passage, but now also shops in the City and Soho. This is the place where the semi-professional patissier comes to buy the best-quality pure Amedei or Valrhona chocolate. The chocolate truffles, all hand-made in the shop, are gracefully crafted and delicious, especially the sea-salted caramel. The small bars of chocolate, featuring complementary combinations such as Szechuan chilli paired with 70 per cent cocoa, or pink peppercorn and white chocolate, make an ideal mid-afternoon snack. Over the summer months the shop (closed on Mondays) offers Paul's homemade ice cream with hot 70 per cent-cocoa chocolate sauce. ◉

The People's Supermarket 72–8 Lamb's Conduit Street, WC1N 3LP
020 7430 1827 www.thepeoplessupermarket.org

Winner of the 2011 Observer Ethical Award in the local retailer category for aiming to be 'a sustainable food cooperative providing healthy food at reasonable prices', this supermarket, set up by Arthur Potts Dawson, is managed and owned by its members. Each member is required to do some voluntary work in the supermarket, benefiting in return from lower prices – an interesting and thought-provoking concept that might be taken up in a more sustainable format by the big supermarkets. ◉

St. Pancras Grand Champagne Bar & Brasserie
St. Pancras Station, Upper Concourse, Euston Road, N1C 4QL
020 7870 9900 www.searcys.co.uk/st-pancras-grand

The owners claim that this Champagne bar, located in the monumental vastness that is the Barlow Shed, is the longest in Europe. Allowing for poetic licence, it certainly makes an interesting meeting spot. The architectural setting is jaw dropping. At 213 m (698 ft) long, 73 m (240 ft) wide and 30.5 m (100 ft) high at its apex, this was the world's largest enclosed space when it was built. For a period of four years before its completion in 1864, this part of the station employed no fewer than 6,000 men, 1,000 horses and 100 steam cranes. The refurbishment at the turn of millennium took seven years and over £800 million. Is this progress or regression? One feature of the Barlow Shed that would not have been given much consideration when it first came into use would have been the lighting. Today, the lighting is one of its greatest successes, really bringing the structure to life both by day and by night.

Thanks to the talents of the interior designer Martin Brudnizki, there is also a great-looking brasserie opposite, seriously sophisticated, elegant and comfortable – what more could anyone ask? The menu is extensive, as every brasserie menu should be. This is the ideal place to enjoy a huge, world-beating British breakfast before setting off for the land of croissants and café au laits. ◉

Paul Young

Chocolate Vodka Sorbet

Serves 6–8 portions

This intense and chilling sorbet laced with smooth warming vodka is a real adult's dessert. With the huge selection of flavoured vodkas on offer, this frozen and exquisite version will not disappoint even the most discerning palate.

25 g (1 oz) dark pure cocoa powder
450 ml (3/4 pint) water
150 g (5 oz) dark bitter chocolate
125 g (4 oz) caster sugar
50 g (2 oz) glucose syrup
100 ml (3 1/2 fl oz) vodka

Place the cocoa powder and the water in a saucepan and simmer for 5 minutes. Cut the chocolate into small pieces and place it into a mixing bowl with the sugar and glucose syrup. Pour the hot cocoa liquid onto the chopped chocolate mixture. Combine it well so the chocolate melts evenly and then set it aside to cool.

After it has cooled to room temperature, stir in the vodka. Place the mixture in an ice cream machine and churn it, following the manufacturer's instructions. Or, pour the chocolate and vodka mixture into a plastic container with a lid. Seal and place it in the freezer. After 30 minutes remove it from the freezer and give it a stir. Repeat this every 30 minutes or until it is smooth and frozen.

Place some small glasses in the freezer until they are totally cold. Offer this wicked sorbet on its own, scooped into the frozen glasses, and serve with a teaspoon.

Right **Paul A. Young working with chocolate in his Camden Passage kitchen.**

The Sampler 266 Upper Street, N1 2UQ
020 7226 9500 www.thesampler.co.uk

No meal is complete without a bottle of wine to complement it, so it seems to us only right to include this multi-award winning destination, one of the top independent wine shops in London. One of the reasons why The Sampler is so important is that it was the first to introduce the Enomatic wine preservation system to Londoners. Thanks to this system, which involves injecting nitrogen gas into the bottle when wine is drawn off, we can try before we buy. Or maybe just try and not buy. Some 80 wines are available to sample, from iconic vintages to everyday table wines. ◐

Steve Hatt Fishmonger 88–90 Essex Road, N1 8LU 020 7226 3963

The queues from early on a Saturday morning speak volumes about the freshness of the fish available here. This no-frills shop is small, but the stock displayed on mounds of crushed ice is exhaustive. Hatt offers everything from tuna for sushi suppers to monkfish, turbot and sea bass for elegant Islington dinner parties. This is a place to buy proper palourde clams for your spaghetti vongole or oysters and prawns to make your loved one swoon. They also smoke a fine range of fish on site. We can't think of a better fishmonger in all of London. Like La Fromagerie, this is one of the finest food retailers in the capital: if you are planning a special meal you should seriously consider making the journey to Steve Hatt. It will be worth it. Incongruously, during the game season, they also sell a fine selection of birds from the moors and excellent wild duck such as mallard. ◐

Above left **The fresh fish displays are always impressive at Steve Hatt. Many Londoners' believe this is the best fishmonger in the capital.**

Sushi of Shiori 144 Drummond Street, NW1 2PA
020 7388 9962 www.sushiofshiori.co.uk

This must be one of the smallest restaurants in London, with just three seats at the sushi bar and four other seats at a shelf against the shop-front-style window. It's a little like eating in a tiny dry cleaner's, but the quality of the temari canapé-style sushi wins you over. While there is just one chef, the menu is massive. The sushi is delicately and precisely prepared as you admire the skill of the Zen-like master. (PP) I dined on my own: it seemed that the four other people in the room were all doing the same, and we all felt equally comfortable. So if you are stuck in London without friends or a dining partner, or are maybe staying in a nearby hotel, this is the ideal place to take a book and slowly enjoy some delicious sushi. ◐

Trullo 300–2 St. Paul's Road, N1 2LH
020 7226 2733 www.trullorestaurant.com

The more informed in the London food world would argue that the most enjoyable restaurant food is to be had at St. John, The River Café and Moro. Trullo is influenced by all of them, plus the virtuous Jamie Oliver. Head chef Tim Siadatan was one of the stars of the *Jamie's Kitchen* television programme in 2002, and went on to work at St. John and Moro, while co-owner Jordan Frieda (son of celebrity hairdresser John and singer Lulu) worked front of house at The River Café. This excellent pedigree permeates the menu, service and ambience at Trullo.

If it weren't so hard to get a table, this would be the model neighbourhood restaurant. Prices are modest, especially for the wine, and the service is polite and willing. There are no airs and graces, and the love of simple Italian produce and cooking is palpable. Like the reassuringly simple dining room, the menu is quite small, focusing on silky homemade pasta or sparklingly-fresh fish and meat cooked over hot coals. If you're tired of the loud and overblown restaurants in central London, we urge you try Trullo. Located just a few hundred yards from Highbury and Islington tube station, it's easier to reach than you might think. ◐

Right **Catherine Conway at Unpackaged is passionate about excellent food while also operating an environmentally-responsible business.**

Unpackaged 42 Amwell Street, London, EC1R 1XT
020 7713 8368 www.beunpackaged.com

Unpackaged is all about Catherine Conway's passion and drive, combined with a brilliant idea. As the name alludes, the idea is to allow shoppers to buy produce without the packaging. This should mean that the cost is lower, there are no wasted resources and pollution is minimized. We've all heard about the landfill problems that we are suffering and creating for future generations, and this small store is doing its bit to make us think again about unnecessary packaging and its environmental consequences, and at the same time reduce CO_2 and other harmful gases.

The system is straightforward and easy to operate, with shoppers bringing in their own previously used packaging – anything from Tupperware and kitchen jars to brown bags and takeaway containers – and buying products by weight or volume. Unpackaged also sells a range of sealable containers to start customers off. And if all that isn't enough, the products are also all vigilantly selected to be organic, Fairtrade or local, with nothing that carries any air miles. Beautifully fashioned out of an old dairy, the shop is quite small, although the choice and range of products is not. You can buy anything from great breads and pastries to fruit and vegetables, pulses, grains, dried goods, oils and all manner of store cupboard essentials. You can even buy wines decanted from large barrels.

With luck, Catherine will be setting up in larger premises in the not-too-distant future. Watch out for the name and the idea – it can only gain in credibility in the future. ◉

Fitzrovia
Marylebone

Fitzrovia and Marylebone probably have the highest concentration of blue plaques in London, marking the former residences of eminent individuals, matched by an equally large number of top-quality restaurants and food stores. The area has developed rapidly over the past 15 years or so, thanks to its many high-profile restaurants and the foodie reputation of two of its main streets, Marylebone High Street and Charlotte Street.

With the exception of the Wallace Collection, in elegant Hertford House on Manchester Square, the area has few other tourist attractions. Rising at the dividing line between Fitzrovia and Marylebone, the BT Tower now makes a bizarre, rather moribund sight. In the 1960s this was the first tower built to transmit high-frequency radio waves, and it housed a restaurant on the top floor that rotated completely in 22 minutes. How fabulous that must have been. (TC) My children always wanted to celebrate their birthdays there when we lived in Fitzroy Square.

Today, Charlotte Street and its tributary roads cater to creatives with cosmopolitan tastes, while Marylebone High Street has a 'village' feel and is one of the chicest retail destinations in London, offering Scandinavian furniture stores (and of course The Conran Shop), the best cheese shop in London, pâtisseries and antiquarian booksellers. Heading south, turn left into Marylebone Lane and on into St. Christopher's Place for continental-style pavement dining. Over the coming years we should expect to see further development in this corner of London: the former Middlesex Hospital site is still to be developed and the Tottenham Court area is experiencing huge change and investment thanks to Crossrail.

Busaba Eathai 8–13 Bird Street, W1U 1BU
020 7518 8080 www.busaba.com

Young, trendy staff serve food that, while it may not strictly speaking be authentically Thai, is certainly moreish, and ideal for a quick, large, one-course bowl of noodles, stir-fry or great Asian curry. There are now several branches of Busaba around town, and although some say that they've lost a little of their cool edge now that founder Alan Yau is no longer involved, we still think they are good in their class. The interior design is mainly of dark teak and large square communal tables, with central low lamps and bench seats. It has a no-bookings policy, but while there are normally queues at other branches, here it's easier to get a seat here. Try the juices and power drinks, such as carrot, apple and celery with dandelion and nettle extract: they must be good for you. ◗

Carluccio's Caffè St. Christopher's Place, W1U 1AY
020 7935 5927 www.carluccios.com

Il Negozio, the shop, buzzes with shoppers from early morning, and the outside seats at this flagship location are occupied all day. The business originally created by Antonio and Priscilla Carluccio is now an international brand, managed by businessmen in suits rather than the original creative force – though Antonio does still help inspire and train the young chefs who work at Carluccio's.

The buying teams responsible for the mini-food stores at each of the Carluccio's are assiduous in sourcing ingredients from across Italy, and they stock a great range of own-brand products in stylish packaging. Whether you are searching for special pasta, polenta or biscotti, the selection is inspirational with food displays to match. The décor is casual and bright, with simple stainless steel shelves and black-and-white tiled floors. Essentially, it's a modern version of your favourite old Italian deli with a very enjoyable caffè on the side. As with everything that Antonio touches, you can always be assured of a great selection of fresh and dried mushrooms. ◗

Giancarlo & Katie Caldesi

"

For something competely different from our own Italian cooking, we like to escape to the exotic surroundings of Chor Bizarre with Depinder's wonderful authentic Indian flavours.

Owners of La Cucina Caldesi

Above **Each Carluccio's includes a small shop with carefully sourced Italian groceries.**

La Cucina Caldesi 4 Cross Keys Close, W1U 2DG
020 7487 0750/6/8 www.caldesi.com

In the 1980s, it seemed that every successful chef aspired to establish his or her own cookery school. Very few now survive: Rick Stein in Padstow and Raymond Blanc at Le Manoir aux Quat' Saisons in Oxfordshire still run excellent schools, and London has La Cucina Caldesi. La Cucina is stylishly appointed, with a technically brilliant kitchen studio suitable for a range of master classes and tutored cookery classes.

In the Tuscan family tradition, Giancarlo and Katie Caldesi share recipes handed down from generation to generation, teaching how to make perfect fresh pasta, 30-minute Italian menus and classic Italian feasts to vegetarian recipes, risottos and pizza. They offer an interesting range of evening, full day or weekend courses year-round, and you can also buy gift vouchers. ●

Dinings 22 Harcourt Street, W1H 4HH
020 7723 0666 www.dinings.co.uk

Reputation, and definitely not location, is the strong suit of this tiny – and we mean *tiny* – sushi joint. The ground floor seats five at a push, all seated at the sushi bar, and downstairs seats a few more in what they call the bunker. It's a little claustrophobic, and the concrete walls don't help, but anyone who really loves great quality Japanese food with modern influences (and in this case a few Spanish interloper elements) should beat a path to Dinings.

(PP) I had terrible trouble finding this place, walking past the entrance – which I assumed was a private doorway – several times. When I did eventually find my way into the ground floor of this Georgian townhouse, I sat at the sushi bar and was in raptures, thanks to my prime position from which I could watch the chefs at work and enjoy the extraordinary quality of their food. The menu is huge, especially given the size of the place. The foie gras sushi roll in sweet soy sauce was mesmeric, and the sea urchin out of this world. ●

This page **Giancarlo Caldesi at his cookery school that offers a wide range of different culinary courses and classes for children and adults.**

244 **Fino** 33 Charlotte Street, entrance on Rathbone Street, W1T 1RR
020 7813 8010 www.finorestaurant.com

Two hispanophile brothers, Sam and Eddie Hart, are responsible for this
restaurant offering excellent Spanish food in comfortable surroundings.
While Barrafina, the sister tapas bar in Soho (see page 199), has recently
attracted more attention, Fino remains popular with those who want to
enjoy great tapas in a more relaxed setting. Start with some delicious
Joselito jamon, and try the seafood cooked on an authentic Spanish plancha. The restaurant has made a significant contribution
to the re-emergence of sherry on the London scene, and their selection is
outstanding. The Iberian wine list is also very enjoyable. ●

Above **Sam and
Eddie Hart outside
Fino, their first
London restaurant.**
Above right **Spanish
scenes and the
kitchens inside Fino.**

Galvin 66 Baker Street, W1U 7DJ
020 7935 4007 www.galvinrestaurants.com

Sibling success is the key ingredient at Galvin. Chris Galvin has more
than 30 years' experience in top kitchens, having gaining a Michelin star
at Orrery and launched The Wolseley as head chef. Jeff Galvin has cooked
at The Savoy, with Marco Pierre White and Nico Ladennis. They now
cook simple bistro food, to a chorus of approval throughout London.
The brothers call it a *bistrot de luxe*, and we wouldn't demur. You can eat
and drink in traditional French bourgeois manner for very good value, as
the *prix fixe* menu is a great deal. The menu is full of simple classics such as
snails, oysters, steak tartare, calf's liver with bacon and crème brûlée.
(PP) The tarte au citron is the best I have ever tasted. The brothers have
gone on to open other restaurants, but this remains our first choice. ●

Galvin Lemon Tart

Serves 8

juice and grated zest of 10 organic
unwaxed lemons (450 ml/³/4 pint juice)
500 g (1 lb) caster sugar
1 litre (1³/4 pints) double cream
6 eggs
6 egg yolks, beaten
icing sugar, to dust

For the pastry

200 g (7 oz) plain flour
pinch salt
75 g (3 oz) icing sugar
100 g (3¹/2 oz) unsalted butter,
at room temperature
seeds from ¹/2 vanilla pod
1 egg, lightly beaten
2 egg yolks

First make the pastry, sieve the flour into
a medium bowl with the salt.

Using a food processor with a paddle
attachment on a medium speed, beat the
icing sugar, soft butter and vanilla seeds
together until pale in colour.

Gradually add half the egg, then half
the flour, then the rest of the egg, followed
by the last of the flour.

Tip the dough on to a board and knead
the mixture until you have a smooth dough,
but do not overwork it. Cover it with
clingfilm and refrigerate for 1 hour.

Roll out the chilled pastry on a lightly
floured board to about a 32 cm-diameter
(13-inch) round, then line a deep flan tin
25 cm (10 inches) in diameter, 4 cm
(1¹/2 inches) deep, leaving the pastry
hanging over the edge, to be trimmed after
cooking. Refrigerate for 25 minutes.

Line the inside of the tart case with
greaseproof paper, fill it to the top with
baking beans (if you don't have any you can use rice),
and bake in a preheated oven, 180°C (350°F),
Gas Mark 4, for 18–20 minutes. Remove the
greaseproof and baking beans, and cook for
another 4 minutes to finish cooking the pastry.

While still hot, brush the inside of the
tart with some of the beaten egg yolks, and
bake for a further 2 minutes. Lower the
temperature of the oven to 110°C (225°F)
Gas Mark ¹/4.

To make the filling, bring the lemon juice
and sugar to the boil in a small pan, then
remove from the heat and stir in the lemon
zest. Allow to infuse for 3–4 minutes, then
pass through a fine sieve.

In a separate pan, bring the cream to
the boil and allow to cool slightly.

Break the eggs into a large mixing bowl,
add the egg yolks and whisk together. Pour
the lemon juice and sugar mixture on to the
eggs while still whisking, then whisk in the
double cream. Pass again through a fine
sieve into a jug, and skim off any bubbles
that form on the top.

Place the tart case on a baking tray and
place on the oven shelf, then carefully pour
in the filling mixture to the very top of the
tart case being very careful to avoid any
spillages. Carefully slide into the oven and
bake for 40 minutes or until set. When the
tart is cooked, the middle should still wobble
like a jelly.

Remove from the oven and cool on the
baking tray for at least 3 hours at room
temperature (do not put in the refrigerator,
as the pastry will go soggy).

When cool, trim the excess pastry from
the edge, remove from the tin and cut the
tart into 8 wedges. Dust with icing sugar
and caramelize the top with a blowtorch.

Serve with a raspberry sauce, made by
pushing raspberries through a sieve to extract
their juice.

Tim Wilson

As a farmer and butcher it is my duty to provide my animals with good husbandry, then I can provide my customers with quality items and a clear conscience.

Owner, The Ginger Pig

The Ginger Pig 8–10 Moxon Street, W1U 4EW 020 7935 7788

This meat-lover's paradise is how the archetypal local butcher's shop should look, smell and sound. Located at the epicentre of foodie Marylebone, it has now properly established itself and feels as though it has been around for 50 years or more. Tim Wilson presides over one of the best food retail experiences in London, with diagrams on the walls indicating the various cuts of meat, a huge walk-in cold room with countless carcasses awaiting the knife of consummate professionals in bloodstained white coats, and the smell of game pies baking in the oven. Longhorn cattle – the oldest domestic beef cattle breed in Britain – Dorset and Swaledale sheep, and several rare-breed pigs including Tamworths (the original ginger pig) all come from Tim's organic farms (he has three) on the Yorkshire moors. Free-range geese, chickens and turkeys are sourced from the 500-acre Belvoir Estate in Rutland, and game is from the most reputable shoots. The extensive selection of sausages, bacon, hams, terrines and pies is not cheap, but the value lies in the flavour. (PP) Do try the epic sausage roll. ○

Above **The hanging room at The Ginger Pig is visible from the shop and skilled butchers are always in hand.**

Hakkasan 8 Hanway Place, Hanway Street, W1T 1HD
020 7927 7000 www.hakkasan.com

Seminal Hong Kong meets Chinese cuisine in glamorous surroundings. When it opened in 2001, this was the first Hakkasan, the place where world-renowned designer Christian Liaigre, in partnership with Alan Yau, imparted a nightclub feel to modern Asian cuisine. The same 'modern ethnic' style has been adopted for all of the new Hakkasans, in Miami, Abu Dhabi, Mumbai and a second London location in Mayfair.

Tong Chee Hwee, the original chef and now the master of the Hakkasan kitchens, deserves a very special mention: this restaurant won a Michelin star in 2003 and has retained it ever since.

If you can't get a table, try the Ling Ling bar for a wide menu of great cocktails. The interior is sleek, stylish and atmospheric, so sit back and admire the design details, especially the evocative lighting scheme with light levels that change subtly throughout the evening, designed by leading light designer Arnold Chan. ○

Above and right
Inside the Christian Liaigre-designed Hakkasan.

Kaffeine 66 Great Titchfield Street, W1W 7QJ
020 7580 6755 www.kaffeine.co.uk

Another Antipodean independent coffee bar where the bean is worshipped and cherished: the influx of these coffee entrepreneurs from Australia and New Zealand has given a welcome fillip to the scene and provides an excellent counterblast to the proliferation of the big chains. It lies directly opposite Riding House Café, where the coffee is good but not as good as at Kaffeine, so cross the road for a post-lunch espresso. ⦿

This page **Kaffeine is small, but perfectly formed and is an ideal for morning coffee or to call-in after a long lunch at Riding House Cafe.**

Giorgio Locatelli

"The word 'organic' isn't shrugged off as being middle-class neurosis any more and is being accepted as a better option. This shift in the attitude towards food reflects that now, in every part of London (not just the West End), there is a huge variety of good restaurants springing up. London has come a long way since the '80s.

Owner, Locanda Locatelli

Locanda Locatelli 8 Seymour Street, W1H 7JZ
020 7935 9088 www.locandalocatelli.com

Following his achievement at Zafferano, it was inevitable that Giorgio Locatelli's own little inn, or *locanda*, would be a great success. The diaries seemed to be full even as the paint was drying on the David Collins-designed modern and elegant dining room. Along with The River Café in Hammersmith (see page 20), Locanda Locatelli is definitely our top Italian eatery.

You start with a generous basket of beautiful homemade bread, as you'd expect, from a deliciously moist *focaccia* to wafer-thin *pane*, and the tables are also laid with two-foot-long *grissini*. Go with an appetite: it would be a shame to have anything less than four courses. The menu is vast. Antipasti deliver artichokes, mozzarella, seasonal insalata, scallops, and on my last visit a thinly sliced calves' head *lampascioni* with rocket, parsley and capers. Then you struggle to select a pasta dish from a perfect selection of about a dozen, followed by an exceptional choice of main courses from wild sea bass to chargrilled lamb. *Zucchini fritte* must be the essential contorno and to finish, it has to be the pick-me-up tiramisu.

The front of house, overseen by Plaxy Locatelli, is also close to perfect, marked by an almost uncanny blend of intuition and anticipation. The specials are recommended with such passion, and you feel that while every member of the team is the ultimate in professionalism, they also live and dine together as a happy family. ◉

Above **Giorgio Locatelli making foccacia.**

Spaghetti 'Latini' alla Vongole

(Spaghetti 'Latini' with Clams)
by Giorgio Locatelli

Serves 4

75 ml (3 fl oz) extra-virgin olive oil
3 garlic cloves, peeled and finely chopped
1 chilli, finely chopped
1 kg (2 lb) veraci clams (palourdes or carpetshell)
1/2 wineglass of dry white wine
400 g (13 oz) spaghetti 'Latini'
1 handful of parsley, finely chopped

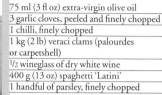

Place a large pan of lightly salted water over a high heat and bring it to the boil. Meanwhile, heat half of the olive oil in a large sauté pan over a medium heat. The aim is to cook the garlic (so that it is digestible) but not burn it (or it will be bitter), so it is a good idea to tilt the pan a little. This way, the oil flows to one spot. Place the garlic and chilli into the oil so they can cook in this depth and will be less likely to burn. Cook gently for a few minutes until they start to colour.

Place the pan back down fully onto the stove and add the clams. Cook them for about 30 seconds and then add the white wine. Cover the pan with a lid to allow the clams to steam open. After about one minute or up to 90 seconds, remove the lid and discard any clams that haven't opened.

Leave around one-quarter of the clams in their shells, but scrape out the rest, discarding the shells. Turn off the heat.

Once the large pan of salted water has come to the boil, place the pasta into it and let it boil for about a minute less than the time given on the packet (usually 5–6 minutes), until al dente. Drain the pasta, reserving the cooking water.

Add the pasta to the clams along with the remaining oil and toss thoroughly for about a minute to let the pasta absorb the flavours and allow the starch to thicken the sauce. If you need to loosen it slightly, add a little cooking water from the pasta. You will see that the sauce starts to cling to the pasta, so that when you serve it the pasta it will stay coated. Sprinkle with chopped parsley and serve straight away.

252 **Marylebone Farmers' Market** Cramer Street Car Park,
off Marylebone High Street, W1U 4EW
Sunday 10 am–2 pm

Marylebone High Street already has its full complement of food stores,
but when the market comes to town on Sunday the vast choice is enough
to sate any foodie's deepest desires. The Marylebone market is London's
largest *exclusively* farmers' market, with between 30 and 40 stalls; Borough
Market is significantly larger, but it doesn't follow the strict rules set
down by the London Farmers' Market Association (whose website,
www.lfm.org.uk gives information about other London markets).

(PP) It's always enjoyable to visit these markets and talk with the
farmers, growers, fishermen and producers themselves. Over time, I have
learned to focus my purchasing on meat, game, fruit, vegetables and salad
leaves. The cheese is eclipsed by the selection at nearby La Fromagerie or
Neal's Yard Dairy, and the cakes are better from other specialist shops. ○

Allan Pickett

I love visiting the Marylebone
farmers' market – I love to buy the
fresh bread and a dozen oysters.
It's also a good chance to see what
other vegetable are in season.

Head chef, Plateau

Orrery Restaurant and Epicerie
55 Marylebone High Street, W1U 5RB
020 7616 8000   www.orrery-restaurant.co.uk

Named after the mechanical device that illustrates the relative positions
of the planets in the solar system (also the name of the second Conran
restaurant in 1954, as it happens), Orrery has several noteworthy features.
The restaurant space – long, narrow and very attractive – sits above The
Conran Shop as part of a converted stable building, with large arched

Above **The cheese
trolley at Orrery
is one of the
restaurant's
highlights.**

Left above **Mickael Weiss, the head chef at Coq d'Argent, helping out in the Orrery kitchens.** Left **Chefs taking a deserved meal break in the restaurant at Orrery.**

windows overlooking the carefully tended grounds of the churchyard opposite and a row of banquette seating on the facing wall. This really lovely dining room is at its best at lunch. It is also complemented by the unique summer terrace upstairs, which not too many people know about. Orrery delivers on several levels; most exciting, however, is its award-winning cheese trolley. If you are serious about cheese (and we are, very), this is the place to dine. There is also a blockbuster wine list.

The Epicerie, on the ground floor, stocks a fine selection of olive oils, truffles, coffee, viennoiserie, madeleines and fleur de sel from the Camargue. *Traiteur* dishes influenced by the cooking of south-west France, such as cassoulet, pot au feu and confit de canard, plus its renowned saucissons, terrines and rillettes, are definitely worth adding to any larder.

If it weren't for the fiddly style of food that has taken over the restaurant in recent years, this would be a flagship destination. **○**

Le Pain Quotidien 72–5 Marylebone High Street, W1U 5JW
020 7486 6154 www.lepainquotidien.co.uk

In the words of the founder Alain Coumont, 'the idea behind "Le Pain Quotidien" is simply to make a good daily bread: a hand-made bread with a good crust and a firm slice, the kind of bread that makes great tartines; bread not only to nourish the body but the spirit as well; a bread best shared around a table to be savoured among friends.' High ambitions indeed.

This branch of the international chain occupies a favoured corner position at the top end of Marylebone High Street, perfectly placed for many local residents to call in for their daily bread. Or perhaps to take time out from the demands of London life to dine at the communal table and enjoy the pastries, tarts, brownies, cakes and meringues. All of the breads are hand-made using just three ingredients, water, stone-ground flour and salt, and baked in stone ovens.

It sounds simple, but the care and skill required to bake such bread are enormous. And it does make great tartines. **○**

Right **The wine list at Orrery is one of the longest in London and is administered by skilled sommeliers.**

The Providores 109 Marylebone High Street, W1U 4RX
020 7935 6175 www.theprovidores.co.uk

Twenty-eight-day-aged Longhorn beef fillet with Sichuan-pickled shiitake mushrooms, chilli-glazed carrots, onion purée, a walnut brioche croûton and béarnaise butter; or cassava, quinoa and wasabi-crusted smoked Dutch eel with saffron lotus root, cucumber, pickled kohlrabi, bean sprouts, green tea jelly and maple teriyaki: just two of the main-course dishes from the huge menu at The Providores, which say more than we can write about the overall direction of the restaurant. Fusion chefs have been much maligned over recent years, but New Zealander Peter Gordon seems to have been the exception. Instead, his menus garner high praise.

The ground-floor Tapa Room, named after a wood-fibre ceremonial cloth used throughout the Pacific for celebratory feasts, offers probably the most innovative breakfast brunch menu in London. Dishes include French toast stuffed with banana and pecans with grilled smoked streaky bacon and vanilla verjus syrup, or kumara, caramelized red onion, kawakawa and feta tortilla with Turkish yogurt, piquillo peppers and rocket. If you find it difficult to secure a reservation at The Providores and don't want to queue for the Tapa Room, a sister restaurant under the same management, Kopapa, has recently opened on Monmoth Street in Covent Garden.

(PP) Even if you're like me, and fusion food isn't top of your list, I would still highly recommend the Tapa Room. Plus you've got to admire the procurement and knowledge of ingredients and combinations of flavours demonstrated by this kitchen. ◐

Peter Gordon

I have two favourite London food shops: the first would have to be Food World on Kilburn High Road which has the most fabulous range of Indian and Middle Eastern spices, grains, vegetables and fruit. I head there as soon as I get a whiff of the arrival of the Alphonso mangoes – there's always something new to discover. My second would be Brindisa at Borough Market, which is great for easily accessible Spanish produce, which I use a lot of, and the Sunday Farmers' Market in Marylebone has to be one of the best of its kind in London.

Head chef, The Providores

Above left **Peter Gordon in the upstairs dining room at The Providores.**

changa
Turkish Eggs

The Providores have worked with changa restaurant in Istanbul since 1999. This is a dish we have eaten many times in Turkey and it is one of our most popular dishes at breakfast time in the restaurant. In Turkey the yoghurt has raw garlic beaten into it but we've found that's a bit too much for the English breakfast palate.

Serves 4

300 g (10 oz) thick yoghurt
^{1}/2 teaspoon fine sea salt
1 garlic clove, peeled and finely chopped (optional)
75 ml (3 fl oz) extra virgin olive oil
75 ml (3 fl oz) white vinegar
8 medium or large eggs
50 g (2 oz) butter
1 teaspoon kirmizi biber (dried Turkish chilli flakes)
2 tablespoons roughly chopped parsley
wholewheat sourdough toast

Beat the yogurt with the salt, garlic and ^{1}/2 the oil and divide ^{2}/3 of it amongst 4 bowls.

Bring a deep pot (about 3 litres/6 pints in capacity) of water to the boil. Reduce the temperature so the water just simmers and add the vinegar. Crack the eggs in one by one and poach them until the whites are set but the yolks are still runny. This should take about 5–7 minutes.

Meanwhile, heat the butter in a small pan until it turns pale nut-brown. Add the chilli flakes and let them sizzle. Then remove them from the heat, add the remaining olive oil and set aside.

Carefully lift the eggs out of the pot with a slotted spoon and place 2 in each bowl, on top of the yoghurt. Spoon the remaining yoghurt on top of the eggs. Give the chilli butter a good stir and spoon this on top.

Scatter with the parsley and serve the toast on a separate plate.

Fitzrovia / Marylebone

255

Left **The communal
table at Riding
House Café
featuring salvaged
theatre seats.**

Left **The bar at Riding House Café with the kitchen behind a glass screen in the background.**

Riding House Café 43–51 Great Titchfield Street, W1W 7PQ
020 7927 0840 www.ridinghousecafe.co.uk

The cheeseburger is brilliant, excellent value and the epitome of the place. The whole ensemble, from the design details to the attitude of the staff, seems to be trying so terribly hard to be New York-esque, and in the main it works. It's a great meeting point and informal gathering place for the ad agency and design kids on the block. And it has the now-ubiquitous small plates, the essential component for any new concept-above-content all-day operation. We recommend this place highly for a weekend breakfast, brunch or late lunch, or maybe an early evening drink and a first date.

The easy-on-the-eye design is strongly reminiscent of the various Soho House operations, especially Shoreditch House, but it also seems to be trying too hard to be stripped-back and basic (though it has some pleasant touches, not least the leather cladding and the saddle stitching on the furniture). We can't help wondering whether this design approach might be becoming a little trite before it's even got off the ground. ○

Above **The bar and dining area at Riding House Café has a New York feel.** Left **A view through to the kicthen.**

Roka 37 Charlotte Street, W1T 1RR
020 7580 6464 www.rokarestaurant.com

Launched after its renowned sibling Zuma in Knightsbridge (see page 85), Roka is generally perceived as a less serious offering, but in our view it is much better and we prefer the ambience and interior at Roka. Japan's esteemed Super Potato and Noriyoshi Muramatsu collaborated on the architecture and design. Light floods through the window walls during the day, creating perfect conditions in which to admire the food. An abundance of natural materials, especially timber, combined with pickling jars on shelves, completes the interior design. The principal feature is the central Robata grill, a type of Japanese barbecue. This open kitchen allows guests to observe the chef preparing lamb cutlets with Korean spices, tiger prawns with ginger, yuzu and mirin or scallop skewers with wasabi and shiso. The menu includes sashimi, nigiri and much more. The desserts are particularly good and the presentation is inspired.

Named after Japanese spirit, the Shochu Bar in the basement is sexy and cool. Unlike sake, which is brewed, shochu is distilled to produce an alcohol content of about 25 per cent. The cocktail list has elevated the drink to new heights; expertly devised and perfectly executed, a drink downstairs before or after your meal upstairs is a must. ●

Peter Gordon

When it comes to eating out, I love the tea room and dim sum at Yauatcha, the rice and wasabi tobiko pot at Roka and the Kiwi Burger at GBK restaurants.

Head chef, The Providores

Selfridges Food Hall Selfridges, 400 Oxford St, W1A 2LR
08708 377 377 www.selfridges.com

Every possible gourmet comestible is to be found in Selfridges Food Hall, now the best department store food hall in London. Alongside the great choice of ingredients are some very interesting concessions. The fishmonger is pretty good, and Jack O'Shea, the celebrity Irish butcher, is a huge draw. The range of restaurants and cafés, meanwhile, has been put together by a management team with their finger on the pulse. Mark Hix has opened a restaurant and the choice of other eateries ranges from Obika – specializing in mozzarella in different forms (smoked, grilled etc.) – to Lola's cupcake café. The wine department is also exceptional. ●

Above left **The entance to Roka.** Above **Chefs work in a completely open kitchen at Roka.**

More places to visit in the area

Le Comptoir Libanais
65 Wigmore Street, W1U 1PZ
020 7935 1110 www.lecomptoir.co.uk
Lebanese-style cooking and deli at very affordable prices in a funky modern setting. Lots to like, not least the flavours.

Pied à Terre
34 Charlotte Street, W1T 2NH
020 7636 1178 www.pied-a-terre.co.uk
Two Michelin stars and very fancy: take those who like a bit of showing off.

Royal China Club
40–42 Baker Street, W1U 7AJ
020 7486 3898
www2.royalchinagroup.biz/
Authentic Chinese food from the best exponents of this style of food to be found in the capital. It's also a very flash and shiny setting.

The Sea Shell
49–51 Lisson Grove, London,
NW1 6UH 020 7224 9000
www.seashellrestaurant.co.uk
The world's most Michelin-starred chef, Alain Ducasse, says this is the best battered fish and chips in London.

Villandry
170 Great Portland Street, W1W 5QB
020 7631 3131 www.villandry.com
An all-day café, bistro and food store. Go for the Aspen fries in the bistro: hand-cut chips tossed in Parmesan and white truffle oil. Once you start there's no stopping.

Vinoteca
15 Seymour Place, W1H 5BD
020 7724 7288 www.vinoteca.co.uk
Sister of the original Vinoteca near Smithfield, with cooking that we think may be slightly better. The menu is pleasingly small and the wine list pleasingly long, with plenty available by the glass.

Above **A hearty sandwich from Selfridges Food Hall.**

Mayfair
Piccadilly
St. James's
Westminster

Named after the May Fair that was held in the area that is now Shepherd Market for two weeks every year between 1686 and 1764, Mayfair is now home to the highest concentration of luxury hotels and prestigious retail brands in London. It's also still a very smart residential area, although many of the grand houses have been converted to offices for the wealth management companies, private banks and corporate HQs that have proliferated in the area (earning Curzon Street the sobriquet 'Hedge Fund Alley'). Five-star hotels – the best being The Connaught and Claridge's, both of which have been given a contemporary revamp – have long catered for the rarified habitué, and now they are joined by some great restaurants. The arrival of Scott's on Mount Street has proved a catalyst for change: the fusty galleries and tired old brands on this once rather sleepy but very prestigious street have now given way to exclusive fashion brands such as Marc Jacobs and Balenciaga, giving the nearby New Bond Street and Burlington Arcade a run for their money.

This part of London still retains it aristocratic character, defined by its bespoke Savile Row suits, full-handle umbrellas from Swaine Adeney Brigg on St. James's, shirts from Jermyn Street, tweeds from Cordings and antique guns and rifles from James Purdey & Sons. This is also the heart of British haute cuisine, the required address for any noble wine merchant or gentlemanly cigar shop.

Mayfair is the smartest address in the metropolis. Its solitary Achilles' heel can only be its shortage of the humble (and often most enjoyable) things in life.

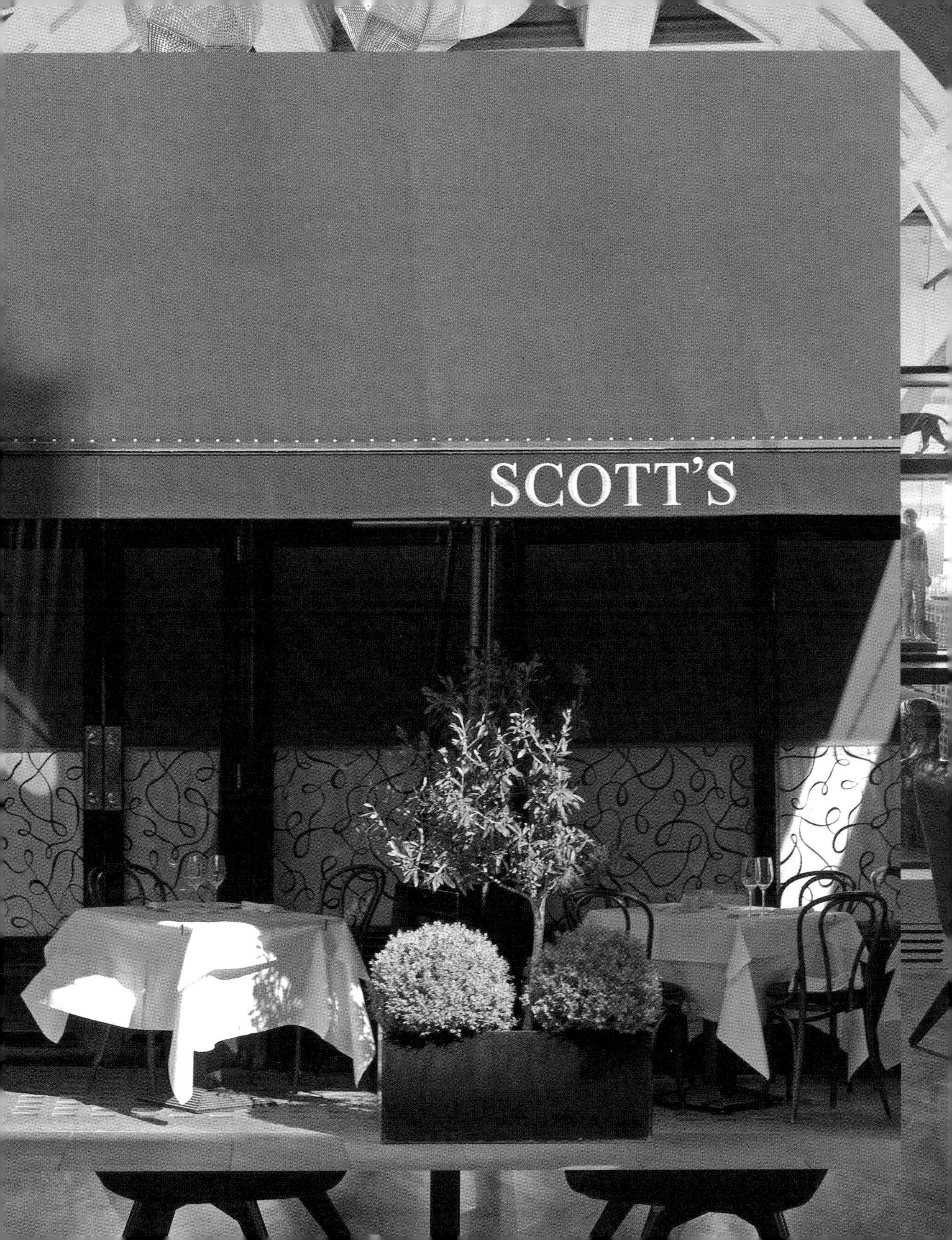
SCOTT'S

Allen's 117 Mount Street, W1K 3LA
020 7499 5831 www.allensofmayfair.co.uk

London's oldest butcher, Allen's has been selling top-grade meats, poultry and game to the 'Mayfair Set' for almost 200 years. This is one of the few places where you can find gulls' eggs during the short May season. The worn octagonal butcher's block in the centre of the shop dominates the space, and unusually very little meat is actually on display: it's best to call ahead and place an order. In 2006 the business was on the brink of bankruptcy, when a commercial butchers from south-east London acquired the company. This change of ownership has brought some positive changes, although some might say it has made it too commercial. ◉

Bellamy's 18–18a Bruton Place, W1J 6LY
020 7491 2727 www.bellamysrestaurant.co.uk

Simple French menus delivered with poise and a certain *je ne sais quoi*.
Incongruously among otherwise humble ingredients, the centrepiece of the menu card is a selection of caviar – a pointer to the old-school society clientele that this restaurant attracts. Owner, Gavin Rankin, was previously involved in various private members' clubs and many of the clientele have followed him. The adjoining shop sells the finest comestibles that the grand homes of Mayfair cannot afford to be without. ◉

Benares 12a Berkeley Square House, Berkeley Square, W1J 6BS
020 7629 8886 www.benaresrestaurant.com

Atul Kochar's subtly spiced Indian recipes are perfectly executed, with a menu that includes a large proportion of premium-catch seafood. Alongside high-quality meats are lobster, bass, scallops and turbot, none of which is ever overwhelmed by the Indian seasonings and accompanying ingredients. While the prestigious Berkeley Square address is a restaurateur's delight, the space has no windows, but despite this the designers have created an attractive series of rooms (though the water feature is a little over the top for us), as well as a chef's table and a sommelier's table. Many top restaurant critics believe that Atul Kochar is the best Indian chef in London. ◉

Above left **Whole beasts hanging in the shop at Allen's.**
Above right **French savoire faire at Bellamy's.**

Tim Hughes

"

My favourite London food shops are St. John's Bakery – they make fantastic bread, have loads different varieties, and personally I think their sourdough and Chelsea buns are amazing; Paxton & Whitfield on Jermyn Street – they pay meticulous attention to detail, and their knowledge arrangement and selection of cheese is unbeatable, and Maison Bertaux in Soho sell pastries to die for.

Chef director, Caprice Holdings

Above left and far right **The marble oyster bar at Bellamy's.** Right **Preparing dessert at Bentley's.**

Bentley's Oyster Bar and Grill 11–15 Swallow Street, W1B 4DG 020 7734 4756 www.bentleys.org

Bentley's is a civilized restaurant serving mainly fish and crustacea, conveniently positioned on a narrow street between Regent Street and Piccadilly. The ground-floor oyster bar menu features a fine selection of bivalves. You can also find really good smoked salmon from Ireland, smoked eel or kippers, fried squid, crubeens (pigs' trotters cooked in traditional Irish fashion), posh fish and chips with mushy peas and tartar sauce good enough to eat on its own, and noble Dover sole. The fish pie is very luxurious, and pricey. Sit at the marble bar and chat with the shuckers, dressed in traditional white coats, while sipping a chilled Chablis grand cru. To finish, the brown sugar meringue with strawberries and Jersey cream is celestial.

The upstairs Grill and Rib Rooms offer a more extensive menu, including both fish and meat. Meat main-course highlights include a mixed grill featuring a pork and sage sausage, sirloin of beef, belly of pork and lamb chops. The grilled West Cork beef with béarnaise and chips is also very tempting. While Bentley's has been trading on this site since 1916, over recent years its reputation became seriously eroded. Richard Corrigan's new energy in the kitchen has saved the restaurant for another generation and brought a calmer influence to the interior design, with an attempt to incorporate a William Morris Arts and Crafts theme.

The outside terrace is also worth a visit on a hot summer's day. ◉

C London 23–5 Davies Street, W1K 3DE
020 7399 0500 www.cipriani.com

When this restaurant opened in 2004 it was called Cipriani, but a High
Court judgment in 2010 forced it to change its name (we're not making
this up). Part of the global Cipriani empire, this is one of those restaurants
that you should make an effort to try just once – although it has to be said
that the true experience is to be found just off the Piazza San Marco in
Venice. (PP) I've visited the London restaurant a couple of times as well
as New York and Hong Kong: all of the dining rooms are very elegant,
and the waiters' gallant white uniforms set the tone to a tee. Remember to
order the beef carpaccio – you will be eating a piece of culinary history. ○

Le Caprice Arlington House, Arlington Street, SW1A 1RJ
020 7629 2239 www.le-caprice.co.uk

Located behind The Ritz (or would it be more germane to say that it is
to the rear of The Wolseley?), Le Caprice is a sister restaurant to The Ivy,
J. Sheekey and Scott's among others in Richard Caring's group of
restaurants. Legendary maître d' Jesus Adorno oversees the unflappable
service, as he has done since the restaurant opened in 1981 (it celebrated
its thirtieth birthday on 1 September 2011).

It is extremely difficult to secure a table during the week, but easier
for Sunday brunch, from 11.30 am to 5 pm. If you go during the week
you must have the salmon fishcakes with buttered spinach and sorrel
sauce; at the weekend it's got to be the brilliant eggs Benedict. ○

Above **Classic
monochrome
interiors at
Le Caprice.**

Cheesecake with Poached Rhubarb

Serves 8

450 g (15 oz) cream cheese
450 ml (3/4 pint) double cream
100 g (3 1/2 oz) caster sugar
seeds from 1 vanilla pod
12 rhubarb stalks, peeled and cut into 1 cm (1/2 inch) lengths
100 ml water
100 g (3 1/2 oz) caster sugar
1 1/2 teaspoons liquid glucose syrup

For the crumble

200 g (7 oz) sugar
200 g (7 oz) butter, at room temperature
200 g (7 oz) plain flour
200 g (7 oz) ground almonds

To make the crumble, put the sugar and softened butter in a bowl and beat until smooth, then add the flour and the ground almonds and beat again until smooth. Pour on to a baking tray and flatten the dough out with your hands to make a sheet 1 cm (1/2 inch) thick. Bake in a preheated oven, 180°C (350°F), Gas Mark 1/4, for 18 minutes, taking it out every 6 minutes to crumble and break up the dough. Leave to cool slightly.

Put the cream cheese, cream, sugar and vanilla seeds in a bowl and whisk for 1–2 minutes by hand or 30 seconds with an electric hand whisk.

Press the cooked crumble evenly into the base of a 23 cm (9 inch) springform cake tin and pour the filling on top. Leave to set in the refrigerator for 2 hours.

Meanwhile, make a syrup by mixing together the water with the sugar and liquid glucose. Put the rhubarb and syrup in a vacuum-sealed bag and boil in water for 3 minutes, then allow to cool. Serve the cheesecake with the poached rhubarb piled on top and juices spooned over.

Cecconi's 5a Burlington Gardens, W1S 3EP
020 7434 1500 www.cecconis.co.uk

If Curzon Street is Hedge Fund Alley, this is the managers' dining room,
especially at breakfast time. As a result, you can also find some very
glamorous ladies hanging out at this easy-on-the-eye setting. The alluring
dining room and bar were designed by Ilse Crawford in partnership with
Nick Jones and his Soho House group: the marble floor and lush green
leather chairs are particular stylish. In the 1980s this was *the* socialite
restaurant, then it lost its way in the 1990s. Now Nick Jones has worked
his magic, and it is again one of the hottest destinations for those with
very deep pockets.

(PP) They make a great negroni cocktail, as you might expect at a
Venetian-inspired restaurant, and I would also rate the excellent lobster
spaghetti. On my last visit, the waiter brought some white truffles to
the table and kept shaving and shaving and shaving. I hope the chef
didn't find out. ●

Martin Williams

My favourite place for breakfast
is Cecconi's – apple juice and
hot chocolate, followed by
eggs Benedict.

Operations director, Gaucho Grill

Above **The
reception desk
at Cecconi's.**

Left **In the kitchens at China Tang.** Right **The beautiful China Tang bar and below it, the equally impressive dining room.**

Left **Special equipment was imported from China for the kitchen and a fierce gas supply was arranged.**

China Tang at The Dorchester Hotel 53 Park Lane, W1K 1QA
020 7629 9988 www.thedorchester.com/china-tang

There are some absolutely horrible places within the Dorchester Hotel (particularly the hideous Bar and The Grill, the worst offenders, both harmful to the eye). China Tang is the arch-opposite and a beacon of good taste: it offers an enchanting blend of chinoiserie and 1930s Art Deco. Having worked closely with Sir David Tang on the development of the Tang Suite at Boundary Hotel and also been fortunate enough to have visited his private residences in Hong Kong, we can say that he is enormously talented in every aspect of life. Whether it is a matter of cultural or social etiquette – as confirmed in his weekly *Financial Times* column, or an interior design or food issue, he is the most informed and learned person you could ever meet. The Cantonese food here is excellent and the Peking duck is essential. They do not use any MSG although, they have been known to use one or two other controversial ingredients (they once offered shark's fin soup), only in their efforts to deliver an authentic experience. ◉

Claridge's Brook Street, W1K 4HR
020 7629 8860 www.claridges.co.uk

(PP) As a former employee of Claridge's (well before Gordon Ramsay), I have a soft spot for the hotel. The hall porters and concierge are peerless: they can get anything the world has to offer and are regularly put to the test. Upstairs, the bedrooms and suites offer some of the most spacious hotel accommodation and the décor is just wonderful (with the glaring exception of the series of bedrooms and suites designed by Diane von Furstenburg). Before you reach the Gordon Ramsay restaurant you could call in on the Art Deco bar, or book a table for afternoon tea in the foyer, under the magnificent Dale Chihuly chandelier. The Art Deco theme continues in the restaurant, with eye-catching three-tier lampshades, etched glass and elements of the original Basil Ionides 1920s clean lines and columns. Thierry Despont's redesign has delivered a lavish yet respectful space. Huge comfortable armchairs, exquisite tableware and enthusiastic staff make the occasion. ○

The English Tea Room at Brown's Hotel Albemarle Street, W1S 4BP
020 7518 4155 www.brownshotel.com/dining/the-english-tea-room/

If you don't fancy The Ritz (and who would?), this is a great and less tourist-oriented place to enjoy a classic and sedate English afternoon tea, maybe with visiting grandparents or mature visiting friends. Comfortable armchairs, pressed linen, silver multi-layer cake stands and ornate teapots, deep carpets, a fire crackling in the background and a pianist on the ivories – it's all very cosseting while you enjoy your finger sandwiches, dainty cakes and pastries, not forgetting the quintessential scones, clotted cream and strawberry jam. And maybe a glass of pink fizz for mother. ○

Fortnum & Mason 181 Piccadilly, W1A 1ER
020 7734 8040 www.fortnumandmason.com

In 1707, William Fortnum and Hugh Mason founded a grocery store that has become an iconic British institution. Fortnum's is probably even more renowned in the eyes of overseas visitors than it is for Londoners. The Scotch egg was invented here in 1851, and in 1886 this was the first place in Britain to sell Heinz baked beans. Today it is grocer to Her Majesty, and is more commonly associated with its loose leaf teas, its confectionery and its amazing collection of hampers, ranging from the picnic variety that are the envy of all at Glyndebourne and Henley to luxury versions at £5,000. In 2007 the store received a revamp and introduced a few new concepts, including the '1707 Wine Bar', where you can order wine from the adjacent wine department and pay a fixed £10 corkage charge. ○

Above and right
**Afternoon tea
and cakes at
Brown's Hotel.**

Soufflé Suissesse

Serves 6

140 g (5 oz) butter
65 g (2¹/₂ oz) flour
700 ml (1 pint plus 3¹/₂ oz) milk
5 egg yolks
1 litre (1³/₄ pints) double cream
6 egg whites
200 g (7 oz) grated Gruyère
or Emmental cheese
salt and freshly ground black pepper

To make the soufflé mixture, melt 65 g (2¹/₂ oz) of the butter in a saucepan set over low heat. Using a small whisk, stir in the flour. Cook gently for 2 or 3 minutes, stirring continuously.

Take the pan off the heat and leave the roux to cool slightly. In another pan, bring the milk to the boil and then pour it over the cooled roux, whisking all the time. Set the pan over high heat and, stirring continuously, bring the mixture to the boil and cook for 3 minutes.

Take the pan off the heat and stir in the egg yolks. Season to taste with salt and pepper. Dot the surface with 1 tablespoon of the butter, cut into small pieces, to prevent a skin from forming. Set aside at room temperature.

Meanwhile, chill 12 round 8 cm (3¹/₂ inch) tartlet tins in the refrigerator or freezer for a few minutes. Remove and immediately grease them generously with softened butter and arrange them on a baking sheet.

To assemble the soufflé, pour the cream into a gratin or Le Creuset dish. Lightly salt the cream, then warm it gently without letting it boil. Beat the egg whites with a pinch of salt until they form stiff peaks. Pour the soufflé mixture into a wide-mouthed bowl. Using a whisk, quickly beat in about one-third of the beaten egg whites, then using a spatula carefully fold in the remainder. Using a tablespoon, heap up the mixture in the tartlet tins to form 12 moulds.

Bake the soufflés in a preheated oven, 200°C (400°F), Gas Mark 6, for 3 minutes, until the tops begin to turn golden. Remove them from the oven and, protecting your hands with a cloth, turn out each soufflé into the dish of warm cream. Sprinkle over the Gruyère or Emmental and return to the oven for 3 minutes.

The soufflé must be taken to the table immediately.

Tom
Aikens

"Le Gavroche is my favourite restaurant for French food – still remains one of the best in London.
Owner, Tom Aikens and Tom's Kitchen

Le Gavroche 43 Upper Brook Street, W1K 7QR
020 7408 0881 www.le-gavroche.co.uk

No restaurant has won more awards than Le Gavroche, and we don't just mean from the Michelin man – although it is worth noting that in 1982 Le Gavroche became the first restaurant in the UK to be awarded three Michelin stars. Most of the awards it receives are voted for by industry peers, as testament to their admiration for the kitchen and front-of-house teams. More to the point, the restaurant is one of the best in London.

First established in Lower Sloane Street in 1967 by brothers Michel and Albert Roux, the restaurant moved to its current location in 1981. When Albert's son, Michel Jr, took over the kitchen in 1991, he subtly modernized the menus and gradually ushered in lighter elements. The rich cheese soufflé recipe (see page 270) is not of the latter variety, however.

Silvano Giraldin, the front-of-house maestro, has also been a major contributor to the restaurant's success. He has been with the Roux brothers since 1971 and is now a director of the company, though over recent years he has stepped back a little.

Another admirable feature of Le Gavroche is the attractively priced all-inclusive lunch menu, including three courses, mineral water, wine, coffee and petits fours. ●

The Greenhouse 27a Hay's Mews, W1X 7RJ
020 7499 3331 www.greenhouserestaurant.co.uk

This is serious fine dining where no expense is spared, and chef Antonin Bonnet has limitless potential. The restaurant's head sommelier appears to have an even bigger budget and more lavish expenditure, however. The Greenhouse has one of most extensive wine lists in the world and in 2005 won the Wine Spectators Grand Award, one of only four restaurants in the world to have done so. ●

Hélène Darroze at The Connaught Carlos Place, W1K 2AL
020 7499 7070

Hélène hails from south-west France where her family are renowned restaurateurs and also produce one of the best Armagnacs on the market, so there is naturally a large selection on display here. Also on display in the restaurant as you enter is a table piled with brilliant butter in large churn-size blocks, alongside cured hams and cheese truckles – an unusual feature for a dining room of this calibre, and something to be applauded. A visit must involve sampling the food from her native Gascony, including duck foie gras followed by Landais chicken.

The old Connaught dining experiences are long gone. This new version may not be to everybody's liking, but it is much invigorated and opens a new chapter in the illustrious history of this once noblest of hotels.

(PP) On my second visit to this restaurant the head sommelier, a confident and passionate young man, gave me a personal tour of the magnificent Connaught cellars, which contain the highest concentration of expensive wines I have ever seen in one place. The Connaught also has a private internal cigar room. A closely guarded secret. ●

Left **Making the soufflé suissesse at Le Gavroche.** Above **Claridge's hotel doormen at work.**

Hibiscus 29 Maddox Street, W1S 2PA
020 7629 2999   www.hibiscusrestaurant.co.uk

This much-admired restaurant appears on the famous World's 50 Best Restaurants list, and it also has two Michelin stars. Founded in Ludlow, Shropshire, by the very experienced chef patron Claude Bosi, the whole operation moved to London in 2007, continuing to trade under the same name and with many of the original staff.

One of the very interesting features of Hibiscus is its wine list, masterminded by Isabelle Legeron MW, generally known as 'that crazy French woman' and one of the leading proponents of the natural wine movement. The list at Hibiscus consists almost exclusively of wines in this category, which is interesting in itself and even more so in this setting. It also has a section devoted to orange wines, which are made like red wines but using only white grapes. The grape skins, pips and stems are macerated in their own juices, and the results are unusual and worth trying.

(PP) I was quite disappointed by my only visit to this restaurant. Lots of friends had told me it was really excellent and I would certainly have a great meal. Sadly I didn't. And my dining companion, who knows a great deal about gastronomy, was even more disappointed, giving the whole experience a meagre 4 out 10. My experience suffered further by comparison with dinner next day at the newly opened Dinner by Heston Blumenthal (see page 69). While everything I tasted at Hibiscus, which included a roasted lobe of foie gras and a saddle of hare, seemed to have less flavour than it really should, at Dinner everything was oozing with it. ○

Hix at The Albermarle Brown's Hotel Albemarle Street, W1S 4BP
020 7518 4004   www.thealbemarlerestaurant.com

This is a very grown-up British dining room, with elegant plaster detailing on the ceiling, wood panelling, agreeable light and very generous space at the table. The room's design is by Olga Polizzi, who with her brother Rocco – who runs Brown's Hotel in which this restaurant is located – is a scion of the Forte family of hoteliers. Mark Hix oversees the British menu, and although it's not as gutsy as his other places, it's still very pleasing and not at all bad for a hotel dining room. The adjoining Donovan Bar, named after the photographer Terence Donovan and lined with his black-and-white photographs, makes a discreet central London meeting point. ○

Ikeda 30 Brook Street, W1K 5DJ 020 7629 2730

(PP) Back in the early 1990s, this was one of the first Japanese restaurants I visited. Within six months of my first visit, Mr Ikeda and I worked together on a special event for the Japanese royal family, plus a memorable wedding attended by a number of British and European royals. The sushi is that good. I don't get the opportunity to visit as often as I would like, but friends tell me it remains a consistently good Japanese restaurant with intrinsically traditional virtues. Ikeda has a great deal to offer, even if you don't fancy sushi, especially if you want a substantial lunch at very reasonable prices. Ask for the *omakase* menu, which translates loosely as 'I'll leave it to the chef to decide'. ○

Simon Wadham

My favourite London café is Inn The Park in St. James's park. It is of a higher standard than many of the cafés you will find around, and of course there are the beautiful views.

Head chef, Rivington Grill

Above **A foot guard from the Welsh Guards in traditional uniform.**
Right **St. James's Park.**

Above left **The Michael Hopkins-designed structure in St. James's Park that houses Oliver Peyton's restaurant.** Below **An apposite message on the staff uniforms at Inn The Park.**

Inn The Park St. James's Park, SW1A 2BJ
020 7451 9999 www.innthepark.co.uk

The royal parks of London are among the capital's greatest assets, and the addition of a restaurant in St. James's Park has increased their value enormously. What was once a dreary park café, with poor-quality ice cream, bad snacks and not much else, has undergone a complete transformation. The architect Michael Hopkins has created a timber building with a turfed roof, with fittings from Tom Dixon, and the whole operation is afforded the careful attentions of restaurateur and television personality Oliver Peyton. The food is the best of British, as befits the location. ◐

Momo Restaurant Familial / Mo Tearoom and Bazaar
25 Heddon Street, W1B 4BH 020 7434 4040 www.momoresto.com

Mourad 'Momo' Mazouz has recreated the Maghreb in a small cul-de-sac off Regent Street. The cuisine and culture of this atmospheric collection of North African nations are combined here with beautiful staff, electro world music and souk-like interiors. Endless artefacts, antiquities and objects collide with a lively, sometimes loud, evening crowd to create an eclectic ambience. The menu displays the fruits of energetic research, with a broad and judiciously applied range of herbs and spices. It may not be strictly authentic, but some would say it is all the better for that, as it benefits from superior ingredients.

Next door, the Mo Tearoom and Bazaar is always busy with fashionistas sucking on shisha pipes or tucking into *kemia* (Arab tapas). ◐

Mount Street Deli 100 Mount Street, W1K 2TG
020 7499 6843 www.themountstreetdeli.co.uk

If you can't get a table at one of Richard Caring's group of eternally modish restaurants, then you can taste a little of what you are missing at his deli. The Mount Street Deli stocks shepherd's pie from The Ivy, J.Sheekey's fish pie, Mark's Club Scotch eggs, Annabel's club chocolate cake and Scott's carrot cake. Mr Caring is rapidly becoming the Blofeld of the food world, aiming at nothing less than world domination. Whatever next? ●

Murano 20 Queen Street, W1J 5PP
020 7495 1127 www.muranolondon.com

Angela Hartnett has spent much of her career working with Gordon Ramsay, and it has often been said that she was the star of a nebulous bunch. Since leaving the GR group Angela's reputation has grown, and while the food is not a million miles from what you'd expect (it certainly doesn't shout Italy) it was perfectly executed and well-balanced. Plus the service was friendly and perceptive. The head sommelier, Marc-Andréa Levy, is one of the restaurant's most impressive assets: I dined with two friends and we each had different foods. Despite this challenge, Marc-Andréa matched each dish with a different wine and all of the wines were a perfect match. ●

Nobu 19 Old Park Lane, W1K 1LB 020 447 4747

This is the restaurant that put black cod on the culinary map. The illustrious Nobu Matsuhisa opened the first European branch of his now global empire on the first floor of the sophisticated Metropolitan Hotel in 1997, since when it has been a perpetual success. (PP) I remember visiting in the early days when the staff were exclusively models dressed in designer clothes – it was revolutionary. Almost ten years on it's still a challenge to secure a table, and the paparazzi are regularly camped out on the doorstep. The interior design is quite dry (they call it minimalist), and don't be swayed by the hype surrounding tables with 'views over Hyde Park': firstly it's actually a view over the traffic of Park Lane, and secondly it's much better to sit at the sushi bar or the chef's table at the far end of the restaurant. Here you are away from the noise and posturing of the main restaurant – where so many of the diners spend the evening checking out their fellow diners – and you get a chance to watch the sushi masters at work. ●

Nobu Berkeley St 15 Berkeley Street, W1J 8DY
020 7290 9222 www.noburestaurants.com/

After a few visits to this second London restaurant, it's clear why the Nobu group has grown so rapidly. The restaurants are money machines (although curiously the Canary Wharf branch was not a success and closed in 2008). This site seats 200 people and is always packed, with tables being turned many times over. The menu and drinks are not exactly inexpensive, so it's very easy to spend a lot, but they are still very good value for money. The quality of service, style, menu and quality of the food are second to none in this category of restaurant. This restaurant also has a large bar, with no windows but very good views. And the martinis are seriously good. ●

Above **The Mount Street Deli counter, and right, they also serve breakfast and lunch.**

La Petite Maison 53–54 Brook's Mews, W1K 4EG

020 7495 4774 www.lpmlondon.co.uk

Beautiful tomatoes, artichokes, peppers, baby courgettes, aubergines, olives and their oil, soft herbes de Provence, tapenade and pissaladière all speak of the brilliant cuisine of Nice and its region. The full range of Mediterranean seafood is also available at this charming dining room, and whole roast Black Leg chicken with foie gras is another highlight (cooked to order, so be sure to let your waiter know the moment you are seated). ○

Pollen Street Social 8 Pollen Street, W1S 1NQ

020 7290 7600 www.pollenstreetsocial.com

This is not generally our style of restaurant, but some of the food is very good. And the launch was one of the most hyped of 2011. Its quirks, twists and gimmicks can be intensely annoying, but underneath them all lies the good intention of providing an interesting meal experience. The 'deconstructed' (chef-speak for the bastardization of a classic dish) English breakfast served in a martini glass seems like a copy of the Caesar salad that chef Jason Atherton served at Maze, his previous restaurant. Although intensely annoying, it does involve a great deal of technique and skill. Jason is renowned as the first British chef to work at El Bulli, the high temple of molecular gastronomy in Roses on the Costa Brava, and this is his latest venture without his former partner Gordon Ramsay. The interior is pleasingly simple, with some interesting details, though it can get a little loud. Jason also claims to have created London's first dessert bar, seating just six. Some influential people have suggested that this restaurant will go on to be one of the best in London. We don't agree, but perhaps you should judge for yourself. ○

Quaglino's 16 Bury Street, SW1Y 6AJ

020 7930 6767 www.quaglinos-restaurant.co.uk

Quaglino's opened on Valentine's Day 1993, an incarnation loosely based on the earlier version opened in 1929 by Giovanni Quaglino, combined with the scale of La Coupole in Paris and the spirit of other famous Parisian brasseries. The 1993 opening sent shockwaves across London: this was the first of a new breed of restaurant, on a scale that eclipsed anything London had seen before. Quaglino's was the most sought-after restaurant in London when it opened, and still regularly manages to thrill almost 500 people on a Saturday night. Along the way it seemed to become *de rigueur* to pinch one of its famous ashtrays. Now managed by a company called D&D London, Quaglino's is trying to regain some of its past glamour. ○

Right **The legendary Quaglino's ashtray, now owned by most of the population of London.**

The Ritz 150 Piccadilly, W1J 9BR
020 7493 8181   www.theritzlondon.com

'Gentlemen are required to wear a jacket and tie … jeans and sport shoes are not permitted': a few short words that tell you everything you need to know about The Ritz.

The restaurant is a magnificently regal dining room with furnishings reminiscent of the Palace of Versailles. The food is grand-palace-style cooking by John Williams, a veteran of Claridge's and the Savoy Group. Service is by would-be footmen. The Palm Court is eternally popular for afternoon tea, so you need to book months in advance. (PP) Before touring the restaurants of Russia, I would have said that The Ritz restaurant is one of the most impressive in the world – but that was before I saw Turandot in Moscow, a £50 million restoration masterpiece. ○

Royal Academy of Arts Burlington House, W1J 0BD
020 7300 8000   www.royalacademy.org.uk

The Royal Academy of Arts is one of London's discreet treasures. Founded in 1768 by George III, with 34 founding members including Sir Joshua Reynolds, it mounts a range of important exhibitions. In 1997 it brought Charles Saatchi to prominence with his *Sensation* exhibition, introducing the likes of Tracey Emin and Damien Hirst. Academicians include sculptors, painters, engravers, printmakers and – importantly – architects. The shows are always interesting, including the famously mixed bag Summer Exhibition, which displays the work of artists of distinguished merit.

The standard of in-house dining and grazing at all of London's major museums and galleries is now much higher than it has ever been. In recent years, Oliver Peyton, a seasoned restaurateur, has moved to monopolize the restaurants at several of these venerable institutions, including the National Gallery and the Wallace Collection. With designer Tom Dixon, Mr Peyton has created an attractive dining room. The food is perfectly decent, and we recommend a visit on a Friday when the gallery remains open until quite late in the evening: an ideal end to the working week. ○

Left and above
The Tom Dixon-designed interior of the Royal Academy restaurant, managed by Oliver Peyton.
Right **Black truffle, about to be shaved.**

Left and right
Making fresh pasta ravioli.

Fillet of Cod with Padrón Peppers and Chorizo

Serves 4

25 ml (1 fl oz) olive oil
2 shallots, diced
1 medium-hot red chilli, finely chopped
100 g (3½ oz) white haricot beans, soaked overnight (or fresh coco beans in season)
25 ml (1 fl oz) white wine
500 ml (17 fl oz) chicken stock
4 x 175 g (6 oz) cod fillets
50 g (2 oz) Padrón peppers (available at some markets and high-quality greengrocers)
75 g (3 oz) cooked chorizo, sliced into 1 cm (½ inch) pieces
20 g (¾ oz) parsley, chopped
1 garlic clove, crushed (optional)
salt and freshly ground black pepper

Heat a third of the olive oil in a large saucepan, add the diced shallots and chilli and cook over a medium heat, being careful not to burn. Drain the haricot beans, add to the pan and sweat down. Season with salt and pepper.

Add the white wine and reduce, then add the chicken stock and cook over a low heat for 45 minutes or until the beans are cooked. Remove from the heat and keep in a warm place.

Heat a non-stick frying pan and add another third of the olive oil. Season the cod fillets with salt and pepper, and place skin-side down in the pan. Cook until the skin is nice and crispy and the flesh has turned white. Turn the cod over and cook for a further 2 minutes.

Put the whole Padrón peppers in a medium saucepan with the remaining olive oil and cook gently until they start to wilt. Add the chorizo to the pan along with the chopped parsley and the garlic (if desired). Cook until the chorizo is heated through.

When ready to serve, spoon the cooked beans on to the middle of warmed serving plates. Sit the cod on top of the beans and pour over the Padrón peppers and chorizo.

Razor Clams with Wild Boar Sausage

Serves 4

1 kg (2 lb) live razor clams (available from good fishmongers)
½ glass white wine
2 sprigs of thyme
3 garlic cloves, peeled and roughly chopped
1 teaspoon salt
1 tablespoon chopped parsley, stalks reserved
60 ml (2½ fl oz) olive oil
125 g (4 oz) cooked wild boar sausages, sliced
50 g (2 oz) butter
salt and freshly ground black pepper

Wash the razor clams in cold running water for 10 minutes. Put them into a large saucepan with the white wine, thyme, garlic, salt and reserved parsley stalks, cover with a lid and cook over a high heat for a few minutes, giving the occasional stir, until the shells open. If any shells do not open, remove and discard. Drain in a colander and leave to cool.

Carefully remove the clams from the shells, keeping the shells intact. Cut away the dark-looking sack and discard. Cut each clam into 4 or 5 pieces and put these carefully back in their shells. Lay the clams in their shells on a baking tray and warm in a low oven.

Heat the olive oil in a pan and add the cooked wild boar sausages on a low heat for 1–2 minutes to heat through. Add the butter and chopped parsley, and season lightly with salt and pepper.

Serve the clams on warmed serving plates and spoon the wild boar sausage mixture over.

Above **Scott's is one of the most in-demand restaurants in London.** Left **The outside dining terrace at Scott's.**

Scott's 20 Mount Street, W1K 2HE
020 7495 7309 www.scotts-restaurant.com

This restaurant borders on perfection. It's great for lunch or dinner, superb for celeb spotting or discreet meetings, fantastic for oysters and seafood. The menu is a joy, and the service is always immaculate. The interior looks ravishing and is also comfortable, the art is engaging, the cocktails spot on and the wine list caters to all tastes. In fact just about everything is present and correct. This could well be the definitive model for success, in every way. We rather like the place, as you may have guessed. ●

Sketch Lecture Room and Library 9 Conduit Street, W1S 2XG
020 7659 4500 www.sketch.uk.com

No other restaurant in London polarizes views like Sketch. You either love it or hate it. Generally, though, everybody has enormous respect for the project's ambition and creativity. The place is full to bursting with ideas, idiosyncrasies and novelty – sometimes a little too much so. The brainchild of Mourad (Momo) Mazouz, who is also responsible for the equally admirable Momo restaurant (see page 273), this project is brave and daring and regularly changes its themes and directions, bringing together the avant-garde from the worlds of art, music, design and food. Pierre Gagnaire, another hugely creative figure, oversees all of the menus, and his experimental food is at its best in the Lecture Room and Library (also known as London's most expensive restaurant). ●

Left **The Umu Chu-toro salad with quail's eggs.** Right **Preparing maki rolls at Umu.**

280

The Square 6–10 Bruton Street, W1J 6PU

020 7495 7100 www.squarerestaurant.com

The Square is consistently one of the most highly praised restaurants in London. It has two well-deserved Michelin stars and Philip Howard, the chef patron, is one of the best in the business. The chefs that we know unanimously respect Philip Howard's cooking (he is truly a chefs's chef), the menu at The Square and the restaurants unfaltering professionalism. The wine list and sommeliers should also be mentioned as excellent. ○

Umu 14–16 Bruton Place, W1J 6LX

020 7499 8881 www.umurestaurant.com

This is London's only Kyoto restaurant, serving exquisite food and stocking the largest sake collection in the capital. When the restaurant opened in 2004, its £200 Kaiseki menu attracted some negative publicity, which sadly seemed to have an impact on the number of diners. We visited the restaurant in the early months of it opening and found it comparatively expensive. However, when you learn that the water the chef uses to make tofu is specially flown in from Kyoto, that the range of fish is unrivalled and that many other traditional ingredients are also imported exclusively for Umu, you begin to understand how the management justifies the high prices, and why Umu cannot be compared with any other Japanese restaurant. The same excellent high standards still prevail today, while the prices seem to be more reasonable. ○

Right **Once a common sight, a gentleman in a bowler hat, a chalk-stripe suit and a long umbrella, is now a rarity, even in Mayfair.**

The Wolseley 160 Piccadilly, W1J 9EB
020 7499 6996 www.thewolseley.com

Behind the listed façade and past the doorman, you enter a world of black, soft gold and brass, Japanese lacquer and large-scale but restrained chandeliers. The clientele is star-studded, and seating positions are all important. The inner horseshoe is reserved for playwrights, knights of the realm, literary agents, leading ladies and the London 'faces' one should immediately recognize. The Wolseley calls itself a Grand Café-Restaurant, and follows the tradition of the great European (chiefly Parisian and Viennese) cafés of the last century. One of its key characteristics is that it is open all day every day, which has led to every other restaurateur wanting to do the same. Unlike the others, The Wolseley addresses the matter lavishly, with an extensive selection of menus to choose from: a chef's nightmare, but a diner's dream. You can have anything here, from an all-day menu, lunch, dinner and afternoon tea to hot breakfasts, grills and crustacea.

The choice offered on each page of the huge *carte* is carefully thought through, and the pricing is fair. This is not gourmet food, but that is not to detract from its excellence. Dishes range from French coq au vin or a fish stew to British summer pudding or European Wiener schnitzel, via hamburgers, Jewish chopped liver or chicken soup with dumplings, and a hint of Italian. It all adds up to a résumé of the best of European cooking, based on what people want to eat (and not what the chef wants to serve). ◗

More places to visit in the area

◯ Automat
33 Dover Street, W1S 4NF
020 7499 3033 www.automat-london.com
A notable American brasserie serving New York strip steaks, macaroni and cheese, Caesar salad, chicken noodle soup and great burgers, all washed down with a bloody Mary at weekend brunch.

◯ Boudin Blanc
5 Trebeck Street, W1J 7LT
020 7499 3292 www.boudinblanc.co.uk
At least two of our friends say this is their favourite restaurant in London.

◯ Corrigan's
28 Upper Grosvenor Street, W1K 7EH
020 7499 9943
www.corrigansmayfair.com
Richard Corrigan's flagship dining room.

◯ Hakkasan
17 Bruton Street, W1J 6QB
020 7907 1888 www.hakkasan.com
With this sister to the original in Hanway Place in Fitzrovia, the Hakkasan brand has launched in a location that is probably more suited to its expensive modern Chinoiserie style. This place is great for celebrity spotting, if that's your thing. The menu is massive, from abalone and ostrich to dim sum and sweet and sour pork. Ask the waiter to recommend the house specialities and

you will have a great meal. The wine list at both London Hakkasans should not be underestimated: great care and attention has been given to the selection, and the choice by the glass is ideal. They also make a great martini.

◯ Maze Grill
10–13 Grosvenor Square, W1K 6JP
020 7495 2211
www.gordonramsay.com/mazegrill
A Gordon Ramsay-owned upmarket grill restaurant with grass-fed, grain-fed, corn-fed and Wagyu beef, and much more. The grilled fish and several other items on the menu are also very good.

◯ Ristorante Semplice
9–10 Blenheim Street, W1S 1LJ
020 7495 1509
www.ristorantesemplice.com
Don't let the name mislead you, this is a very chi-chi Italian restaurant. The chef, Marco Torri, has an exceptional CV.

◯ Rose Bakery
Dover Street Market,
17–18 Dover Street, W1S 4LT
Essential information for all fashionistas: head for the fourth floor of the Dover Street Market for a pit stop with exquisite cakes, baked items, salads and soups, plus great coffee. If you're in Paris, search out the cafés in Montmartre and the Marais.

Above **Outside The Wolseley on Piccadilly.**

Southwark

The ancient borough of Southwark may be divided roughly into three separate areas on the south side of the Thames, opposite the City.

Until the early 1990s, Shad Thames, to the east of Tower Bridge, consisted largely of derelict warehouses that had once been used to store the tea and spices shipped into the Port of London. The largest of these was Butlers Wharf, which was to form the centrepiece of Terence Conran's 1980's redevelopment of the area. At the time, many people thought he was mad to even think of opening restaurants, cafés and bars here – but they have been obliged to eat their words. Evocative cobbled streets, warehouse-to-warehouse bridges and high-level walkways make this a highly atmospheric area that is regularly used for photo shoots and filmmaking.

The Borough has been known by this name since 1550, to distinguish it from the City. The undisputed showpiece here is Borough Market. Now recognized throughout the world, the country's best-known fine foods market is an unmissable destination for foodies and visitors alike.

The third area is Bankside, inextricably linked with Sir Giles Gilbert Scott's power station, which since 2000 has housed Tate Modern. Nearby are numerous stellar attractions from the worlds of culture and the arts, including Shakespeare's Globe Theatre, the Hayward Gallery, the IMAX cinema, the Oxo Tower and the Royal Festival Hall, to name just a few. In the future, the vertiginous glass-sheathed edifice known as The Shard will shadow over the entire area. Designed by star architect Renzo Piano, this 72-storey building will be Europe's tallest. Love it or hate it, this impressive structure is destined to become as synonymous with London as jellied eels.

Anchor & Hope 36 The Cut, SE1 8LP
020 7928 9898

Unprepossessing portals lead here to some of the best-tasting food in London – just don't expect comfortable surroundings or fawning service. The no-reservations policy means there is sometimes a delay before you are seated, and you often have to share a table with other diners in the rather poky and ear-splittingly noisy dining room. Service is relaxed, but once you get to know the staff perspicacious recommendations are sure to follow.

The menu focuses on earthy and robust flavours and excellent ingredients, cooked with skill but without unnecessary garniture. The dish descriptions may be laconic, but you can be assured of first-class provenance. Expect hearty British favourites, with the occasional French, Spanish or Italian influence. The sharing dishes and large cuts of meat for two, three or four are perfect for this type of setting. Go with friends, maybe after a performance at the Old Vic or the Young Vic, ignore the place's imperfections and just tuck in to some really gutsy food. ○

Baltic 74 Blackfriars Road, SE1 8HA
020 7928 1111 www.balticrestaurant.co.uk

Baltic offers an impressive selection of eastern European cuisines, with a menu that travels through Hungary, Siberia, Poland, Ukraine and Russia. These are not nations generally known for their food, but at Baltic you can enjoy some fine examples of their best-tasting dishes. You can also enjoy great blinis served with smoked fish, marinated herrings, and aubergine or keta caviar.

As you pass the busy bar, which serves one of the largest vodka selections in London, you enter a larger dining room with a high-vaulted glass atrium with exposed beams and a wooden truss ceiling. Simple white-painted walls and interesting art, as here, seem to have become the trademark of most stylish restaurants that serve well-researched foods.

Sunday evenings (always a difficult night for restaurants) are jolly affairs, with background music from professional jazz musicians. ○

Above left **Whole roast Sasso chicken and Caesar salad at Anchor & Hope.**
Above and right **Baltic restaurant.**

Right **Yorkshire veal
'saltimbocca' from
Anchor & Hope.**

Far left **The elevated position above the Design Museum and overlooking the Thames.**
Left **Jeremy Lee, centre.** Above and right **Thonet bentwood chairs at Blueprint Café.**

Blueprint Café 28d Shad Thames, SE1 2YD
020 7378 7031 www.blueprintcafe.co.uk

Blueprint Café's elevated position atop the Design Museum on Shad Thames offers panoramic views over Tower Bridge, The Gherkin, Heron Tower and Tower 42 (and many more skyscrapers to come) to the north, and the vertiginous towers of Canary Wharf to the east. This panorama can all look quite magical by night, if slightly less inspiring and more an expression of corporate ambition by day. On this busy stretch of the Thames, river traffic provides further fascination. Sebastian Conran has thoughtfully designed miniature Blueprint binoculars for each of the tables, so that diners can inspect the urban topography in more focused detail.

While the views are attention-grabbing, most people visit for the food and to enjoy the company of charismatic Jeremy Lee. Blueprint has recently celebrated its 21st birthday, and for over 15 of those years Dundonian Jeremy Lee has been the head chef. As a graduate of the Simon Hopkinson school of gastronomy and having worked with Alistair Little, Jeremy creates food that is intensely seasonal and the embodiment of modern classic cuisine. Drawing influences from Elizabeth David, Jane Grigson and Claudia Roden, the twice-daily changing menu captures the best of European regional cooking while also referencing his native Scotland.

Jeremy is passionate in his support for the food artisans, farmers and fishermen who produce the best-quality ingredients. Often (to the consternation of the company's accountants) Jeremy's menus are dictated entirely by what's seasonal and comes through the kitchen door. Thanks to the excellent relationship that he enjoys with all of his suppliers, deliveries might include rare-breed beasts or whole turbot; his loyal band of regular supporters benefit from this, generally at very reasonable prices thanks to Jeremy's ability to recognize the ingredients' potential and their many and diverse applications.

To get down to specifics, the smoked eel sandwich with horseradish and red onion pickle has recently been a regular on the menu, and although the description sits slightly oddly with the other starters, the dish is delicious. Jeremy's pies are also to be celebrated, particularly his rabbit pie in spring and game pie in season, and his St. Emilion au chocolat sets the benchmark for all other chefs.

With such great views and imaginative cooking, the room has been kept deliberately simple, although it has just had a little spruce-up as part of the birthday celebrations. White walls, a blond-wood floor, Thonet bentwood bistro chairs, linen-free tables, David Mellor cutlery and a few judiciously chosen pieces of wall art – that's all it needs.

A recent initiative from the company that owns the restaurant has introduced a few renowned fine wines at lower than normal mark-ups. This current promotion offers a decent Meursault and a Gevrey Chambertin for a combined price of less than £100.

So, lots to like about this very distinctive restaurant, which comes with our enthusiastic recommendation. ●

Lamb and Asparagus

This is a very fine dish of food to serve heaped on a big plate.

Serves 6

For the lamb

a boned leg of lamb weighing 2 kg (4 lb), butterflied
1–2 sprigs of thyme, leaves picked
1–2 sprigs of marjoram or oregano, leaves picked
juice of 1 lemon
olive oil
sea salt and freshly ground black pepper

For the asparagus

24–30 spears best asparagus (or more), peeled
small bowl cooked and shelled broad beans
small bunch of mint
small bunch of flat leaf parsley
juice of 1 lemon

For the green sauce

12 best anchovy fillets
2 garlic cloves, peeled and roughly chopped
1 tablespoon capers, rinsed well
6 tablespoons olive oil
2 heaped soup spoons chopped parsley

To serve

several bunches of watercress

Heat a heavy cast iron grill pan over a modest flame (a fierce heat will cook the fat too quickly). Liberally salt the fat side of the lamb and lay it on the grill. Grind a heap of pepper over the meat side, followed by a good application of salt. Let it cook at a friendly sizzle (smoke, flame and general bluster are to be discouraged). After half an hour so, turn the meat with great care. After a further 15 or 20 minutes, the meat should be checked fairly regularly to see if it is cooked to your liking by inserting a metal skewer.

When the meat has finished cooking, sit the lamb in a handsome dish and strew with the thyme and marjoram or oregano leaves. Squeeze the lemon over the joint then follow with the olive oil. Cover with foil and keep warm, letting it sit for at least 45 minutes.

Cook the asparagus for a few minutes in plenty of boiling salted water. Cool lightly under cold water and drain thoroughly.

To make the green sauce, pound the anchovies and garlic in a bowl, then add the capers, olive oil and parsley. Pour into a pretty bowl and set aside.

When all is ready, carve the leg into thin slices. Toss the asparagus and broad beans together with lemon juice and olive oil, salt and pepper. Strew watercress over a handsome dish. Lay the asparagus on top, then the slices of lamb. Pour over any lamb juices and serve with the green sauce served seperately.

Sea Bass and Peas

There is a delightful modesty to this dish (though sadly not to its price): a perfect foil to the superb quality of the ingredients that makes this dish so fresh.

Serves 4

4 fillets of sea bass, each about 175 g (6 oz)
8 small handfuls, roughly 750 g (1 ½ lb), freshest peas in their pod
100 g (3½ oz) unsalted butter
a large handful of mint, leaves coarsely chopped
1 lemon
sea salt and freshly ground black pepper

Pod the peas and cook in boiling water until tender.

Slice the sea bass fillets and lay them in a wide cast-iron baking dish. Add enough cold water to just cover the fish. Dot with the butter, then add salt and pepper to season. Bring this to a simmer on the stove, then transfer to a preheated oven, 200°C (400°F), Gas Mark 6, for 10 minutes until just cooked.

Remove the dish from the oven, and check the fish is cooked – it should flake easily. Drain the peas in a sieve, return to their pot then add mint and lemon juice and shake the pan gently to mix. Pour these over the sea bass, shake once or twice to settle, then eat without delay.

Borough Market 8 Southwark Street, SE1 1TL
020 7407 1002 www.boroughmarket.org.uk

Over 10,000 visitors flock to Borough Market every weekend to enjoy one of the best food experiences in the country, if not the world. Not only is the food and drink selection excellent, the feel-good factor is palpable seeing small artisan producers in such atmospheric surroundings.

Historically focused around a wholesale fruit and vegetable market, the weekend fine-foods market has over 70 stalls. Between them these offer delights ranging from olive oils, herbs, spices and dried fruits and patisserie to regional British dairy products and the best fish, shellfish, aged beef, rare-breed pork and game birds. All manner of lovingly prepared foods are to be found here. Many stalls sell only one product, such as Isle of Wight tomatoes or single cheeses.

As you stroll along the cramped and crowded walkways, you might find yourself bumping into a whole roe or buck deer, straight from the fields and hanging on a railing awaiting the knife. Pheasants in full plumage, huge monkfish, mounds of oysters, truckles of cheese: all these and much more are to be found at Borough Market in a very raw and tempting state.

The market also makes a great brunch or lunch destination, with plenty of excellent stalls offering real meat burgers, lamb koftas and proper pizza slices, or you can simply gorge on the many free tasters on offer.

As Saturdays have now become so busy, more and more traders now operate earlier in the week, when many Londoners now prefer to go. ◉

Butlers Wharf Chop House
The Butlers Wharf Building, 36e Shad Thames, SE1 2YE
020 7403 3403 www.chophouse-restaurant.co.uk

Reminiscent of a cricket pavilion or boat shed, the Chop House sports walls, floors and a slatted ceiling of English oak. With heavy timber furniture, and zinc and marble tops, it looks the same today as when it opened over a decade ago, and we hope it will look the same for many years to come.

The cooking is true best of British. Steak and kidney pudding is a signature dish, alongside fish and chips with mushy peas. The choice of meats from the charcoal grill ranges from Barnsley chop to a veal T-bone or porterhouse steak, all served with chips or mashed potatoes, bone marrow, watercress and a choice of sauces. Follow your meal with a hefty English pudding or large plate of British cheeses and oatcakes. A good selection of English wines is available, alongside an extensive list from the Old World and a fine range of eccentrically named English ales.

The outside tables are particularly romantic on a summer's evening. ◉

Above **Borough Market is located under the railway viaducts.**

Above and right **Everything from fresh fish to chorizo burgers can be found at Borough Market.**

Left **Baked goods from De Gustibus.**

Left **The Garrison is a well-managed neighbourhood pub.**

De Gustibus 4 Southwark Street, SE1 1TQ
020 7407 3625 www.degustibus.co.uk

An excellent artisan bakery on the edge of Borough Market, De Gustibus is open all week and also has a stall within the market selling home-made breads, from Mediterranean ciabatta and foccacia to San Francisco sourdough and bagels. ◉

The Garrison 99–101 Bermondsey Street, SE1 3XB
020 7089 9355 www.thegarrison.co.uk

A lovely neighbourhood public house with a menu that outdoes most other attempts at gastropub grub. The prices are competitive and the French-bistro-meets-American-diner dishes are prepared with some skill. The space is decorated in an eclectic fashion with mostly reclaimed and intentionally distressed furniture, sensitively juxtaposed with a few modern pieces. The slightly raised seating booth overlooks the kitchen and provides a cosy spot for a weekend brunch.

The basement houses a mini-cinema, available for private hire and ideal for birthdays. ◉

Maltby Street SE1 3PA
www.maltbystreet.com

Visitors here will feel that they are in at the start of something important. Frustrated by the high rents and general direction that nearby Borough Market is adopting, a breakaway group has formed a collective trading under the Maltby Street banner. The layout isn't obvious, or not yet at least, with the traders spread between the railway arches. Check out the website and take a street map, as the various outlets are not adjacent to each other and may be located on different sides of the tracks.

One of the stars of this enterprise is Booth's, the most acclaimed fruit and vegetable retailer in London, located on Druid Street. ◉

Monmouth Coffee Company 2 Park Street, SE1 9AB
020 7645 3585 www.monmouthcoffee.co.uk

Southwark has two branches of this business that is ultra-serious in its pursuit of excellent coffee. The Park Street coffee shop, adjacent to Borough Market, has lovely pastries and provides an ideal meeting point before setting off to explore the market, or a haven to which to repair after the onslaught. The second branch, part of the Maltby Street market (see above), includes the roastery and is for the eager bean aficionado. There is also a shop on Monmouth Street in Covent Garden. ◉

Right **Monmouth Coffee Shop at Park Street.**

Mrs King's Pork Pies Borough Market, SE1 1TL
Thursdays 9 am–5 pm, Fridays 9am–6 pm, Saturdays 8 am–5 pm
www.mrskingsporkpies.co.uk

It was in 1853 that Elizabeth King set up her family business in the village of Cotgrave, at the heart of Melton Mowbray country. The trio of brothers who have owned Mrs King's since the 1980s continue to champion her original recipes, and these authentic pies have now attained virtually cult status among the pie-lovers of London.

The meat comes only from the shoulder of pigs fed on whey from the nearby Stilton dairies, and the hot-water crust is formed without the assistance of a tin. Everything is handmade, and the jelly is derived from boiled-down trotters (the heads and spleen are no longer used for jelly since the BSE crisis of the late 1990s – much to the disappointment of Ian Hartland, who mans the market stall each week).

In 2008, Melton Mowbray pork pies were awarded Protected Geographical Indication, which means that only pie-makers who are situated within the designated area and who use the specified techniques can call their pies Melton Mowbray. Mrs King's now also offers a few variations on the original recipes, but our favourite is the simple pork pie, with its peppery back note, especially as part of a ploughman's lunch or partnered by good English ale.

You can also buy Mrs King's pies from Selfridges (see page 258). ●

Neal's Yard Dairy 6 Park Street, Borough Market, SE1 9AB
020 7367 0799   www.nealsyarddairy.co.uk

Quite simply the best place in London to buy British cheeses, this shop is a retail experience of considerable note where you can be assured of peerless cheese in perfect condition. The original shop opened in Covent Garden in the 1980s, and when the Borough warehouse shop opened in 1996 the company was catapulted to a position of pre-eminence in the cheese world. Randolph Hodgson has been largely responsible for this, and his name is now synonymous with the making and maturing of fine British cheese.

Keen's, Montgomery's, Isle of Mull, Westcombe and Daylesford seem to be the most popular Cheddar styles. The wealth of other cheeses – hard, soft, blue and washed rind, made from cows', goats' and sheep's milk – comes from 70 cheesemakers in Britain and Ireland. Neal's Yard also operates a burgeoning wholesale arm and a worldwide mail-order service. They also sell a few other dairy and creamery offerings, such as good butter, cream, crème fraîche, eggs and milk. During winter they sometimes have a raclette stand outside the shop for an Alpine-style cheese indulgence. ●

Randolph Hodgson

"

My favourite restaurants include Clarke's (Sally Clarke was one of my first restaurant customers) and I like Anchor & Hope and St. John for their no-nonsense approach and gutsy cooking.

Owner, Neal's Yard Dairy

Top left **Mrs King's pork pies at Borough Market.** Above **Truckles of cheese at Neal's Yard Dairy.**

Le Pont de la Tour

The Butlers Wharf Building, 36d Shad Thames, SE1 2YE
020 7403 8403   www.lepontdelatour.co.uk

The South Bank is now blessed with many excellent restaurants, and one of the first of these was Le Pont de la Tour. In the 1980s, when Terence Conran was masterminding the Shad Thames redevelopment and turning derelict warehouses into cool riverside apartments, it was Le Pont de la Tour – with its bar, grill, deli, bakery, wine shop and 'posh' French brasserie – that lay at the heart of this transformation, the first Conran gastrodrome.

The bar and grill serves plateaux de fruits de mer arranged on a three-tier stand. The dustbin-lid-sized trays of oysters, lobster, cherrystone clams, Dorset crab, langoustines, mussels, cockles, winkles and whelks are all set on ice and served with shallot vinegar, a large lemon and mayonnaise. Simple grills and salads are also served, and a pianist adds to the mood in the evenings.

The main restaurant, with its understated luxury, is reminiscent of the dining room on an elegant ocean liner. The menu tries hard to impress – perhaps too hard – with a roll-call of top-end ingredients, from caviar and foie gras to lobster and Dover sole.

Most people know Le Pont because of its outside dining terrace, one of the best al fresco dining spots in London. Open for almost six months of the year, thanks to extensive awnings and outdoor heat lamps, it affords tremendous views of Tower Bridge and the river traffic, as well as of the endless streams of people strolling along the river, like an urban version of the Promenade des Anglais.

The adjoining wine shop offers a vast collection of the finest wines and rare *grand crus*, in addition to a small tasting table where private events can be arranged. The Salon Privé features a large map of Burgundy etched on to the window, with poster-sized framed labels from the legendary châteaux of the region. The Foodstore supplies a range of bakery breads, cured meats, fresh fish and French cheeses as well as takeaway meals. **○**

Roast   The Floral Hall, Borough Market, Stoney Street, SE1 1TL
0845 034 7300   www.roast-restaurant.com

There could hardly be a more perfect location for a restaurant dedicated to the best of British cooking than this cast-iron and glass structure above the stalls of Borough Market. The salvaged and restored portico, formerly the entrance to the Floral Hall at the Royal Opera House, Covent Garden, now crowns the market entrance on Stoney Street. With Borough Market drawing thousands of people every weekend, the new portico is sure to be an enduring commercial and architectural success.

Iqbal Wahhab OBE, the restaurant's founder, and Lawrence Keogh, the head cook, belive that British produce is the best in the world and are on a mission to elevate the profile and quality of British ingredients. In addition to its enticing lunch and dinner menus, Roast also offers a breakfast menu of considerable choice and great popularity. **○**

Above **The terrace at Le Pont de la Tour.** Left **Roast restaurant is located on the first floor above the salvaged portico.**

Skylon Royal Festival Hall, Belvedere Road, SE1 8XX
020 7654 7800 www.skylon-restaurant.co.uk

If you have a preference for mega-restaurants with a capacity topping a few hundred, Skylon is definitely for you. The ceilings are high, the dimensions wide and long, and the huge windows add further depth to this unique space. The designers have cleverly divided up the single room by creating three distinct offerings.

A central raised island bar serving expensive and creative cocktails, complemented by excellent table service from girls wearing statement uniforms, makes an ideal meeting point before or after a concert, talk or dance performance in the vibrant Royal Festival Hall.

Flanking the bar are a grill and a smarter restaurant with linen napery, gueridon service and other fancy touches. Whichever you choose, the views are fantastic and this is an ideal venue to choose for entertaining.

Skylon takes its name from the futuristic structure that was built alongside the Royal Festival Hall for the Festival of Britain in 1951: a fascinating event well worth reading up on. ◉

Tapas Brindisa 18–20 Southwark Street, SE1 1TJ
020 7357 8880 www.brindisa.com

Housed in a converted potato warehouse on the edge of Borough Market, this small bar and dining room delivers an authentic tapas experience. The name Brindisa derives from the Spanish *brindis*, meaning a drink or toast. In celebration of all things Spanish, we suggest you raise a small glass of fino, manzanilla or oloroso over a simple plate of hand-carved Joselito. You can stand in the bar and jamoneria (traditional ham-carving corner) and enjoy grilled anchovies, salt cod or croquettes, or take a seat under the shelves of specially imported products and order a range of small individual plates of montadito tapas.

Underneath Roast restaurant along Stoney Street, Brindisa also has a small shop, open Tuesday to Saturday, selling an extensive range of Spanish tinned fish, olive oils, hams and innumerable Iberian delicacies. ◉

Above left **The Royal Festival Hall's brutalist facade overlooking The Thames.**
Top right and right **The Skylon Restaurant and Grill.**
Above **View towards the London Eye.**

Helena Puolakka

Ottolenghi on Ledbury Road is my favourite London café. The neighbourhood restaurant I like to visit most is Sonny's.

Executive chef, Skylon

This page **Typical and authentic Spanish food from Brindisa.**

Tate Modern Bankside, SE1 9TG
020 7887 8888 www.tate.org.uk

In the 1990s, the Victoria and Albert Museum press office proudly
declared that it had an ace café with a good museum attached. Since then,
dining in museums and galleries has been as good as on the high street,
and in many cases significantly better. Certainly all of the Tate cafés and
restaurants are professionally managed.

The menus might not demonstrate creativity on a par with many of
the Tate's esteemed artists, but they are good solid affairs none the less, and
you certainly don't need to leave the gallery to enjoy a tasty meal or snack.

The restaurant on level seven of Tate Modern has an eclectic modern
menu with lots of great British ingredients, plus an innovative wine list.
The café on level two is a simpler refuelling point before taking on Dali
and Surrealism or Lichtenstein, Warhol and Pop Art.

The restaurant dining room has spectacular views north and south
across London, plus a huge mural, *Cold Mouth Prayer*, by James Aldridge.
This mural is changed on a regular basis: previous works have been by
Brazilian artist Beatriz Milhazes, Fiona Rae and Hamish Fulton. ◗

Village East 171–3 Bermondsey Street, SE1 3UW
020 7357 6082 www.villageeast.co.uk

Whether it is thanks to gentrification or simply its pleasant environment,
Bermondsey Street – just a short walk from London Bridge or Butlers
Wharf and the Thames – is a feel-good area. Like nearby Shad Thames, it
has historic links with food warehousing, and Bermondsey is inextricably
linked with chocolate. Many of the original warehouses are now trendy
apartments or hip creative design offices. Add a little green, a florist, some
quirky retailers including Zhandra Rhodes' Fashion, Textile and Design
Museum, and you have a magnet for serious urbanites.

Village East has certainly helped to put Bermondsey Street on the
map of places to go. The owners of this style-led, multi-faceted operation
who also run the nearby Garrison gastropub (see page 291), describe
Village East as a 'New York warehouse-style brasserie restaurant'. The
menu includes lots of things you want to eat in this type of setting, from
a great burger served with foie gras to a choice of steaks including bavette,
rib-eye, fillet and chateaubriand, plus fish and chips and grilled lobster.

Chi-chi cocktails, Scandinavian furniture, oversized lampshades
and a 100-plus wine list all contribute to the statement being made here.
The artistic graphics on the literature are testimony to the owners' creative
flair. And Village East offers a great brunch and Sunday roast menu. ◗

Above **The view
from, and the 7th
floor restaurant at
Tate Modern.**
Right **The Turbine
Hall at Tate Modern.**

Wright Brothers Oyster and Porter House 11 Stoney Street, SE1 9AD
020 7403 9554 www.thewrightbrothers.co.uk

From Cromer crabs, Poole Bay prawns, Dorset lobsters and the world's finest langoustines, fished from icy Scottish waters to a fine range of oysters sourced from around the coastline, humble mussels, clams, shrimps, cockles and whelks, Wright Brothers Oyster and Porter House is a celebration of all British seafood.

Behind the business are Ben Wright and Robin Hancock, two family friends (not brothers) who share a passion for oysters and who have previously grown, imported and supplied oysters to London's top chefs. Their restaurant seems set to become an essential London experience.

The tiny dining space consists essentially of an L-shaped counter overlooking the oyster display and shucking activities, a few raised long tables with stools, and a tiny open kitchen for preparing the few cooked dishes on the menu. The exposed brick walls and electrics suggest a hint of Manhattan fused with the classic signwriting of a Parisian zinc bar.

The choice of oysters is extensive, with a range including specialities such as French spéciales de claire, rocks from Cornwall and natives from Mersea Island in the Thames estuary near Colchester. You can enjoy your oysters *au naturel* or garnished by delights such as Kilpatrick (smoked bacon), New Orleans (deep-fried, tartare sauce), Spanish (chorizo) or Japanese (wasabi, soy and ginger).

The menu, written on the blackboard above the counter, also includes delicious oyster rarebit and a steak, oyster and Guinness pie. ◗

Right **A happy chef with a tray of oyster at Wright Brothers.**

Zucca 184 Bermondsey Street, SE1 3TQ
020 7378 6809 www.zuccalondon.com

The River Café experience and quality for half the price: a succinct endorsement of this highly rated Italian restaurant that cherishes simplicity and taste. We stress, the prices are very reasonable. A recent supper including the mandatory *zucca fritti*, excellent bread, San Daniele ham and pigeon crostini, a braised rabbit main course with deliciously sloppy white polenta, a pasta main course with pork and fennel ragù, plus a side of borlotti beans, two puddings and two glasses of wine produced a modest bill of less than £60. Stunning value, with no compromises on the quality or service.

The opening of Zucca confirms Bermondsey Street's burgeoning reputation as a foodie alley. While other restaurants on the street cater for the locals, this is most certainly a restaurant to travel to. The only negative is the difficulty one might experience in securing a table. On a recent occasion we couldn't get a table at Zucca, yet managed to find one at The River Café. Which speaks volumes. ◉

Sam Harris

"

My favourite bakery in London is St. John on Maltby Street – go on Saturday mornings. Wyndham House in Fulham is my favourite butchers – they sell great game and veal – ask for Paul, he's a legend. And Steve Hatt is still the best fishmonger in town.

Head chef, Zucca

Above left **Bermondsey Street is now a hot dining and drinking destination.** Left **The Zucca dining room.** Right **Sam Harris in his kitchen at Zucca.**

Zucca
Linguine with Squid, Chilli and Lemon

Serves 4

500g good-quality dried linguine
extra virgin olive oil (not too strong,
ideally Ligurian or Sicilian)
2 garlic cloves, peeled and finely chopped
1 large red chilli, finely chopped
a handful of flat leaf parsley,
roughly chopped
4 medium squid, cleaned, scored on
the inside and cut into very thin strips
(ask the fishmonger to do this)
1 large Amalfi lemon

Bring a large pot of salted water to the boil, add the linguine and cook according to the packet instructions. When the linguine is about half-way through cooking, take a large deep-sided frying pan, add a few tablespoons of olive oil and fry the garlic, chilli and half the parsley over a medium heat, being careful not to let the garlic colour.

Add the squid strips to the garlic, chilli and parsley pan, increase the heat and stir for a minute, then add the undercooked linguine with a ladleful of the pasta water (the idea is that you want to finish cooking the pasta in the pan juices of the squid). Keeping the heat high, stir vigorously to combine. As the water is absorbed by the pasta, add another splash of water and the juice of half the lemon. Cook for a minute longer and test the pasta. If it is still not cooked, add a little more pasta water, keeping the pasta moving constantly.

When the linguine is cooked, turn off the heat and add another squeeze of lemon, the remaining parsley and a good glug of olive oil. Serve on warm flat plates.

Above **Sam cooking linguine.**

Vanilla Pannacotta

Serves 6

2 vanilla pods
700 ml (1 pint 4 fl oz) double cream
300 ml (½ pint) milk
100 g (3 ½ oz) caster sugar
2½ leaves gelatine
poached fruit, to serve

Split the vanilla pods in half lengthways and scrape out the seeds. Put the cream, milk and sugar in a large saucepan and stir in the vanilla seeds. Bring to the boil over a high heat, then reduce the heat and simmer for 5 minutes.

Remove the pan from the heat, stir in the gelatine leaves until they dissolve, then allow the mixture to cool slightly.

Pass the mixture through a fine seive into a jug, then pour the mixture into 6 moulds.

Cover each mould with clingfilm and chill in the refrigerator until set, ideally overnight.

Serve chilled with seasonal fruit, either fresh or poached in a light sugar syrup.

Zucca Pistachio, Lemon and Almond Cake

Serves 10

125 g (4 oz) shelled unsalted pistachio nuts
1 1/2 vanilla pods
375 g (12 oz) butter, at room temperature
360 g (11 3/4 oz) caster sugar
5 eggs, at room temperature
finely grated zest of 1 1/2 lemons
200 g (7 oz) ground almonds
60 g (2 1/2 oz) plain flour

For the topping
150 g (5 oz) shelled unsalted
pistachio nuts, roughly chopped
finely grated zest and juice of 1 lemon
100 g (3 1/2 oz) caster sugar
juice of 1/2 orange

Whizz the pistachio nuts in a food processor until they become a very fine powder and set aside. Split the vanilla pods in half lengthways and scrape out the seeds.

In a free-standing mixer, cream the butter and sugar together until very light and fluffy – this will take at least 15 minutes. Reduce the speed to low and add the eggs one at a time, making sure each egg is fully incorporated before adding the next one. If the mixture starts to split, add a small spoon of the flour and continue mixing.

Add the lemon zest and vanilla seeds to the mixture, then gradually add the ground almonds and pistachios. Finally add the flour just to combine.

Let the mixture rest in the bowl for 5 minutes. Butter a 28 cm (11 inch) cake tin with a removable base and line with parchment paper.

Spoon the mixture into the tin and bake in a preheated oven, 160°C (325°F), Gas Mark 3, for 40–45 minutes or until a skewer inserted into the centre comes out clean.

To make the topping, put the pistachios and lemon zest in a bowl and set aside. Put the sugar, lemon and orange juices in a small saucepan over a high heat. When the sugar has dissolved and the mixture comes to a boil, remove from the heat and immediately pour over the pistachio nuts, stirring to coat.

Once the cake is cooked remove from the oven and whilst still warm pour the pistachio nut topping over the top of the cake, then leave to cool in the tin.

More places to visit in the area

Above **Sam Harris (centre) in his open kitchen at Zucca, one of the best new restaurants in London.**

Brasserie Joël
Park Plaza Westminster Bridge, SE1 7UT
020 7620 7272 www.brasseriejoel.co.uk
This completely bizarre setting in a typical mass-market hotel conceals an amazingly talented chef, Joël Antunes. Ignore everything else, just go for the food.

Brew Wharf
Brew Wharf Yard, Stoney Street, SE1 9AD
020 7378 6601 www.brewwharf.com
As the name implies, Brew Wharf boasts its own micro-brewery.

José
104 Bermondsey Street, SE1 3UB
020 7403 4902 www.josepizarro.com
This already bustling sherry and tapas bar – another welcome addition to the Bermondsey Street scene – is brought to you by José Pizarro. Look out for this name and expect more in the future.

Magdalen
152 Tooley Street, SE1 2TU
020 7403 1342
www.magdalenrestaurant.co.uk
A restrained and confident menu with lots of lovely ingredients that we love to eat, from a husband-and-wife team in the kitchen. This small and elegant restaurant, which opened in 2007 to critical acclaim, is equidistant between Tower Bridge and Borough Market.

M. Manze Pie and Mash
87 Tower Bridge Road, SE1 4TW
020 7407 2985 www.manze.co.uk
Only a few pie and mash shops survive in London; Manze's is one of the best.

Oxo Tower Restaurant and Brasserie
Oxo Tower Wharf, Barge House Street, SE1 9PH 020 7803 3888
www.harveynichols.com/oxo-tower-london
The Oxo Tower has attracted occasional criticism for its sky-high prices. Here restaurant dining is all about occasions, special dates and the odd honourable proposal, while the brasserie offers simpler fare. But there is no doubt: the views across the river towards the architecture of the capital are amazing.

Real Food Market at South Bank Centre
Royal Festival Hall, SE1 8XX
Friday–Sunday
This weekly market at the rear of the Royal Festival Hall bypasses the middlemen to connect the UK's best artisan food and drink producers with the consumer. Open Friday to Sunday.

Vinopolis
1 Bank End, SE1 9BU
020 7940 8322 www.vinopolis.co.uk
A wine and drinks expo located under a railway viaduct.

Index

Staff, Service Charge and Tipping

Throughout this book we have extensively discussed the people aspects to our business and how quirky personalities, world-class chefs, distinguished maitre d's and influential proprietors can make or break a business. The other essential ingredient is, of course, great staff. We cannot forget the pivotal role staff play in the attainment of their leader's crusade to provide the best service.

Good staff can make or break a business, irrespective of who sits at the top of the tree or wears the toque. The best staff gravitate to the most professional employers and it is down to the management to hold on to these star performers. Ultimately, the retention question can only be answered with fair pay, good conditions, clear policies, the opportunity to learn and civility amongst colleagues, not to mention the odd laugh and an off-duty beer.

Service charge and tips are invariably a component of the waiters pay, and in some situations, the chefs remuneration can also include a direct contribution from their patrons. Many London restaurateurs have sought to overcome awkward situations by introducing a discretionary service charge that will allow reasonable funds to be raised so that the staff can receive a relevant wage commensurate with the experience provided at the table.

Excepting a few, the standard service charge percentage added to the customer bill is 12.5%. A sum that, even at the most successful restaurants, only covers a small percentage of the total labour payroll cost. Therefore, you can be quite sure that in most circumstances all of the money ultimately makes its way to the staff – if in a sometimes convoluted fashion.

It is worth mentioning the service charge is discretionary and optional, if you don't believe the service warrants that amount, then simply speak with the manager and remove or reduce the amount. Don't be afraid or embarrassed. This is something that every manager is legally obliged to do without any qualms or hesitation. Hopefully, the message will proficiently permeate to the staff and they will realise that the service at the table directly impacts their pay.

These words only scratch the surface of a huge subject area, however, one thing is for certain, if the employers pay a decent wage and provide an enjoyable environment, it will hopefully become manifest at the table.

Acknowledgements

First, I must thank one person that has helped enormously with this project and is likely to receive the least recognition. David Hawkins, the designer, has done a brilliant job with this second book, as he did with the first.

Lisa Linder's photographs are spectacularly good and were often taken with just a moment to prepare and in difficult circumstances.

Sybella, at Octopus, has brought everything together and kept the team on the straight and narrow, very hard work indeed.

A special mention for our project manager is important; Charlotte Pennington helped coordinate the photo shoots and liaised with the chefs and restaurateurs. I can assure you, this is no easy task, and it was done with great confidence.

And finally, but certainly not the least important, I must thank Terence for his perpetual support in all aspects of our work together. *Peter Prescott*

Second edition published in 2012
by Conran Octopus Limited
a part of Octopus Publishing Group
Endeavour House, 189 Shaftesbury Avenue
London WC2H 8JY
www.octopusbooks.co.uk

An Hachette UK Company
www.hachette.co.uk

Text copyright ©
Conran Octopus Limited 2012
Recipes copyright ©
individual copyright holders
Photography copyright © Lisa Linder 2012

British Library Cataloguing-in-Publication Data. A catalogue record for this book is available from the British Library.

Publishers Lorraine Dickey & Alison Starling
Senior Editor Sybella Stephens
Art Director Jonathan Christie
Art Direction and Design Untitled
Photography Lisa Linder
Production Caroline Alberti

ISBN: 978 1 84091 583 9
Printed in China